ATTRIBUTING

An Intro

Recent literary scholarship has seen a shift of interest away from questions of attribution. Yet these questions remain urgent and important for any historical study of writing, and have been given a powerful new impetus by advances in statistical studies of language and the coming on line of large databases of texts in machine-searchable form. The present book is the first comprehensive survey of the field from a literary perspective to appear for forty years. It covers both traditional and computer based approaches to attribution, and evaluates each in respect of their potentialities and limitations. It revisits a number of famous controversies, including those concerning the authorship of the Homeric poems, books from the Old and New Testaments, and the plays of Shakespeare. Written with wit as well as erudition, *Attributing Authorship: An Introduction* will make this intriguing field accessible for students and scholars alike.

HAROLD LOVE is Professor of English at Monash University. He has written extensively on early modern English literature and the history of the performing arts in Australia. He has edited the works of Thomas Southerne with R. J. Jordan and recently published a complete scholarly edition of the works of John Wilmot, second earl of Rochester.

ATTRIBUTING AUTHORSHIP

An Introduction

HAROLD LOVE

Monash University

CAMBRIDGE UNIVERSITY PRESS
Cambridge, New York, Melbourne, Madrid, Cape Town, Singapore,
São Paulo, Delhi, Dubai, Tokyo, Mexico City

Cambridge University Press
The Edinburgh Building, Cambridge CB2 8RU, UK

Published in the United States of America by Cambridge University Press, New York

www.cambridge.org
Information on this title: www.cambridge.org/9780521789486

First published 2002

A catalogue record for this publication is available from the British Library

Library of Congress Cataloguing in Publication data

Love, Harold, 1937–
Authorship and attribution: an introduction / Harold Love.
p. cm.
Includes bibliographical references and index.
ISBN 0 521 78339 9 – ISBN 0 521 78948 6 (pb.)
1. Authorship, Disputed. 2. Style, Literary. 3. Language and languages –
Style. I. Title.
PN171.F6 L68 2002 809 – dc21 2001052854

ISBN 978-0-521-78339-2 Hardback
ISBN 978-0-521-78948-6 Paperback

Contents

Acknowledgements

To list all the individuals who have contributed over the years to the preparation of this book is unfortunately impossible, but I must particularly mention Felicity Henderson for her assistance with the assembling of sources and Meredith Sherlock whose long-standing knowledge of my bad habits as a writer allowed her to suggest many improvements in matters of style and exposition. John Burrows, Hugh Craig, Robert D. Hume and Keith Walker all generously agreed to read the book in draft and A. R. Braunmuller did the same on behalf of Cambridge University Press: their comments were of great value for the preparation of the final version. Peter Groves gave much appreciated assistance with the discussion of metre and Ada Cheung, Wallace Kirsop and Constant Mews with other specialised questions. However, my greatest debt is, as always, to my wife Rosaleen, who, having abandoned academia for a successful career as a full-time writer, has been my expert and unfailing guide to the realities of the profession of letters.

Work on this book was encouraged by a three-year Australian Research Council large grant awarded to myself, John Burrows and Christopher Wortham to investigate the authorship of seventeenth-century scribally circulated satires.

Abbreviations

BSANZ Bulletin	*Bibliographical Society of Australia and New Zealand Bulletin*
CHum	*Computers and the Humanities*
E&F	David V. Erdman and Ephim G. Fogel, eds., *Evidence for Authorship: Essays on Problems of Attribution* (Ithaca: Cornell University Press, 1966)
IE	Schoenbaum, Samuel, *Internal Evidence and Elizabethan Dramatic Authorship: An Essay in Literary History and Method* (London: Edward Arnold, 1966)
LLC	*Literary and Linguistic Computing*
MLR	*Modern Language Review*
N&Q	*Notes and Queries*
PMLA	*Papers of the Modern Language Association of America*
SB	*Studies in Bibliography*
TLS	*Times Literary Supplement*

Introduction

This book sets out to mediate from a literary perspective between the impressive computer-based work on attribution studies which has been done over the last four decades and a much older tradition of such studies, which, considered as an organised scholarly enterprise, reaches back as far as the great library of Alexandria and embraces the formation of the Jewish and Christian biblical canons. It is not the work of a specialist in attribution but of a scholar for whom the determination of authorship has repeatedly been a crucial element in other kinds of investigation. In reviewing the existing literature I soon realised that fundamental questions concerning criteria of proof in establishing attributions remained unexamined: these are addressed in my concluding chapter. It was also a surprise to find that a discipline whose subject matter was individual authorship had given very little attention to what it meant by individualness – a matter that I also try to remedy. The book is directed equally at those who need to orientate themselves in the field in order to investigate particular cases and those whose primary interest is in wider issues of argument and methodology.

My first practical involvement with questions of attribution arose during many years of work on the thousands of political and libertine satires that circulated in early-modern and Enlightenment Britain, for the most part anonymously and in manuscript. This corpus was considered in broad outline in a chapter of my *Scribal Publication in Seventeenth-century England*[1] and from the perspective of the best-known author of such pieces in my edition of *The Works of John Wilmot, Earl of Rochester.*[2] It will also be the subject of a further study now in preparation. These satires emerged from a culture in which personal safety demanded that authorship should be concealed, but in which speculation about it was intense. The Rochester edition raised the additional problem of presenting an author, for whom even major and long-accepted ascriptions were frequently unprovable, to present-day readers who not only desired a canon which would offer a secure basis for interpretation but were often drawn to Rochester by a strong interest in his personality. Neither kind can have been very pleased with the result, which left several key attributions undecided.

A second personal involvement arose from the writing of two books on the performing arts in nineteenth-century Australia whose primary materials were unsigned notices in newspapers.[3] From their origins in the late seventeenth century until within living memory, newspapers and magazines presented the bulk of their contents as the anonymous voice of the organ or under pen-names. Any attempt to write the life of a major author of that period is likely at some point to strike against the problem of unattributed journalism, either in defining the canon or in establishing whether the person concerned really held particular views. For minor literary authors and politicians and all professional journalists, the determination of authorship is often crucial to whether a career can be mapped out in the first place. In the case of metropolitan journals, surviving archival sources and financial records may sometimes permit attributions to be established; but the more one moves away from the metropolis towards the ever-advancing frontier of European expansion, the more likely the researcher is to be left with bare columns of newsprint without either internal documentation or much in the way of complementary book publication. Daily, weekly and monthly journalism is the largely unmapped *terra incognita* of attribution studies.

A need to move beyond traditional techniques for dealing with such cases led me to the genial door of John Burrows, who from the Centre for Literary and Linguistic Computing at the University of Newcastle, New South Wales had established a position of world leadership in computational stylistics. By working with John on problems from the Rochester canon and then on a wider range of attribution questions from scribally circulated satire, which produced joint papers on Shadwell and Aphra Behn, I was able to watch his methods in action and encouraged to explore the work of a lively and disputatious group of international scholars who, over the last half-century, have applied statistical and computer-based methods (two categories which, despite overlap, are not synonymous) to the determination of authorship. My interest in computer applications in the humanities is a long-standing one, my first contribution having been published as long ago as 1969, but had been until then chiefly applied to scholarly editing. In our joint work on Rochester the new methods were applied alongside the old, sometimes producing the same identifications and sometimes differing ones which then had, if possible, to be reconciled. John more than anyone else provided the inspiration for this book; however, I must absolve him from any complicity in the positions it maintains, which several times depart from what I know to be his.

My movement from a practical to a theoretical study of attribution has taken place during an era of searching philosophical enquiry into the nature of authorship, a matter famously brought to the forefront of literary studies at the close of the 1960s by Barthes's 'The death of the author' and Foucault's response in 'What is an author?' and far from concluded by Seán Burke's *The Death and Return of the Author*.[4] It may disappoint some readers that the issues raised in this debate are not, by and large, given much consideration in what follows. This is not because of any lack of interest on my part but because a study of attribution practice had to maintain a precise focus on the question of how personal responsibility for given aspects of given texts might be distributed. My approach acknowledges from the start that there are many texts and aspects for which no sure answer can be given to this question and has no desire to reinstate what is referred to by a convenient shorthand as 'the myth of the Romantic author'. Its arguments are more often disintegrationist than integrationist, maintaining, with the tradition of editorial theory inaugurated by Jerome McGann, that most literary creation is to a greater or lesser degree co-operative, if not collaborative, in nature. Authorship so conceived is a form of intellectual work which for good practical reasons (even if they are as mundane as determining the address to which the royalty or copyright cheques should be sent) needs to be credited to those craftspersons who perform it. It is true that for many of the texts considered in this book that responsibility has been evaded, but it is equally true that this has often been done unwillingly. The great majority of writers wish passionately to assert their responsibility for their creations – whether in the form of 'an ill-favoured thing, sir, but mine own' or *quod scripsi scripsi*.

CHAPTER ONE

Individuality and sameness

The subject of attribution studies is the uniqueness of each human being and how this is enacted in writing. One determinant of uniqueness is biological: at the moment of conception a mingling of genetic information occurs which is unprecedented and unrepeatable. This mingling is partly a rule-governed and partly a random process. The rule-governed part ensures a degree of resemblance between siblings and close relatives and of uniformity over the race and species: individuality is never absolute. But then neither is it ever absent: in the most inbred of populations there will still be immeasurable possibilities of variation. Nature's poker machine never gives the same prize twice.

Even in the brains of identical twins, formed when the zygote divides after conception, tiny irregularities in the laying down of neural pathways become magnified into differences in the ways by which the brain, as a self-organising system, coordinates its vast assemblage of centres and individual neurones in the acts of knowing, speaking and writing. Experience stocks all brains with different knowledge, perceptions and attitudes. On the other hand, since language is also a shared possession with communal as well as self-expressive functions, what nature and experience individualise will often be overwritten by socialisation.

A fable may help to clarify the roles of the individual and the communal. A wise queen in ancient times established a college of philosophers. Because her dominions covered many lands in which many different tongues were spoken, her first instruction to this college was to devise an artificial language, free from all anomalies, which would permit all the members of her far-flung dominions to converse freely with each other, and with the tax-gatherers. There were a hundred philosophers in the college – all of them, sadly, male – and each one was told to perfect a language and devise a script in which it might be written. One year was allowed for this and a handsome prize promised to the winner. Differences both of nature and nurture combined to produce a variety of artificial languages which were, of course, mutually incomprehensible. The judgement of the prize was made by a senate of savants from all the lands concerned, none of whom were themselves members of the college; but the winner, who came from a distant, minority people, was so resented by his rivals that, as he made his way to the throne to receive his prize, he was seized by them and torn to pieces.

Horrified by this dreadful crime, the queen banished the entire college to an island where they were to live the remainder of their lives in isolation. Here the philosophers continued to compose and copy works of learning; but, from obstinacy, each of them did this in his individual invented language, convinced that this was the most perfect and should have been awarded the prize. Even in the daily affairs of life they would condescend to speak only in their own languages, with the result that there was no possibility of meaning being communicated. It became a matter of pride that messages were transmitted only in this self-defeating way: even the universal language of mimicry and gesture was avoided. Instead, the philosophers always held their arms absolutely rigid and never changed the expressions of their faces from an unyielding frown.

The resultant society was profoundly dysfunctional; but it would have offered no problems at all for the determination of attribution. A work encountered in this island must have been written in one of its ninety-nine different artificial languages with their characteristic scripts: it was only a matter of discovering which one. With the aid of a grammar and dictionary of that language, which the inventor was always willing to supply, it might even be read by someone who was determined enough, though it is not recorded that this ever happened.

The reverse case is shown by the subsequent history of the nation. On the death of the queen, her realm was threatened with civil war over the succession. In order to avert this it was concluded that one of the exiled philosophers should be chosen by lot and made absolute monarch. The new king commenced his reign by sentencing all his fellow philosophers to death, with the mitigating clause that they were each permitted to utter a speech of farewell in their own artificial language outlining its excellences. His second measure was to make the speaking of his own invented language compulsory for all official business throughout the realm. To this end schools were established in which the language was taught; moreover, it was taught in a particularly pure and regulated way from which no departure was permitted. Innovations were punished by death; even unintended solecisms might lead to imprisonment.

At the end of ten years the new language was taught in every corner of the realm but in a way that left no possibility for individual difference except in vocal pitch and timbre, and even here an attempt was made to avoid this by close imitation of the speech of the inventor. It was also required that in speaking this language one should adopt the 'philosophical facial expression' as described above and refrain from movement of the limbs. Writing, similarly, became so uniform that it was a matter of the greatest difficulty to tell one person's hand from another's. In this society the determination of attribution became a matter of the most acute difficulty, with the result that when satirical poems about the monarch began to circulate it was impossible for his spies to identify their scribes or authors. Even to overhear one being recited would not necessarily allow one to identify the speaker since everyone present spoke in exactly the same way. The finest minds of the country were therefore enroled into a corps of attributionists charged with overcoming this problem: inevitably, they found, there were always minute differences between individual performances of the common language.

The exiles' island and the philosopher's kingdom represent on the one hand a total individualisation and on the other a close-to-total uniformity in language behaviour. Fortunately in real life these two tendencies are never so extreme. For communal, civic and national tasks to be performed efficiently requires enforcement of common linguistic rules and meanings at every level; yet in everyday speech there will always be countervailing processes of adaptivity and invention, as a result of which the speech of the young may cease to be intelligible to the elderly, even when familiar words are being employed.

> Those who came of age in the 1960s think of those who came of age in the 1990s as 'Generation X', as being characterized by an unknown factor. Although they both use the same language in everyday speech, these generations supposedly talk past each other because their words refer to different things, different experiences, different texts.[1]

One would expect a greater stability of the formal 'grapholects', specialised forms of language, such as that in which this book is written, whose raison d'être is to be read rather than spoken. These are conservative, highly artificial forms of a language that require many years of training if they are to be written with assurance. A newspaper editorial from any part of the world in which English is spoken or read is likely to be written in a common style whose historical origins lie in the prose of the eighteenth-century periodical essay and the early nineteenth-century review. (It is only half a century ago that aspiring leader writers were instructed to model themselves on the prose of Lord Macaulay.) Since such leaders are always by convention anonymous and cultivate a studied impersonality (the voice of the paper rather than any individual) they are a fruitful field for attribution studies. A leader writer once confided to me that he could always pick his own work because he was the only one of three regular editorialists to make generous use of the semi-colon; but, apart from that, even he could not readily recognise his own writing once memory of the subject matter had faded. But this is a practical difficulty rather than a theoretical one: leader-writers' English is simply another version of the idea of the invariant philosophical language, and, however determined the attempt to repress individuality, will always betray its authorship to a skilled enough investigator with sufficient data to work from. Dr Johnson may be allowed the final word on this topic: 'Why, Sir, I think every man whatever has a peculiar style, which may be discovered by nice examination and comparison with others: but a man must write a great deal to make his style obviously discernible.'[2]

The individualist position has not been a popular one in the humanities in recent years. In its reaction against the nineteenth-century and modernist cult of the author as cultural hero, the 1960s turned to ways of defining the workings of language that disregarded the agency of the author in order to present a purely linguistic model of text creation: language giving rise to language. As a heuristic device this proved productive in the same way as non-Euclidean geometries have proved productive, that is by bringing processes to our attention that were not otherwise visible and allowing us to articulate these both practically and theoretically. Yet this erasure of the author has remained paradoxical, not least because it was powered by the creativity of a number of profoundly individualistic thinkers and writers. There was never any doubt as to where royalty cheques for Barthes, Foucault, Lacan, Kristeva and Derrida ought to be sent: they reasserted heroic authorship even in their questioning of it. Attribution studies demands that we attend to the notion of individual agency in a way that cannot be fully satisfied by structuralist and poststructuralist epistemologies because it raises questions which they have no capacity to address. Even to think from within poststructuralist discourse about 'the individual' as a reality rather than a concept can only be done through the most tortuous of theoretical convolutions, a predicament which is an unavoidable consequence of the Saussurean distinction between *langue* and *parole*.

Saussure's distinction has recently been revisited by sociolinguists interested in individual performances of language. The earlier tendency was to categorise *parole*, which would include the variants of a language spoken, or written, by individuals, as somehow inferior to or derived from the generalised *langue*. Barbara Johnstone argues that if *langue* is identified as 'true' language, then *parole* which departs from it (as most do) comes to be seen as either deviance or immaturity.[3] But this *langue* is at best an uneasy back-formation from the innumerable varieties of *parole*, which in themselves can never claim more than a temporary stability because of the continual pressure to innovation in the language behaviour of individuals as they respond to changes in their immediate environments or simply assert their uniqueness through linguistic play. The moment linguistics admits a model of language as a mode of individual self-expression, the received view immediately starts to crumble. A Saussurean explanation of the phonetic changes that turned Latin into French would be that they were deterministic products of a synchronic system which could not have adjusted itself in any other way. This is a very hard proposition to swallow and would probably not have been swallowed if it had not appealed to the prejudices of educational bureaucracies wedded to the promulgation of a particular standardised version of the national language.

Johnstone, the most outspoken advocate of the new individualism in linguistics, cites one of the great pioneers of the modern discipline, Edward Sapir, in support of her claim for the necessary uniqueness of the idiolect. In his paper 'Speech as a personality trait', Sapir wrote: 'There is always an individual method, however poorly developed, of arranging words into groups and of working these up into larger units. It would be a very complicated problem to disentangle the social and individual determinants of style, but it is a theoretically possible one.'[4] In *The Linguistic Individual* Johnstone takes up exactly this problem of disentangling the social from the individual in ways that are of great interest to attribution studies. 'Linguistic behaviour', as she sees it,

> varies statistically with social factors – sociolinguistic research has made this abundantly clear – and with psychological factors, as well as with changes in rhetorical situation. But none of these factors *causes* people to talk one way or another. (p. 55)

To the structuralist, language is a rule-generated system; but in Johnstone's and Sapir's linguistics the 'rules' are nothing more than an oversimplified *post hoc* record of the innumerable things individual people actually do with language in order to represent themselves to each other and communicate meaning. Elsewhere Johnstone summarises Sapir:

> If one looks at culture from the perspective of a child acquiring it . . . one sees that culture is not a unitary whole. Each individual's culture is different . . . . In his writings he points out again and again that the abstractions studied by anthropologists and linguists – cultures and languages, in other words – should not be taken as real. (p. 20)

Against 'laws of syntax' Sapir set 'the stammerer who is trying to "get himself across" ', denying that the former had any 'higher reality' and calling for 'a minute and sympathetic study of individual behavior . . . in a state of society' (p. 21).

A second critique of Saussurean linguistics, this time of its insistence on the arbitrariness of the sign and the generation of meaning through differentiation, is offered by the work of cognitive linguists, for whom language is an embodied function of the individual human brain. In *Shakespeare's Brain*, Mary Crane explains:

> From a cognitive perspective, language is shaped, or 'motivated', by its origins in the neural systems of a human body as they interact with other human bodies and an environment. This theoretical position has profound implications for postmodern concepts of subjectivity and cultural construction. In the first place, although the relationship between a particular phoneme *tree* and the concept that it represents is arbitrary, the meaning of the concept itself is grounded in the cognition and experience of human speakers and is structured by them. Cognitive subjects are not simply determined by the symbolic order in which they exist; instead, they shape (and are also shaped by) meanings that are determined by an interaction of the physical world, culture, and human cognitive systems. In Terence Deacon's formulation, the human brain and symbolic and linguistic systems have coevolved, and each has exercised a formative influence on the other.[5]

The brain and its functioning are exactly what was banished from Saussure's immaterialist model of linguistic process, as it was from those of Foucault, Derrida and Lacan, but, like Banquo's ghost, it refuses to stay away from the party. To reinstate it and its operations at the centre of linguistics is also to reinstate the reality of human agency as, in Crane's words, 'a constitutive feature of the human experience of embodied selfhood and a basic building block of thought and language' (p. 20). This realisation is likely to be of great practical as well as theoretical importance for attribution studies.

To reject certain reigning epistemologies as irrelevant to the tasks of attribution studies is not, however, to step back into a positivist golden age. Because these epistemologies have come into existence, and have enlarged our sense of the complexity of any socially situated act of writing, it is impossible simply to revert to older, naive conceptualisings of authorial agency. It is misleading, therefore, to salute the rebirth of the author: the author as conceived by positivism remains dead. What is happening is closer to 'The author is dead: long live the author' with the nature and lineaments of the new successor still fully to reveal themselves. What attribution studies, cognitive science and the new sociolinguistics maintain is that language is also languages and that there are as many of these as there are individuals. We should add to this the self-evident rider that the search for aspects of language behaviour that are unique to specific individuals cannot be undertaken without a belief in the reality of individuality. Those who do not believe in the individual and the individual's power to originate language will, presumably, reject the project, and deny its results, even when these are addressed to their own texts.

This distinction in viewpoints is further illuminated by Don Giovanni from Mozart's opera. That the Don is driven by an insatiable hunger for sexual conquests is obvious enough; but the reasons for this have been much debated. The central issue is again one between sameness and uniqueness. Giovanni may want endless women because he does not really notice their individual differences. In Congreve's words from *The Old Batchelour*:

> Men will admire, adore and die,
> While wishing at your Feet they lie:
> But admitting their Embraces,
> Wakes 'em from the golden Dream;
> Nothing's new besides our Faces,
> Every Woman is the same.[6]

Conversely, he may want endless women because he is acutely aware of their individuality and variety – sexual and spiritual – and the ways in which every one is distinct and different from every other one, instilling each fresh experience with the promise of new knowledge. A way of resolving the matter is suggested by Leporello's catalogue aria in Act I of *Don Giovanni*. The effect of the words is to emphasise the sameness of women. They might differ in nationality, age, hair-colour, temperament and a few other characteristics, but the ground is unvarying: the same woman distributed under a number of classifications but otherwise a constant. This was very probably the view of the matter held by the librettist, Da Ponte, an Enlightenment maintainer of the notion of a universal human nature expressed and constituted through universal passions and therefore reducible to a relatively few variables. (God's formula for individuality would not, in this view, be an overly complex one.) But musically the matter is different. Mozart's treatment of the phrases of the cataloguer is subtly characterising in a way that gestures beyond the Da Pontean category to the possibility of innumerable sub-categories that will conclude in that category of one known as the individual (e.g. Anna, Elvira, Zerlina). The individuating capacities of the music – its unique ability to conduct dialogues between the universal and the personal – point us towards ways in which the same kinds of dialogue can be identified in language – even the language of a catalogue. In some cases individuality separates out from the general fairly easily. 'Harry, a lot of women wear *bal à Versailles*!', says the seductive older woman under suspicion in *Twilight* (Paramount Pictures, 1998). 'Smells different on them', replies Paul Newman as the retired cop. In other cases it has to be searched for more assiduously; but it is never absent.

Another fable. Let us imagine Don Giovanni waking up in the early hours of the morning, realising that he is not alone, and asking 'Now, who on earth is this I am in bed with?' Let us then imagine the means he might use to solve this conundrum. One would be memory. Yes, there was a masked ball last night . . . a number of captivating creatures . . . too much wine . . . a fight as usual . . . an encounter in the street with a woman, also masked, who may or may not have been at the ball . . . following her home through the streets . . . a serenade outside her window . . . badinage . . . admission to the house . . . an erotic conjunction . . . and now steady breathing and the pressure of a warm body in the night. But from whom? The next step might be to try to place the partner within the classifications proposed by Leporello: Spanish, high social rank, of the city not the country, dark-eyed, on the plump side, shortish, early thirties. To which he might add other things: that she was left-handed; witty; laughed engagingly at unusual moments. But, if we have got the Don right, he would also want to ask another question: how is this woman different from every other possible woman in the world? Instinct would give him the answer long before he was able to work it out verbally. In the meantime he lies there in the night using touch and scent and the sound of breathing to give him clues. For if he does not discover it, this will be a lost, a meaningless experience. It will not do to wait until breakfast to explore the matter further, for by breakfast time they will have parted forever.

We must also consider the matter from the angle of his partner of the evening, Donna Olympia, a distant cousin of the high-minded Donna Anna whom the Don plans to visit later in the week. She would recognise his skill as a lover, as he had recognised hers. She will have noticed that he moved his body rather clumsily (the result of too many sword wounds and leaps from high windows). Her first and most powerful knowledge of him was through his voice in that serenade with the arresting rising fourth: an effortless light baritone with a hint of restrained power in the lower register. Is it as important to her as to him that he should be different from all her other lovers? Why should we think otherwise? Might she too lie awake asking the same questions of him as he is asking of her? Might she realise that she was lying beside the most interesting man she would probably ever meet: one who when, assailed by the hosts of Hell, to a background of sombre trombones and rising and falling harmonic minor scales on the violins, would refuse the offer of redemption transmitted by the stone agent of Heaven? If she did realise something of this before his hasty early-morning departure via the balcony, we would congratulate her. But it is possible that she had no wish even to enquire, or that her interest was in men in a general sense rather than the particular Giovanni.

Language is only one of a number of factors expressing individuality in this imagined encounter, possibly one of the less important. But it will serve to illustrate the will to individualise which stands opposed to the will to deindividualise which has stood at the centre of most literary thinking over the last forty years. There will always be scholars and thinkers for whom the genus is of greater interest than the particular case. For these attribution is probably not a subject of great interest.

MEASURING INDIVIDUAL DIFFERENCE

For the several reasons given I personally have no difficulty with the axiom presented by Joseph Rudman as the 'primary hypothesis' of attribution studies: 'that every author has a verifiably unique style'.[7] That, in his view, 'This hypothesis has never been tested, let alone proven' is a problem only in the 'verifiably' – the issue is not whether individual idiolects and grapholects are indeed different but how these differences are to be detected with a certainty that permits the confident ascription of works to authors. What follows in this book will be a history of the many attempts that have been made to arrive at this goal. They range from the traditional categories of internal and external evidence to current techniques based on Principal Component Analysis and neural networking. An attentive reader should be able to learn enough from the case studies considered, and from the sources to which reference is made, for it to be usable as a manual for the application of these methods. There will also be much cautionary advice against assuming too much from particular findings. But what I hope the book offers to attribution studies as a discipline, and where its contribution may be seen as constitutive and original, is in its raising of broader questions concerning the assessment of evidence and the ways in which data give rise to conclusions. It will therefore be concerned as much with the nature and logic of attributional reasoning as with the practical matter of determining authorship in particular cases. The reader is invited to watch attributionists at work and to assess the persuasiveness of their arguments. When I have had to criticise particular methods or scholars it has not been without respect for the courage with which they have addressed themselves to significant problems in a collective enterprise in which failure has often been as instructive as success.

CHAPTER TWO

Historical survey

This chapter does not offer a comprehensive history of scholarly attempts to establish attributions but simply seeks to identify a number of fields in which interesting problems of this kind have been recognised and addressed. Erudite disputes over the identity of the creators of texts are probably as old as writing, and may well predate it. Many ancient, orally transmitted works descended along with the names of their presumed originators, which must sometimes have been questioned, as happens to present-day 'Beecham' and 'Churchill' anecdotes when they are told (often with greater authority) about other conductors and politicians. Writing, and the storing of records together in archives, brought the need to identify the physical item by a title or label, which usually included the name of its presumed author.

The scholarly study of attributions made its appearance at a period when literacy had ceased to be the monopoly of small cadres of specialist scribes and reading was for the first time practised by a substantial public, ministered to by booksellers, stationers, scribal publishers, schoolmasters and grammarians. In the Western tradition such a public seems first to have consolidated itself in the fifth and fourth centuries BCE in Athens, contemporaneously with the intellectual ferment aroused by the teaching of the sophists. The study of attribution presupposes the existence of libraries in which texts may be checked against others of known date and authorship and the meaning of allusions ascertained. In the Greek world the most important collection was that of the museum and library of Alexandria, founded by Ptolemy I (reigned 323–283 BCE). Nourished by the aggressive collecting policies of the Ptolemies, this famous institution was the first in the history of Mediterranean civilisation where the historical development of literature, philosophy, science and language could be traced over centuries of development.[1] A famous succession of scholar librarians created traditions of literary research which included the systematic study of attribution. One important project was to distinguish the genuine works of Homer from other works that still at that time went under his name. In the *Poetics* Aristotle had set apart the *Iliad* and *Odyssey* from other epics of the Trojan War cycle on the grounds that they were 'as perfect as possible in structure'.[2] The Alexandrian editors Zenodotus and Aristarchus argued on this basis that only these two epics were actually composed by Homer, rejecting the contention of a school of even more radical separatists that they were the work of two different writers. Callimachus, a librarian at Alexandria as well as a great poet of the Hellenistic period, compiled catalogues of writings by eminent Greek authors arranged under genres. This involved him in many speculative attributions left to be argued over by his successors. The Roman writer Vitruvius tells of the librarian Aristophanes of Byzantium, who had such a tenacious memory that he was able to expose plagiarists in a poetry competition by going straight to the shelves and returning with the works from which they had borrowed.[3]

Great was the delight of the Alexandrians when they discovered that their rivals at the library of Pergamum had been duped into paying for an oration, fraudulently attributed to Demosthenes, which was already in their own collection under the name of the less distinguished Anaximenes of Lampsacus.[4] Anthony Grafton has illuminated the motives behind such forgeries, which, besides the legal and commercial, include the humiliation of supposed experts, the projecting of modern values onto an idealised past, and the validation of ancient traditions. An important special case of the last of these was the need of non-Greek peoples to defend their own inherited wisdom against that of the hegemonic culture.[5]

Our best evidence for the methods of attribution current in the ancient world comes from scholarly authors such as Plutarch (*c.*46–*c.*120 CE) and Athenaeus (*fl.* *c.*200 CE) in Greek and Aulus Gellius (died *c.*180 CE) in Latin, whose works reflect a culture of intellectual gladiatorialism in which meetings of the learned were enlivened by competitive displays of erudition. In the third book of his miscellany, *Attic Nights*, Gellius considers the case of the early Roman dramatist Plautus (*d.* 184 BCE) to whom, during nearly four centuries of transmission, some 130 plays had been attributed.[6] Various lists already existed which claimed to distinguish genuine works from spurious: these had been considered and rejected by an earlier authority, Marcus Terentius Varro (116–27 BCE), who identified twenty works as genuine on the grounds of unassailable ascriptions, and was prepared to admit others into the canon on stylistic grounds even when they circulated under the names of other authors.[7] Gellius chose to be guided by an intuitive recognition of 'the characteristic features of his manner and diction'. On reading *Boeotia*, which was accepted by Varro but had been declared spurious by Accius (170–*c.*86 BCE), he was personally convinced that it was a genuine work. The lines of one speech, which he quotes in full, were not simply Plautine but 'Plautinissimi'. And yet Gellius could see that there were problems in attributing an entire comedy on the strength of a few lines, for Plautus, as well as writing works entirely his own, had also worked as a play-doctor revising the scripts of other writers (a problem that bedevils dramatic attributions of all periods). So, while Gellius trusts mainly to his personal stylistic antennae in making attributions, he is also attentive to the judgements of earlier scholars, and acknowledges the special conditions of writing for the theatre. What he does not do is to test systematically for counter-attributions. Although he notes that *Boeotia* had been attributed to Aquilius, he makes no mention of having looked for other plays of that author (assuming they were still to be found). Nor does he invoke Plautine metrical practice, a matter that would be regarded as crucial by any present-day classicist. That he hardly considers dramatic method and structure would follow from the fact that virtually all Latin comedies of Plautus' time were adapted from Greek originals of the New Comedy, and showed originality only in their ingenious intermingling of these materials.

Attributions also exercised the compilers of the Jewish and Christian Bibles, most of whose individual books bear the name of a putative author. It was recognised early that the Pentateuch could not be more than partly the work of Moses, though it was customary to present this fact with some delicacy.[8] The canon of the Jewish Bible was only formalised after the destruction of the Temple in 70 CE, and therefore lacks certain books accepted into the Christian Old Testament, which drew on the more liberal Alexandrian Jewish canon preserved in the third century BCE Greek translation known as the Septuagint. However, these 'apocryphal' books were regarded by many Christians as of lesser authority. Saint Jerome, writing in 403 CE to guide the education of a Roman girl named Paula, cautioned: 'Let her avoid all the apocryphal books, and if she ever wishes to read them, not for the truth of their doctrines but out of respect for their wondrous tales, let her realize that they are not really written by those to whom they are ascribed.'[9] Although Jerome omitted the Apocrypha from his Latin Vulgate, their popularity led to them being restored in later recensions.

The New Testament also took a while to settle into its modern form, which was finally confirmed by the first Synod of Carthage in 393 CE, when a canon of twenty-seven books was declared. The Epistles, being a collection of short texts written from differing theological and ethnic standpoints, were particularly variable in regional traditions. Very early bibles frequently contain epistles of Barnabas and Clement. The Epistle of Paul to the Laodiceans, now regarded as spurious, hovered on the fringe of the canon until the fifteenth century.[10] Debate continues over how many of the canonically 'Pauline' epistles were really written or dictated by Paul. Authorship was not always the main consideration in determining admission to or exclusion from the canon: the basic discrimination was between books not writers, and rested on the sanctity and doctrinal tendency of those books. In some cases the book was in use prior to its being supplied with the name of an author, who was usually an apostle or someone who could have gained information from an apostle, as Luke did from Paul, and Mark, presumably, from Peter.[11] Yet it was not until towards the end of the second century that the gospel of John came to be accepted by most Christians as the work of the apostle of that name. It was evident in antiquity that the Greek of that work was very different from that of the Apocalypse, also claimed for John. Bernard McGinn points out that 'In its Jewish origins, the apocalyptic mode of revelation is always pseudonymous, that is, fictionally ascribed to a long-dead sage in order to provide it with enhanced authority.'[12] The disciple John was not long-dead in this sense but is unlikely to have been the actual author of either text, or of the three epistles that pass under his name. The ascription of the first gospel to the apostle Matthew was possible only on the assumption that it was the predecessor and source for Mark rather than, as is now generally agreed, its successor. When a gospel attributed to Peter that enjoyed popularity in the second century was found to be doctrinally unsound, the attribution also had to be withdrawn.[13]

The criteria applied by Jerome to questions of disputed authorship have been summarised by Foucault:

> How then can one attribute several discourses to one and the same author? How can one use the author-function to determine if one is dealing with one or several individuals? Saint Jerome proposes four criteria: (1) if among several books attributed to an author one is inferior to the others, it must be withdrawn from the list of the author's works (the author is therefore defined as a constant level of value); (2) the same should be done if certain texts contradict the doctrine expounded in the author's other works (the author is thus defined as a field of conceptual or theoretical coherence); (3) one must also exclude works that are written in a different style, containing words and expressions not ordinarily found in the writer's production (the author is here conceived as a stylistic

unity); (4) finally, passages quoting statements that were made, or mentioning events that occurred after the author's death must be regarded as interpolated texts (the author is here seen as a historical figure at the crossroads of a certain number of events).[14]

It should be noted that these criteria are not offered by Jerome himself, but generalised by Foucault from Jerome's discussions of particular problematic attributions. In some cases Jerome allows them to yield to other criteria.[15]

The catastrophic destruction of books and libraries following the collapse of Roman order removed the resources which had permitted systematic study of contested authorship. Mediaeval schoolmen still possessed deliberations over attributions by such venerated predecessors as Jerome and Augustine, but were more inclined to use these to investigate the philosophical nature of authorship than to reopen empirical questions.[16] While some of the ninth-century followers of Alcuin tried to revise the methods of ancient scholarship, their achievement was significant only by the depleted standards of their own time.[17] Robert Holcot in his fourteenth-century review of evidence for the authorship of the Book of Wisdom knew of Jerome's report that it was a compilation and translation by Philo Judaeus of originals by Solomon, and likewise that Augustine had at one stage attributed both Wisdom and Ecclesiasticus to Jesus, son of Sirach and then retracted this view, but lacked the resources to reopen the case for himself.[18] In any case, as with other mediaeval discussions of this attribution, the real issue was the theological one of how to distribute doctrinal authority in cases of collaborative authorship. The ultimate author of Wisdom was, naturally, God.

HUMANIST ATTRIBUTIONAL SCHOLARSHIP

While scholarship is sometimes able to question the authenticity of a work on technical evidence alone, the most fruitful perspective is always a comparative one. The conditions for comparative work were only restored when Renaissance Humanism began to reassemble the surviving ancient writings and the press to make them readily available in editions which also included variant readings, scholia and annotations. The replacing of ecclesiastical with classical Latin in the schools of the Renaissance produced a sharpened sense of the historical evolution of the language, which led in turn to the questioning of numerous long-standing attributions. Lorenzo Valla's *Declamatio de falsa et ementita donatione Constantini*

(1440) may surprise readers coming to it with the expectations aroused by dispassionate modern attributional scholarship. Its form is that of a classical Roman forensic oration, in which the accused (the forger and more generally the papacy) is lambasted at every turn. This is deliberate. Valla, while in later life himself a papal secretary, was at the period of writing in the service of Alphonso, King of Aragon and the Two Sicilies, who was engaged in a territorial dispute with Pope Eugenius IV. The earlier part is largely taken up with imaginary speeches in the manner of the Latin *suasoriae* and *controversiae*, which are designed to bring out the implausibility of Constantine having given his empire to Pope Sylvester. The next section attacks the Donation on various historical and legal grounds. Valla then turns to particular examples of anachronisms, inconsistencies and unclassical Latin. His conclusion is that the Donation was the work of 'some fool of a priest who, stuffed and pudgy, knew neither what to say nor how to say it, and, gorged with eating and heated with wine, belched out these wordy sentences which convey nothing to another, but turn against the author himself'.[19] This and a number of similar exposures of ancient fakes will be considered in Chapter ten.

One of the finest examples of the new scholarly sophistication is to be found in the introductions Erasmus wrote in 1516 to the second volume of his edition of the works of Jerome. It will be helpful to examine his arguments at some length both because they represent a marriage of the intuitive methods of Gellius with mature professional scholarship and because he boldly assumes that a sensitive reader can achieve a communion of subjectivities with a well-loved writer. Jerome was the most universally learned of the Church fathers and a brilliant stylist in the pagan rhetorical tradition. Erasmus, aspiring to the same ideals, applied the methods of Humanism to the work of a man who had himself been an important questioner of attributions. In his view certain works ascribed to Jerome had not been written by him at all while others that were his work had been misascribed to other writers. The function of the introduction was 'first to set forth the causes that give rise to such *spuria* and secondly to demonstrate the signs and inferential evidence by which false attribution may be detected'.[20]

The first stage of his demonstration is a survey of already accepted examples of false attribution. Among classical writers, works attributed to Homer, Aesop, Theocritus, Plato, Aristotle, Plutarch, Lucian, Phalaris, Plautus, Cicero, Virgil, Quintilian, Seneca and Boethius had all been declared spurious by reputable scholars of his own or earlier times. A discussion then follows of sacred writings, including some from the Bible itself, which could not be by their presumed authors (Jerome had himself supported some of these deattributions). Next comes a survey of some of the causes of error. A work might be attributed to someone else of the same name: in the case of the *Hierarchies* of the pseudo-Dionysius, three historical individuals seem to have been conflated. Note-takers might link together fragments from a number of writers without indicating that this had happened. Since Jerome wrote summaries of the books of the Bible, summaries by others might be attributed to him. Works of Anselm might be ascribed to Augustine (or vice versa) because their styles were similar. Authorship might be assigned on pure whim to some anonymous work. Declamations in which the speaker assumed the persona of an author might be mistaken for the real thing. Booksellers might add a famous name to increase their profit. Authors might appropriate a name to commend their own ideas or to spread 'doctrinal poison' (pp. 71–5).

As a result of these possibilities it was folly to trust to title-page ascriptions: 'the man who is satisfied with the name of the author on the title-page regardless of how it got there will read fourteen Gospels, I think, instead of four. Nothing is easier than to place any name you want on the front of a book' (p. 75). 'Wrongness of time' and 'inconsistency of doctrine' were indications of spuriousness, but the most significant was 'the character and the quality of speech' (p. 76). Jerome himself had made attributions purely on the basis of 'the flavour or, as he puts it, the taste of the language and the style' (p. 76). This was not to deny that the style of a writer might change during his lifetime or as he moved from subject to subject; but the basic singularity would remain, much as we recognise a well-known face although it is changed by strong emotion or the passage of time. If in doubt one should seek the advice of an expert on the writer concerned. Some writers could be identified through individual habits of language: so, Quintilian uses *interim* where most Latin writers would use *interdum*. Others were marked by the way they constructed their sentences or drew out their arguments. Augustine 'uses with some frequency the rhetorical figures that put words with similar endings or words with similar inflections in parallel positions' (p. 78). Style includes a great variety of separate attributes which Erasmus proceeds to detail: many are ethical qualities of the individual:

> The term style comprehends all at once a multiplicity of things – manner in language and diction, texture, so to speak, and, further, thought and judgment, line of argumentation, inventive power, control of material, emotion, and what the Greeks call ἦθος, – and within each one of these notions a profusion of shadings, no fewer, to be sure, than the differences in talent, which are as numerous as

men themselves. One may have greater charm, another more conscientiousness, still another more simplicity, another a more vivid personality, another more gentleness, another more intensity; one man may be marked by austerity, another by kindliness, one by loquacity, another by conciseness, one by learning, another by holiness, one by copiousness, another by force and vigour. Finally, to keep this within bounds, style is at once an imaging of the mind in its every facet. It is like physical propagation, where parental features appear in the offspring. (pp. 78–9)

Style then is very much *l'homme-même*:

As each individual has his own appearance, his own voice, his own character and disposition, so each has his own style of writing. And the quality of mind is manifest in speech even more than the likeness of the body is reflected in a mirror. (p. 76)

In Augustine, again, 'we find a certain flowery and picturesque quality, a Carthaginian quality, . . . a not unpleasant subtlety' (p. 90). Jerome's personal characteristics include 'an inborn vitality of mind which I may call preternatural, a marvellous fertility, an incomparable fervour, eloquence, sanctity, a knowledge of Sacred Scripture, a passionate application to study', all existing in 'a happy union' (p. 79).

In short, Jerome has a special quality about him, a kind of mental savour and temperament, a quality which may be felt rather than explained. After a detailed scrutiny of all the works which truly represent the godlike man, I have duly assigned them to his authorship, stripping from the others the false title. In these determinations I relied . . . on the intimacy which repeated readings of Jerome's works gained for me just as face-to-face association with him might have done. (For even in the past in my youth I found an uncommon delight in his writings . . .) (p. 80)

In further support of his deattributions Erasmus points out that Jerome repeatedly cites his own writings but never the works which were now deleted from the canon.

The basic appeal, then, is to the experienced reader's deep interiorisation of the style (in all its complexity) of a much-loved writer who is known as well as any other close friend is known. This involves what David Greetham characterises as 'a speculative, personal, and individual confrontation of one mind by another'.[21] However, an attribution so arrived at would always be vulnerable to a counter-attribution by another scholar who claimed the same privileged insight. Erasmus concedes as much in his rather uneasy alternation between abuse directed at potential critics and a stressing of his personal modesty and the tentativeness of his attributions.

The other striking aspect of Erasmus's introductions is his attribution of a number of the rejected works to an 'impostor' who used the name of Jerome to draw attention to his own worthless writings. The impostor is a poor Latinist and ignorant of theology. His writing manifests 'no weight of aphoristic expression, no refinement of language, no charm, no subtlety, no learning, in fine, no trace of a sound mind'. It also 'abounds with grammatical blunders and the most debased words and recent coinages'. Further investigation suggests he was a member of 'that breed of men who are popularly called Augustinians sometimes and sometimes Eremites' (pp. 84, 88). This is both a description by negatives of the style of the true Jerome and an exercise in attribution in its own right. The motivation of the forgeries was the desire to advance the standing of the Eremite order by making both Jerome and Augustine members of it before its creation. (Attributionists over the centuries have been rather given to conspiracy theories of this kind.) There seems to be no subsequent work on the identity of Erasmus's 'impostor' or whether the works he attributes to him are truly of the same authorship.

This example has been examined with particular care, as it represents both a summation of ancient practice and a distinctly modern attempt to ground attribution in an unmediated apprehension of interiority. The method of Erasmus recognises a distinction between internal and external evidence, but places its greatest reliance on the intuitive responses of an experienced scholar. Arthur Koestler offers an analogy:

> A locksmith who opens a complicated lock with a crude piece of bent wire is not guided by logic, but by the unconscious residue of countless past experiences with locks, which lend his touch a wisdom that his reason does not possess.[22]

Erasmus is able to identify the stylistic idiosyncrasies of the major Latin authors, but is otherwise prepared to rest at the level of impressionism. He has little conception of what might be learned from the systematic, quantitative analysis of language, though scholars of a slightly later generation did begin to publish very detailed examinations of style and idiom.[23]

HUMANIST BIBLICAL AND HOMERIC SCHOLARSHIP

Erasmus also contributed to a new questioning of the authorship of New Testament books and epistles which had begun in the fifteenth century when the Council of Florence (1439–43) finally rejected the Epistle to the Laodiceans. Cajetan (Thomas de Vio), who as a papal representative tried to make peace with Luther, had earlier questioned the apostolic authorship of five further epistles: Hebrews, James, Jude and John 2 and 3.[24] Jerome had already queried all these ascriptions, but in the case of Hebrews Cajetan went further, first rejecting Jerome's argument that the epistle might have originally been written in Hebrew and then advancing both textual and theological arguments to show that it could not be by Paul.[25] In the prefaces to his edition of the Greek Testament, published in 1516, Erasmus, accepting these deattributions, queried the authorship of 2 Peter. He also insisted that the Apocalypse could not be by the same author as the Gospel of John.[26] Unlike Cajetan, who argued that if Hebrews was not by Paul it could not be accepted as a guide to faith, Erasmus accepted the sanctity of the text as existing independently of the attribution. The early Protestants continued the work of deattribution: Luther's German translation of the Bible, published in 1522, questioned both the authenticity and the doctrinal value of Hebrews, James, Jude and the Apocalypse. However, Protestantism, in basing its faith upon the Bible rather than on the authority of the Church, left itself open to scholarly attack from both Catholics and freethinkers.

The most famous of these attacks was that of Spinoza, who, in Chapters eight to ten of the *Tractatus Theologico-politicius* (1670), argued on the basis of a close philological examination of the Old Testament and a more cursory one of the New that the Biblical text was 'faulty, mutilated, adulterated and inconsistent, that we possess it only in fragmentary form, and that the original of God's covenant with the Jews has perished'.[27] His position was a disintegrationist one, argued from the incompleteness and incoherence he detected in the existing books and their incorporation of materials from lost sources and other books; however, he became an integrationist in arguing that Genesis through to 2 Kings was the work of a single compiler, whom, following Jewish tradition, he identified as Ezra, and attributing Daniel, Ezra, Esther and Nehemiah to another compiler.[28] His views found a necessarily cautious echo in the Catholic, Richard Simon's *Histoire critique du vieux testament* (1678), which, while suppressed at one period in France, appeared in English translation as early as 1682 with a commendatory poem by Dryden.

The importance of Simon's work lies not so much in his questioning of attributions, which were of little concern to him, as in his insistence on the collaborative nature of the process by which the sacred writings had been compiled. He accepted Spinoza's view that the Old Testament as we have it was the product of a process of reconstitutive editing, supervised by Ezra, which took place after the disruption of the Exile had led to the loss of many foundational documents; but he also regarded the original composition of the earlier books as, in many cases, having been performed not by their reputed authors but by a class of 'écrivains publiques', drawing on carefully preserved national chronicles.[29] Simon did not see this as detracting from the inspired status of the work, regarding not only the original authors but 'les Auteurs de ces Reformations' as inspired by God.[30] In this way he opposed Spinoza's claim that what was merely of human authority in the Bible possessed only a contingent and temporary sanctity.[31] His view was one of texts that grew and matured through history within a sanctifying social framework. Simon expressed interest in the view of the Jewish scholar Isaac Abravanel that Samuel had compiled Joshua and Judges and that Jeremiah had written Samuel and Kings – this being simply an extension of the theory of 'public writers'.

Simon's work, and that of freethinkers such as John Toland who drew on his findings, pointed towards what are still active traditions of Biblical scholarship known as Source Criticism, Historical Criticism and Redaction Criticism. Source criticism concerns itself with the preceding documents drawn on for particular Biblical books as we now have them. It was apparent from an early date that Genesis incorporated two separate accounts of the Creation and the Flood and used two different names for God in different passages. Isaiah is another book recognised as a compilation from elements of different periods. Hypothesised sources for the New Testament Gospels include, firstly, each other (with Matthew and Luke drawing on Mark and a lost source 'Q'); secondly, individual shorter narratives and collections of sayings ('pericopai'); and thirdly such non-narrative documents as Testimony Books listing the Old Testament predictions of the life of Christ. The search for traces of these tributary genres is called Form Criticism. Historical criticism is concerned with the milieu in which a work was assembled and quickly leads to a concern with the particular crisis in the life of nation or church to which it was addressed; so, Mark is seen by some as directed to Roman Christians suffering under the Neronian persecutions. Redaction criticism looks for evidence of the editing process by which material from earlier stages of transmission was reordered, expanded and explicated to make it accessible to new generations of readers. Some books are believed to have passed through more than one process of redaction, each characterised by a different point of view and polemic aim. The effect of such analyses has been in many cases to replace personal authorship with a much more complex process of progressive compilation.

These approaches are also applicable to secular texts. Among more recent works whose original form can be traced through the reworkings of a redactor are the many stage revisions of Shakespeare's plays. This process, which had begun within his own lifetime, soon led to such radical reworkings as the Dryden and Davenant *Tempest* (1667) and Nahum Tate's version of *King Lear* (1681) with its abandonment of the original tragic conclusion. The process continues every time a director constructs a new acting script. In the case of Shakespeare and Fletcher's *Cardenio*, which survives only in an eighteenth-century rewriting by Lewis Theobald as *Double Falsehood, or the Distrest Lovers*, the original no longer exists for our comparison; in other cases, fortunately, it does, allowing us to observe every move made by the redactors and revisers. By the time Marlowe's *Dr Faustus*, first performed around 1594, finally appeared in print in the quarto of 1604, it had already suffered some degree of revision. A second version published in 1616 is even more heavily transformed. Further changes can be followed step by step through William Mountfort's heavily cut-down reworking of 1686 to nineteenth-century pantomime versions. In dramatic traditions closer to the present day, documentation often survives of a collaborative process by which performers, assistants, dramaturges and editors modify and extend the authorial text.[32]

The Enlightenment questioning of the idea of a unitary historical author with total responsibility for the inherited text was also undertaken with many classical and mediaeval works. The most famous of these demonstrations was Heinrich Wolf's *Prolegomena ad Homerum* (1795). Convinced that the Homeric text was composed before the invention of writing, Wolf argued that the poems as we have them must be regarded as an assemblage of songs or short sagas that had originally existed separately. Wolf thought these materials had been brought together in the sixth century BCE under the supervision of Peisistratus. A more developed form of the same argument put forward by the great textual critic Karl Lachmann in 1837 and 1841 broke up the *Iliad* into sixteen constituent pre-texts, together with bridging passages and smaller interpolations. Opponents of this view follow Aristotle in pointing to the thematic coherence of the poem and the subtlety of its organisation, which they deny could have arisen from a process of patching and joining. So E. V. Rieu in the introduction to his widely read prose translation of the *Iliad*, first published in 1950:

> It will astonish people who know nothing of the 'Homeric question' to learn that these splendidly constructed poems, and especially the *Iliad*, have in the past been picked to pieces by the men who studied them most carefully and should presumably have admired them most. They alleged certain incongruities in the

> narrative and argued that the *Iliad* is the composite product of a number of poets of varying merit, who had not even the doubtful advantage of sitting in committee, but lived at different times and each patched up his predecessor's work, dropping many stitches in the course of this sartorial process.[33]

For Rieu (a 'Unitarian' responding to 'Analysts') the strongest argument for a single author is the epic's 'consistency in character-drawing'. The process of reasoning is essentially that used in the 'argument from design' for the existence of God and has the same weakness. The key issue is whether a coherent, elaborately integrated work of art could have arisen from a prolonged process of collective composition. The existence of mediaeval cathedrals suggests that the hypothesis is not an inane one. Modern understandings of Homer, following the path marked out by Milman Parry, draw on extensive research into those traditions of oral epic which survived into the modern period, especially in the Balkans and Africa.[34] This offers a picture of works being reimprovised around inherited, mnemonic patterns by drawing on an extensive repertoire of stock phrases, lines and passages. By this account 'Homer' was simply the improviser whose version of 'the wrath of Achilles' was for some unknown reason selected for preservation, first by rhapsodes and then in writing. So far so good; but when the same reasoning is applied, as by John Michell, to Shakespeare, making him no more than a sewer-together of others' fragments, the result (properly in my view) is outrage.[35] The Homeric question must still be regarded as unsettled.

There was also much debate over whether the *Odyssey* was the work of the same poet as the *Iliad*. Richard Bentley believed that a single poet had written the *Iliad* for male listeners and the *Odyssey* for women. Samuel Butler in the nineteenth century was convinced that the *Odyssey* had actually been written by a woman.[36] The present-day consensus is that the two works reflect the social practices of two distinct historical periods.

THE ATTRIBUTION OF ENGLISH TEXTS

Scholarly investigation of the authorship of texts written in Britain had its origins in the work of post-Reformation clerics on the ancient traditions of the English church and seventeenth-century lawyers on the origins of the English common law and representative government (a somewhat myth-laden quest which sought for origins as far back as the ancient Britons). Both of these enquiries were highly politicised and their disputes often fought out with intemperate bitterness.[37] An early achievement of British historical scholarship was the exposure of the fraudulent nature of the mythical history of pre- and post-Roman Britain narrated by Geoffrey of Monmouth and still widely accepted by readers of Shakespeare's time (the legend of King Lear was a part of this history). However, at the same time as accurate ascriptions and datings for mediaeval chronicles were slowly being established, the new writing of the scholars' own days was laying up problems for future enquirers. For a variety of reasons, only one of which was political censorship, many seventeenth-century writers of verse and polemic and historical prose preferred to distribute it by manuscript circulation rather than through the press.[38] Very little of Donne's or Marvell's verse, for instance, appeared in printed form during their lifetimes. Much of this scribally published work bore no author's name to begin with, and names supplied during transmission were not necessarily the correct ones. Guessing at authorship became a social game, as in 'Timon' (1674):

> He takes me in his Coach, and as wee goe
> Pulls out a Libell, of a Sheete or Two;
> Insipid as the Praise, of Pious Queenes,
> Or Shadwells, unassisted former Scenes;
> Which he admir'd, and prais'd at evr'y Line,
> At last, it was soe sharpe, it must be mine.
> I vow'd, I was noe more a Witt than he,
> Unpractic'd, and unblest in Poetry:
> A Song to Phillis, I perhaps might make,
> But never Rhym'd but for my Pintles sake;
> I envy'd noe Mans Fortune, nor his Fame,
> Nor ever thought of a Revenge soe tame.
> He knew my Stile (he swore) and twas in vaine
> Thus to deny, the Issue of my Braine.
> Choakt with his flatt'ry I noe answer make,
> But silent leave him to his deare mistake.
>
> (ll. 13–28)[39]

Aphra Behn has a poem 'To *Damon*. To inquire of him if he cou'd tell me by the Style, who writ me a Copy of Verses that came to me in an unknown Hand.'[40] When such works were eventually transferred to print (sometimes years or decades after their original composition) they often did so under incorrectly ascribed names, or were supplied by the bookseller with any name that was considered good for sales. This has given rise to problems of attribution which are still far from resolved and in some cases may never be.

Printed works might also be issued anonymously or pseudonymously. Anthony Wood in his *Athenae Oxonienses: An Exact History of all the Writers and Bishops who have had their Education in the Famous University of Oxford* (London, 1691–2), having set himself the task of listing the complete productions of several hundred learned writers, had to deal summarily with many cases of uncertain authorship. His younger contemporary, Pierre Bayle, was at the same time performing a similar task for European *eruditi* in his great *Dictionnaire historique et critique* (1697–1702). The luxury not available to Wood of extensive (some would say incontinent) footnoting allowed Bayle to follow up a number of these cases in great detail. A more specialised production of the same period was Gerard Langbaine's *An Account of the English Dramatic Poets* (1691), which had originally appeared in 1687 as *Momus triumphans, or, the plagiaries of the English stage: expos'd in a catalogue of all the comedies, tragi-comedies, masques, tragedies, opera's, pastorals, interludes, &c. both ancient and modern, that were ever yet printed in English: the names of their known and supposed authors, their several volumes and editions: with an account of the various originals, as well English, French, and Italian, as Greek and Latine, from whence most of them have stole their plots.* Langbaine's demonstration of the sources from which dramatists of his own time had drawn their materials, and sometimes whole plays, was an early example of the study of influences, but one which also reflected a growing cultural disapproval of plagiarism that was to have important implications for the future of both authorship and attribution.[41] Each of the three writers mentioned had discovered a reason for a new exactitude in attribution. In Wood's case it was the honour of his university and in Bayle's, very often, a need to establish responsibility for doctrinal points raised in Protestant–Catholic polemic, though he is also concerned to act the part of a moderator in scholarly disputes of every kind. Langbaine's motive is less clear; but since he was a lawyer it may well have been an inchoate sense that these texts were a form of property that might someday become a concern to his profession. He certainly reflects a growing demand that authors should be original rather than simply giving a new cast to materials handed down by their predecessors.[42] There was a precedent for his scarifying of theatrical plagiarists in such lost ancient texts as Latinus' *On the Books of Menander That Were Not By Him* and Philostratus' *On the Thefts of the Poet Sophocles*.[43]

Langbaine's work represents a coming into print of what must have been a common subject of discussion in the literary coffee-houses of the time, which were also centres for the circulation of pamphlets and manuscripts. Elkanah Settle's attempt to unravel the authorship of *Notes and Observations on the Empress of Morocco*, an attack on his tragedy of 1673, employs a colloquial, *ad hominem* manner reflecting a kind of coffee-house punditry in which point-scoring is more important than the facts of the matter.[44] The late eighteenth-century controversies over the authenticity of the Ossianic and Rowley poems represent a meeting of this agonistic oral tradition with a more judicial, scholarly one in which authors strove at least for the appearance of impartiality.

One of the longest running and most bitterly fought debates over the authorship of an English text was that concerning *Eikon basilicon*, a collection of prayers and religious meditations attributed to Charles I, which was deeply revered by Civil War Royalists and their Tory successors. Questions about the authorship of the work were originally raised when Milton pointed out that a prayer added in the second edition had been plagiarised from a secular work, Sidney's *Arcadia*. Hard on the heels of this came evidence that the work may actually have been composed by one of the king's chaplains, John Gauden. Since an ingenious Tory counterthrust held that Milton had himself inserted the plagiarised prayer, the debate developed two strands, one concerned with the probity of Milton and the other with that of Charles. One of Milton's defenders, John Toland (1670–1722), also raised questions concerning the authorship of the gospels.[45] For Toland and those who opposed him the questioning of Charles's authorship was also a questioning of powerful political and religious interests.

Throughout the early modern period the law had interested itself in questions of attribution as they affected documents regarded as libellous and treasonable. In libel cases some show of evidence was usually required, but where treason was suspected the unsupported testimony of two witnesses or even one would be sufficient. In the case of seditious writings circulating in manuscript, mere possession of such a work, if the accused was not prepared to reveal the source, was enough to constitute constructive authorship. Blasphemy and pornography were originally dealt with by the clerical courts, before moving into the secular jurisdiction during the seventeenth century. Pornography was not the major department of the book trade it has since become: English readers of the Renaissance and early Enlightenment were satisfied with a small body of texts surreptitiously reprinted.[46] Prosecutions for blasphemy were brought against a number of works of an anti-Christian tendency, but providing those who held such positions were urbane enough to insinuate their views rather than proclaiming them directly they were not much troubled. Genuine persecution of the kind that gave rise to the surreptitious printing of pseudonyma and anonyma was reserved for outspoken Non-conformist and Catholic books.

From 1694, when the legislation enforcing pre-publication censorship in England lapsed for the last time, there was an outpouring of printed poems and pamphlets in a quantity which had not been known since the similarly uncontrolled Civil War years. Defoe, Swift, Pope and Fielding were all masters of writing under assumed polemic identities, the first two publishing relatively little under their own names. Addison and Steele presented the most famous series of periodical essays as the work of an eponymous 'Mr Spectator', thus encouraging the establishment of the convention under which all contributors to a periodical or newspaper concealed their own personalities under that of a collective 'I' or 'we'. One famous instance of pseudonymous journalism was the series of vituperative letters signed 'Junius' which appeared in the *Public Advertiser* between 1769 and 1772 in defence of the Whig position. Curiosity about Junius's carefully concealed identity spawned a long series of studies in support of various candidates.[47] But this is no more than a single snowflake on the tip of an iceberg. Of all the tasks facing attribution studies, that of uncredited journalism and pamphleteering from the eighteenth to the mid-twentieth century is the most daunting.

Even as late as 1800 attributional work on English texts still had a residue of the amateurish and the gladiatorial; yet, by the mid-nineteenth century, the major problems in the attribution of plays from the Elizabethan, Jacobean and Caroline stage had at least been identified, if not always solved, and the Shakespearean canon had assumed its modern shape. Later nineteenth-century attributional scholarship was able to draw on a greatly enlarged body of source materials, the product of devoted archival work which bore fruit in the *Historical Records Commission* reports, the *Calendars of State Papers*, the *Oxford English Dictionary*, the *Dictionary of National Biography*, the publications of numerous record and reprint societies, the British Museum Library's catalogues of printed books and manuscripts, and, of greatest significance for the present study, Samuel Halkett and John Laing's *A Dictionary of the Anonymous and Pseudonymous Literature of Great Britain* (Edinburgh, 1882–3), which in its current form as the *Dictionary of Anonymous and Pseudonymous English Literature*, together with the contributions of two further generations of editors, fills a hefty nine volumes. Halkett and Laing is a dictionary of titles. The reader encountering an anonymous work consults it to see whether there is a recorded attribution. In the two most recent volumes, edited by Dennis Rhodes and Anna Simoni, an authority is always given for an attribution, although in most cases it is simply a library catalogue (chiefly the British Library and the Library of Congress). The only attempt made to generalise about the materials collected are observations on the ways by which authors devised pseudonyms (often using ingenious transformation of their own names) and some common-sensical remarks on the reasons why authors should omit their names from their books:

> Anonymous and pseudonymous books and pamphlets may be grouped, in the first place, according to the motive which led to the suppression of the author's name. Generally the motive is some form of timidity, such as (a) diffidence, (b) fear of consequences, and (c) shame.[48]

To which we should add shameless dishonesty and the desire to present the reader with an amusing puzzle. As the product of industrious data-collection, Halkett and Laing is true to its nineteenth-century origins, and therefore provides a suitable termination for this preliminary survey. Some of the more interesting cases from among those discussed will be revisited in subsequent chapters.

CHAPTER THREE

Defining authorship

'Authors', Mark Rose proposes, 'do not really create in any literal sense, but rather produce texts through complex processes of adaptation and transformation.'[1] The study of the practice of such transformations is different from the study of 'authorship' as 'a free creative source of the meaning of a book', which, Diane Macdonnell avers, 'is not a concept that exists within discourses that have developed recently'.[2] James Clifford reports that 'The general tendency in modern textual studies has been to reduce the occasion of a text's creation by an individual subject to merely one of its generative or potentially meaningful contexts.'[3] Yet Edward Said, for one, demurs from this orthodoxy:

> Textuality is considered to take place, yes, but by the same token it does not take place anywhere or anytime in particular. It is produced, but by no one and at no time. It can be read and interpreted, although reading and interpreting are routinely understood to occur in the form of misreading and misinterpreting . . . . As it is practiced in the American academy today, literary theory has for the most part isolated textuality from the circumstances, the events, the physical senses that made it possible and render it intelligible as the result of human work.[4]

To identify authorship as a form of human work is to validate individual agency. Said also tells us that 'literature is produced in time and in society by human beings, who are themselves agents of, as well as somewhat independent actors within, their actual history'.[5] In cases where such a thing is possible, attribution studies attempts to distinguish the traces of agency that cohere in pieces of writing, sometimes discovering one singular trace, but often a subtle entanglement of several or many. (This play was a collaboration between Fletcher and Massinger with later revisions by Shirley and minor alterations by a scribe and two compositors.) Where that is not possible, its aim becomes one of contextualisation – locating the text within time, place, a culture, a genre, an institution, as precisely as the evidence permits. (This treatise is by an Augustinian disciple or disciples of Hugh of St Victor, writing in Paris in the mid-twelfth century.) In all cases it requires a model of authorship, not as a single essence or non-essence but as a repertoire of practices, techniques and functions – forms of work – whose nature has varied considerably across the centuries and which may well in any given case have been performed by separate individuals. This chapter will try to give some sense of the richness of that repertoire.

COLLABORATIVE AUTHORSHIP

Much consideration of authorial work still takes as its model the single author creating a text in solitariness – Proust's cork-lined room, Dickens's prefabricated Swiss chalet, Mary Ward's elegant study at 'Stocks'. In doing so it restricts itself not just to a particular kind of authorship but to a particular phase of that kind of authorship. It omits, for a start, all that precedes the act of writing (language acquisition, education, experiences, conversation, reading of other authors); likewise everything that follows the phase of initial inscription while the work is vetted by friends and advisers, receives second thoughts and improvements, is edited for the press, if that is its destination, and given the material form in which it will encounter its readers. Moreover, the 'solitary author' model is often not an accurate description even of what we will shortly describe as the 'executive' phase of authorship. Consider this description of the creation of a late seventeenth-century translation of Terence:

> But to come now to what we have done; 'tis not to be expected we shou'd wholly reach the Air of the Original; that being so peculiar, and the Language so different; We have imitated our Author as well and as nigh as the *English* Tongue and our small Abilities wou'd permit; each of us joyning and consulting about every Line, not only for the doing of it better, but also for the making of it all of a piece.[6]

The collaborative process here described was also that used by the committees of clerics which produced the Authorised Version of the Bible and would be recognised today by many writers for film and TV. If we happened to know who the 'we' who translated Terence were, which we more or less do, but were to proceed on the supposition that they had worked in isolation on individual scenes instead of 'consulting about every Line', we would emerge with a completely fallacious picture of the distribution of work.

Collaborative authorship is both widespread and highly variable in its workings. Writers from the ancient world were prone to claim all authorship as collaborative, in the sense that the speaker or writer was the channel for meanings conveyed from a higher being or from forerunners. At the beginnings of the *Iliad* and the *Odyssey* the poet addresses a question to the muse: the rest of the poem is, formally speaking, the muse's reply to that question. The Old Testament prophets insisted that they were inspired by God: they did not claim to speak with their own voices; or if they did it was to deliver a message that God had given them through dreams or by the mediation of an angel. That they might also insist on their own individuality and historicity as prophets (as Jeremiah does in Chapter one) does not detract from their insistence on the derived nature of their message.

An author's choice of a particular technology of writing and reproduction will often involve a surrender of control over some aspects of the finished text. We do not know how Jeremiah composed; but the model of an author inscribing words on a surface with stylus or pen is quite a late one: virtually all illustrations of writers from Graeco-Roman civilisation show them dictating rather than inscribing. (The famous exception is the 'Sappho' from Pompeii, with her stylus to her lips and a *tetraptychon* in her left hand.) The fourth-century Latin poet Ausonius, in a poem recounting the events of a typical day, records a session of composition in which his words were taken down by a shorthand writer who would often anticipate what he was about to say.[7] In the case of the third-century Biblical interpreter, Origen, we have a contemporary account of the elaborate means used to perform the act of authorship through dictation. His staff, provided by a wealthy patron, consisted of 'more than seven' shorthand writers who relieved each other regularly, 'as many copyists', and female calligraphers. As Harry Gamble describes the process:

> His oral composition was transcribed by trained stenographers; their shorthand transcripts were then converted into full-text exemplars by copyists who could decipher stenographic notes; and from these examplars female scribes produced fair copies in a good bookhand. Origen himself would have revised the exemplars before the copies were made.[8]

The stenographers, using a system far less efficient than Pitman's, are unlikely to have produced a verbally accurate version of Origen's declamation: it would be the task of the intermediate copyists to convert their notes into eloquent Greek prose. Origen's review of the resultant text would no doubt have been careful; but for him to have exercised the minuteness of a present-day author correcting proof would have defeated the whole purpose of the system as it is described. The same uncertainty over verbal detail attends the homilies of Chrysostom and other early fathers, which were memorially reconstructed by believers from addresses delivered during worship, and the long history, commencing with Aristotle and represented in the last century by posthumously published works by Saussure and Wittgenstein, of treatises compiled from students' lecture notes.[9]

In Origen's case we would still concede him the function of author while accepting that some of the expression was probably that of the note-takers who recorded (or misrecorded) what was said and then put it into acceptable form for readers. A mediaeval example is more challenging. Laurence of Durham, in the prefatory letter to his treatise *De tabernaculo et de divisione testamentorum*, tells of being assigned to record the words of the famous theologian Hugh of St Victor (1097–1141). As a member of Hugh's divinity class, Laurence was asked by the other students to 'entrust the same sentences to writing and memory' for their benefit. After he had twice refused Hugh then 'enjoined on us this task of writing and announced his confidence that I would carry it out with great alacrity'. Still diffident, Laurence submitted his tablets once a week to Hugh so that 'by his endeavour anything superfluous could be cut out, anything left out be added, anything put down badly be changed, and if by chance something had been said well, it be approved by the authority of such a great man'. And yet Laurence was still conscious of his own contribution, specifying:

> For I profess to be not the author [*auctor*] of this work, but in a way its maker [*artifex*]. For someone else has thrown certain seeds of sentences; we have put together what has been thrown by another into one body of speech by a kind of labour.[10]

Here we have a division of work between two individuals both of whom could claim a share of authorship in its modern sense. Laurence's 'we have put together' (*nos . . . coniecimus* in the original) suggests that his fellow students contributed to the formation of the verbal text.

It is also common for one person to lay out ideas in writing for a second person to turn into fluent and finished words. Roger North in his memoranda on the life of his brother, Francis, notes that at the height of the Popish Plot agitation of the late 1670s, in order to 'quallifie this distemper of the publik . . . his Lordship applyed himself to prepare instructions for some expert pamfletier, who had a popular style, and address, to treat upon the subject of Oatses plott'. North did this 'after his way of extempory wrighting, which was familiar, and just as he used to speak'. His detailed plan outlined the argument in some detail but 'he stopt at the facts, which were left to the wrighter to deduce as he saw occasion'.[11] North would have been aware of a precedent for this kind of activity in the instructions a solicitor might give to a barrister, but there is no reason to believe that this was solely a legal practice. It was recorded of Sir Robert Walpole's great foe, William Pulteney, that he wrote two of the pieces ascribed to him but that in others he 'assisted only' or merely 'furnished hints'.[12]

Let us look at a more detailed case of how the processes of authorship may be distinguished and distributed in the modern world. The *Boston Globe* of 8 July 1999 contained a report of the decision by Christopher F. Edley junior, a Harvard professor, to resign from his White House position as the official ghostwriter of a book by President Clinton on race relations.[13] The article tells us that

> The book, which Clinton considers a potential cornerstone of his legacy on race relations, had been scheduled for publication in April. But the project has stalled amid internal wrangling among White House aides over issues as politically incendiary as the prospects for affirmative action in the 21st century and as nettlesome as which passages of poetry should be used to underscore the president's positions.

The situation described is one in which the book had been drafted by Edley, in collaboration with a former White House speechwriter named J. Terry Edmonds. It had then gone to the aides for further revision. Clinton explained at a press conference that 'Chris gave me his draft, then the staff looked at it and talked about where it was or wasn't consistent with present policies we are pursuing.' The only thing he had not been able to do was to read it himself: he had been too busy with the Kosovo crisis. This is probably the condition of most authorship by modern, and no doubt many ancient, heads of state. Even Julius Caesar, who was no bad hand at Latin prose, delegated the accounts of his three last campaigns to assistants.

This description is helpful in identifying some of the separate functions involved in collaborative authorship. The source of the ideas is not specified: no doubt Clinton contributed thoughts of his own and there would be a ready supply of White House and Democratic Party position papers. Edley and Edmonds performed a role which was partly that of *auctor* and partly that of *artifex*. Next came an intense process of revision by the collective body of staffers. Clinton's main role in the process of authorship seems to have been that of a validator of the ideas presented, bestowing his name so that the work might perform its political function more effectively. There is a parallel in multi-authored scientific papers to which a senior scientist lends his name in order to secure publication in a prestigious journal. In both cases the role of the named author/co-author is a kind of fostering of a work.

Collaborative authorship is so common, and so often disguised, as to constitute a central concern of attribution studies. Notably, much scholarly work on plays of the age of Shakespeare is concerned not with finding a single author but with teasing out the contributions of two or more working either as collaborators or as original author and reviser. Samuel Schoenbaum notes four different arrangements such a collaboration might take:

> (1) allocation of scenes may be entirely mechanical, e.g., when there are five dramatists, each takes one act; (2) one author may supply the plot, the other(s) being responsible for the execution; (3) one writer may take the main action, another the underplot; (4) or the division may be worked out with reference to the character of the material, one playwright undertaking farcical scenes while another assumes responsibility for tragic or satiric episodes.[14]

To which he might have added (5) 'any other arrangement, imaginable or unimaginable'. (Fritz Kreisler recalled being left by his teacher, Delibes, to continue composing for him when Delibes was off visiting his mistress.[15]) The record for numbers is a lampoon collaboratively written by 'about twenty labouring people from Southwark'.[16]

Yet even when all phases and functions of composition are performed by a single author, we need to recognise that most novels are much more like films than we are prepared to acknowledge in deserving a long roll-out of credits at the end. Occasionally this almost happens. One example is the section headed 'Acknowledgements: research' at the end of Lindsey Davis's *A Dying Light in Corduba*, which includes the confession 'Neither the books I have plundered nor the archaeology I have cribbed will ever be listed as formal sources, because the Falco series is fiction, and meant purely to entertain.'[17] The debts that are acknowledged are chiefly to friends who gave her information on a personal basis, as must happen to all writers of fiction. Neither does she specify any changes made by publishers' editors, apart from a single deletion, because it is a convention that their work should remain anonymous. Clearly if it was the convention for writers of historical novels to detail all their sources and assistants in the way that is compulsory for academic writers, they would also have to supply acknowledgements, a bibliography, and extensive footnotes. In this respect academic authorship, with its often neurotically punctilious instancing of debts to others, is the one kind that betrays the condition of nearly all authorship.

In some cases the aid sought by an author is of a specific kind that does not impinge on other aspects of the writing. Consider Yeats, who derived materials for his late poems from his wife Georgie's spirit writing, and at the other end of the process preferred to delegate the punctuating of his texts to more confident hands. At a later stage still, but one that still affects meaning, decisions were made about how poems should be arranged within particular books and then within the larger unity of the collected works. Warwick Gould has traced how intricate these negotiations were and the multiplicity of agencies that were involved in them.[18] It is a process that continues in the present-day editing of Yeats, which in terms of our work-oriented model has to be regarded as a continuation under delegation of the process of Yeatsian authorship. An attributionist who, unaware of these processes, was to test for Yeats's presence through analysis of punctuation would not get very far. Testing for the recurrence of certain kinds of 'spirit images' would not be misleading in the same way, since other poets did not have access to them, but would not acknowledge their actual origin.

There is another kind of composition for which the process of authorship is never a complete one but passed on from agent to agent, all of whom will subject it to their own forms of alteration. In the modern world this characterises much oral transmission of jokes and urban myths; also written texts passed around on the Internet. We are so familiar with this kind of transmission as an oral phenomenon that we often overlook how frequently written texts enter and exit the oral repertoire. (Our own oral retellings of stories we have read in magazines would be one example.) A mediaeval form of this practice is described by Derek Pearsall, writing of the professional performers of romances, whom he calls '*disours*':

> Whoever composed these poems, whether booksellers' hacks, clerics, or genuine *disours*, they were evidently written for performance, and became to that extent the property of the *disours*. It is their memories of a written text, modified in performance-from-memory (it was no extraordinary feat for many thousands of lines to be recited in such a way), that would provide, directly or indirectly, the basis for the extant written copies. These processes of 'recomposition' do

> not produce garbled texts, or texts necessarily inferior to the original, since the capacities and ambitions of the re-composer are little if at all different from those of the original composer. There is no ideal text from which succeeding copies degenerate by a process of scribal corruption and decomposition: rather the text exists in an open and fluid state, the successive acts of writing down being no more than arbitrary stages in the continuously evolving life of the poem.[19]

The pattern is one of movement from the written to the oral then, eventually, back to the written. Pearsall adds that it tends to be the exciting bits which are the most revised. In transmission of this kind the roles of *auctor* and *artifex* inevitably blur.

FUNCTIONS OF AUTHORSHIP

Examples such as those just given complicate the notion of authorship to a degree that it becomes more helpful to define it in relation to a series of functions performed during the creation of the work rather than as a single, coherent activity. The term 'authorship', as used in this chapter, will not therefore denote the condition of being an originator of works, but a set of linked activities (*authemes*) which are sometimes performed by a single person but will often be performed collaboratively or by several persons in succession. Our model for determining these will be the actual work of authors of various historical periods, which brings the consequence that it will be a variable model requiring to be reformulated for different writing cultures.

There have been many attempts to distinguish the activities involved in authorship. An influential early one was Quintilian's breaking down of the tasks of an orator into *inventio*, *dispositio*, *elocutio*, *memoria* and *pronuntiatio*.[20] In still earlier times there were Athenians who would provide a citizen with a written speech that could be memorised and delivered in the Agora as his own. This meant that the first contributor would do the *inventio*, *dispositio*, and *elocutio* and a second the *memoria* and *pronuntiatio*, which, in the specialised field of oratory, were by no means the easiest bits. But even when Demosthenes, say, performed all these five stages himself, the distinction between them would still exist, along with subsidiary ones such as that by which the oration was built from structural modules, each following its own rules and precedents (Quintilian isolates some of these). In his prefatory letter to *Annus Mirabilis* (1667) Dryden testifies to the persistence of these categories:

> So then, the first happiness of the Poet's imagination is properly Invention, or finding of the thought; the second is Fancy, or the variation, deriving or moulding of that thought, as the judgment represents it proper to the subject; the third is Elocution, or the Art of clothing and adorning that thought so found and varied, in apt, significant and sounding words: the quickness of the Imagination is seen in the Invention, the fertility in the Fancy, and the accuracy in the Expression.[21]

This is still very general, and as expressed here applies only to style, but it points the way towards finer distinctions.

PRECURSORY AUTHORSHIP

For those cases in which a significant contribution from an earlier writer is incorporated into the new work we will employ the term precursory authorship. A precursory author would be anyone whose function as a 'source' or 'influence' makes a substantial contribution to the shape and substance of the work, as Holinshed's *Chronicle* does in most of Shakespeare's history plays and North's *Plutarch* in the Roman plays. Georgie Yeats is in this sense a precursory author of Yeats's later verse; however, Hugh of St Victor's contribution to the tract composed by Laurence extends beyond this to the supply of all the ideas and at least some of the words. The co-presence of a precursory author should not be taken to imply a lack of individuality in the work concerned. A witty musicologist once called Franz Liszt 'a tireless nurseryman for other men's flowers' because of his fondness for paraphrasing and reworking the compositions of others; but even a couple of bars of any of these transcriptions immediately declares the hand of Liszt.[22] In a different way, parodies, which consciously pervert the work of their precursory authors, could not exist without them.

A second mode of precursory authorship is found in works that directly incorporate extensive material from a preceding work into a new one. Even in oral transmission it was possible for longer texts to absorb pre-existing shorter texts: the identification of embedded elements has been an important preoccupation of Homeric scholarship. That literacy created vastly enhanced opportunities for such incorporations can be seen from the transmissional history of the Bible. In cases where an author makes extensive unacknowledged use of the words of other authors we have what is now called plagiarism (still a form of authorship, albeit a discreditable one). A disarming acknowledgement of quasi-plagiarism comes in a late nineteenth-century guidebook. Having conceded that the text of the work was 'in the main a mosaic', the author adds:

> In the process of selection and compression the necessity of 'joining the flats' has occasioned some re-writing; but where no such demand arose, I felt that to paraphrase would be an affectation of original research, for which the writers named have left little room.[23]

Appropriation of this kind is omnipresent in the writing of the Middle Ages and the Renaissance, often being undertaken as a form of deference or loyalty to the precursory author. If Seneca or Jerome had expressed one's meaning fully and perfectly, it was a gesture of respect to employ their words rather than one's own. In most periods there have also been those who deplored such practices, but even these anti-plagiarial arguments belonged to the inherited stock of commonplaces: an accomplished rhetorician should be able to take either side in the debate. It is only with the emergence around 1700 of modern ideas of literary property that the accusation of plagiarism seems to have acquired its present-day moral weight or that authors have been pushed into uneasy defences of their borrowings.[24]

In many cases, the precursory author is a species of collaborator. This becomes particularly so when, following Foucault, we extend the notion of authorship to genres as well as individual works. Mark Rose points out that 'in mass culture the authorial function is often filled by the star': his example is Clint Eastwood.[25] It seems reasonable to say that Eastwood is the *auteur* of the sub-genre of action movies that bears his name: of the genre, that is, not necessarily of individual films. Of course we have to acknowledge that the Eastwood starring role was not his own invention but that of Sergio Leone in the early spaghetti westerns that made Eastwood bankable. Did Eastwood then plagiarise Leone to create his own action movie genre? We might say that: but it seems fairer to say that they were collaborators in those particular pieces of film-genre authorship. Would we then also want to say that Richard Burbage was a precursory author of *King Lear* and *Hamlet*? The answer we give to that would depend on whether we believe that these plays could have been written in anything like the form we give them if Burbage had never existed; or, to look at it from another direction, if Shakespeare was composing around Burbage's stage presence, previous successful roles, vocal skills, favourite catchphrases, skill as a fencer and brilliance at mad scenes, and perhaps supplying new lines at the speaker's suggestion, was Shakespeare plagiarising Burbage, as he plagiarised so many of his historical and literary sources? If so we would need to enrol Burbage alongside Plutarch and Holinshed as a precursory author of certain Shakespearean dramas.

Precursory authorship may be multiple or collective. Consider Synge in the preface to *The Playboy of the Western World*:

> In writing *The Playboy of the Western World*, as in my other plays, I have used one or two words only, that I have not heard among the country people of Ireland, or spoken in my own nursery before I could read the newspapers. A certain number of the phrases I employ I have heard also from herds and fishermen along the coast from Kerry to Mayo, or from beggar-women and ballad-singers nearer Dublin; and I am glad to acknowledge how much I owe to the folk-imagination of these fine people.[26]

This appears to say that the nursemaids, servant girls and tinkers of Ireland, considered collectively, were the precursory author of *The Playboy* and that Synge's role was simply that of an arranger of words and phrases contributed by a host of others. Even the plot turns out to come from a story he collected on his travels. In this he foreshadows the work of subsequent nationalist and left-wing writers who regarded their task as one of articulating the experience of the masses, and would often represent themselves as little better than transcribers. In another direction he anticipates techniques of *collage* and *decoupage* which were to have a long history in twentieth-century avant-garde writing.

There are cases where we may be in doubt as to whether we are dealing with derivation or collaboration. The works of Josephus were written by a native speaker of Hebrew or Aramaic who had become fluent in Greek but who, because he doubted his mastery of Greek literary style, became closely dependent on particular models. The resulting inconsistency of style is so marked in places that Henry St John Thackeray came to believe that sections of *Antiquities* were written by two assistants, one of whom wrote in the style of Thucydides and the other in the style of Sophocles. Tessa Rajak has reinterpreted the evidence as indicating that Josephus wrote with works of other authors dealing with similar topics handy for consultation – a method recommended by Dionysius of Halicarnassus in his *De imitatione* – and that his own style was influenced by whatever author that happened to be.[27]

I cite these examples not to press accusations of plagiarism but to indicate the complexity and indebtedness that attend the assembling of the source- and life-materials utilised in any piece of writing, and some of the ways in which preceding speakers and writers may be participants in the work of authorship. Many novelists speak in interviews of jotting down real-life conversations in notebooks and of cannibalising their friends for characters.[28] It is easy to preserve the ideal of individuated authorship by treating such purloined stories, characters, phrases and intonations as if they were inert counters or building blocks to be manipulated by the writer; and most writers do, of course, give them an individual stamp. No doubt Synge would have argued that since he selected only those found elements that resonated for him in a particular way, his derivations were still intensely personal. The metaphor of digestion is sometimes used for the process by which borrowed work acquires a character individual to the borrower; but writers also often tell us that, from their perspective, the case is the reverse – that these pre-existing materials have an inherent force and trajectory that gives them a shaping power in the construction of the work, much as the opening notes of a chorale harmonised by Bach suggested the tone-row that generated the musical substance of Anton Berg's violin concerto. In many cases the writer's own perceived role is simply one of letting the materials develop under their own impetus with the minimum of interference. In Synge's case it is as likely that the materials, with their inherent shaping power, found him as that he found them, or that the process was one of an intricate interaction of the external with the personal. All these possibilities need to be considered in any investigation into the presence and effects of precursory authorship.

EXECUTIVE AUTHORSHIP

Our second category is that of the maker or *artifex*, whom we will call the executive author – the deviser, the orderer, the wordsmith, or, in the case of Liszt, the reformulator. As we have seen, this function may be performed singly or collaboratively. The executive author may be defined as the compiler of the verbal text up to the point where it is judged suitable for publication in one or another form (all subsequent alterations being classified as revisions). Executive authorship may be either solo or collaborative. In contemporary Western culture the former is the more prestigious mode and the one most likely to be asserted by publishers; the danger is always that it will be too readily assumed.

Collaboration is easiest to unravel when it proceeds section by section, providing it can be ascertained that this really was the case. Eighteenth-century periodical literature yields several cases where two or more executive authors took it in turns to produce numbers: famous examples are the English *Spectator* and the American *Federalist*. A theatrical one is the 1662 translation of Corneille's *Mort de Pompée* by a club of five writers associated with the court of Charles II. Our first clue to their identity comes in letters from Katherine Philips ('Orinda') who was independently working on a translation of the same play. On 10 January 1662 she wrote to a friend at court:

> I have laid out several ways to get a Copy, but cannot yet procure one, except only of the first Act that was done by Mr. WALLER. Sir EDWARD FILMORE [Filmer] did one, Sir CHARLES SEDLEY another, and my Lord BUCKHURST another; but who the fifth I cannot learn, pray inform your self as soon as you can, and let me know it.[29]

Sidney Godolphin and Sir Samuel Tuke were both later proposed as the fifth collaborator. It is not clear from the letter whether Orinda thought that the acts had been assigned in the given order or that she was ignorant of who was responsible for which act, apart from the first. Later Dryden credited Buckhurst (better remembered as the sixth Earl of Dorset) with the fourth act.[30] The case would be a ripe one for stylistic investigation if there was not a problem over obtaining texts for comparison. Sedley wrote another tragic drama, *Antony and Cleopatra*, and evidence from this would seem to point to him as the translator of Act II. Waller's replacement last act for Fletcher's *The Maid's Tragedy* (written to remove the blot of regicide) offers stylistic evidence in favour of Orinda's attribution to him of Act I: her wording would also suggest that the act was being circulated in manuscript with his name on it. Dorset left no drama but quite a deal of verse; however, this itself poses considerable attribution problems and has not yielded a stylistic fix on any particular act. Because Filmer and Godolphin were literary nonentities, there is no way by which their contributions could be distinguished, though if they ever could be it might result in the attribution of further, anonymous work to them. Tuke is credited with a comedy, *The Adventures of Five Hours* (1663), translated from the Spanish; however, one source claims this was a collaboration with George Digby, Earl of Bristol. What is clear, though, is that five translators were indeed involved: the five acts spread apart on a quantitative scatter-plot while Orinda's five acts stay snugly together.[31]

DECLARATIVE AUTHORSHIP

Ex-President Clinton's role in the compilation of his book on race relations introduces a third function, that of the validator or, as we will now call her/him, the declarative author. In his case the placing of a name upon the title-page would not indicate executive authorship but a combination of precursory authorship and a form of sponsorship or fostering.

In early editions of the Bible, the first five books of the Old Testament, known to Christians as the Pentateuch and to Jews as the Torah, are attributed to Moses. (Genesis, in the King James translation, is 'The first book of Moses called Genesis'.) But since Moses cannot have written a work that describes his own death, it is more likely that the name of Moses became attached because he was the greatest of Jewish leaders, and because these books contain the Jewish law, which was the Law of Moses.[32] In the same way the names of the disciples Matthew, Mark and John may have become attached to three of the Christian gospels as a way of conferring dignity on these writings and making sure they were taken seriously. The voluminous works of Josef Stalin are a more recent example of the same principle. In cases such as these, attributionists are unlikely to have the evidence that would permit them to find an alternative named author or authors: their task is rather to identify the institutional sources of the writing and the circumstances of its compilation and revisions. Sometimes it will be possible to establish different chronological layers of composition performed by successive redactors.

A second function of the declarative author is that of 'owning the words' – of appearing in the public sphere as the work's creator, and of shouldering the responsibilities and accepting the benefits that flow from this: indeed, it is only through performing the declarative part of authorship that one can figure oneself as an author or enable a work to activate Foucault's 'author-function'. In two forms of authorship, plagiarism and appropriation by agreement of the work of a ghost-writer, this role is assumed by a specialist who may not perform any of the other tasks of authorship but who still has to be regarded as a participant author under our work-oriented model. Faking (discussed in Chapter ten) makes the same severance of executive authorship from declarative authorship. To complicate matters further, some authors are reluctant to assume declarative authorship and may go to considerable lengths to evade it. Attributionists see the anonymous or pseudonymous work as a vacuum in nature which it is their moral duty to fill with an author. Every time they attach a name to an anonymous text they are making a retrospective bestowal of declarative authorship.

In some cases the role of declarative author is openly or covertly contested. Carl Jung's 'autobiography', *Memories, Dreams, Reflections* presents itself as a summing up of his achieved wisdom written at the age of eighty-three. In fact, while sections of it were dictated by Jung, the bulk of the writing was done by his secretary Aniela Jaffé. Moreover, Jaffé and various of Jung's relatives censored and edited his material heavily in a process that he described as 'auntification'. The typescript of the English translation contains further changes by four different editors. Jung willingly signed a declaration that Jaffé should be credited with authorship; however, once he was dead this was ignored and the book brought out under his own name.[33]

It is necessary to repeat that this declarative role is still a genuine element of the sequence of processes we know as authorship even if the person claiming it has made no other contribution to the creation of the work concerned. It should also be noted that the attachment of a new declarative author's name to a work changes its meaning by changing its context: an epigram bearing the name of the plagiarist Fidentinus does not mean the same as the identical epigram encountered in the works of its true author Martial, because it lacks certain kinds of meaning conferred by its membership of and position in the book or *œuvre*. *Hamlet* by William Shakespeare is a different play from *Hamlet* by the Earl of Oxford or Francis Bacon.

REVISIONARY AUTHORSHIP

Our final category is that of revisionary authorship. In the revising of Mary Barber's poems for their publication in 1735, Swift's friend Patrick Delany, Swift himself, Matthew and Laetitia Pilkington and Constantia Grierson would meet regularly in a sociable '*Senatus Consultum*, to correct these undigested materials'.[34] A. C. Elias believes that Swift's own poems were subject to a similar process of joint editing, for which a present-day analogy would be the workshopping of drafts in a writers' group. Such processes tend to erase idiosyncratic aspects of style and replace them either with more conventional ones or with the style of the dominant personality of the group. Returning to the Clinton account, we should note the intervention of the White House staffers who performed a shaping and revising function exercised after the main phase of executive authorship. It is not hard to imagine another form of 'each of us joyning and consulting about every Line'. Their role was similar to that of publishers' editors or, in another context, of censors. However, executive authors can also, naturally, be their own revisers, the distinction being one of phases, not of persons. With some misgivings I offer the term revisionary authorship for this phase in the composition of the work, the problem being that revision is not always clearly distinguishable from primary composition. The very notion implies a chronology in which either an entire text or a discrete section of text is first created and then polished and corrected. In the days when works were written by hand or typed on manual typewriters and then set in movable type this was still a fair description in that the unit of composition was likely to be the draft or, in the cases of Dickens and Faulkner, the annotated printer's proof. But the process of drafting and redrafting on screen, or in the wax-coated table-book of antiquity, is and was generally much more fragmented than this, involving a mingled alternation of composition and various kinds of alteration, including new spurts of composition inspired by revision.[35] There still has to be a chronology of some kind but it is one whose period may be the sentence or the phrase, rather than, or as well as, the completed draft.

The simplest way out of the difficulty is to consign to the phase of executive authorship all work up to the completion of a text regarded by the author/authors as suitable for sending to a publisher or putting into manuscript circulation, and everything that comes after that to the phase of revisionary authorship, no matter who performs it, but with the caution that special cases may require a different division. Alternatively, we might recognise revisionary authorship as a distinct phase when it can be distinguished as a phase, either by a return to the text, after a gap, by an executive author or by the work being passed to an acknowledged reviser, and delete it from our model on occasions when revisionary activity is integrated into executive authorship. The key issue is that the difference in the nature of the operations should hold even when there is no clear chronological break between them and no matter who performs them.

The clearest cases of revisionary authorship are those in which a second writer or editor remodels a work completed or in some cases abandoned by a first. Among well-known instances are Ezra Pound's editing of *The Waste Land*; Max Brod's preparation of Kafka's manuscripts for the press; the ongoing production of new works from the Hemingway *Nachlass*; and the well-documented interventions of publisher's editors such as Maxwell Perkins in the case of Thomas Wolfe and Gordon Lish in that of Raymond Carver. It is not my purpose to denigrate the work of revisers and editors: many a good book has been improved by a gifted editor and many a potentially good book ruined for the lack of it. Rimsky-Korsakov both maimed and improved Mussorgsky's *Boris Godunov* when he reshaped and reorchestrated it. At the same time, living as we do in a culture which places great stress on individuality, and often being attracted to writers by our perception of that individuality, we have a strong predisposition to prefer the authentic and unpolished over the version perfected by an alien hand. What the cases just mentioned possess in common is that the original documents still survive to be consulted should we so wish. We can purchase printed texts of Wolfe 'revised Perkins' and Wolfe 'unrevised' and CDs of *Boris* Rimskyed and unRimskyed. This is not the case however for many instances from the past. John Sheffield, Earl of Mulgrave, Marquis of Normanby and Duke of Buckinghamshire gave copies of his 'Essay on Satire' first to Dryden and later to Pope to have it polished for circulation; but it is only these revised versions which have survived, not the original.

Writers are most likely to be reliant on editors and surrogates such as manuscript assessors, mentors and agents in early works in which they are still learning their craft. In an article headed 'First novels' published in 1988, forty-three American writers gave brief descriptions of their experiences of working with a professional editor.[36] These were almost all enthusiastic. Jim Anderson wrote: 'Stung by criticism, I look with fresh eyes at what I have written so lovingly. Invariably the cold eye of a good editor improves the writing. I had excellent editorial help both at an early stage, and at the end, after acceptance.' Don Hoover recorded that his editor 'immediately intuited the soul of the book and set about baptizing it. Punctuation and paragraphing were the main foci, with some attention to syntax . . . His impact is therapeutic and spiritual – the sacred feeling that comes from aimed perfection.' When J. Michael Straczynski's typescript came back, 'The margin was littered with repeated similes and misused metaphors like cars rusting in a junkyard'. For Shelly Reuben, 'Submitting my novel . . . was like finding that ephemeral [*sic*] tennis pro against whom I could play and learn and improve my game.' John Ed Bradley saw the ideal editor as a kind of gardener: 'He tidied it up and cleaned out the weeds.' Betty Ann Moskowitz preferred a sexual metaphor: 'Like all virgins, first novelists require gentleness and expertise.' For Robert MacLean the editor was an authoritarian mother:

> You scream indignantly. Your expressionless editor lifts you from the toilet, adjusts your clothing, waits while you persist with a button. Downstairs, she manhandles you into your snowsuit. You work your fists in protest, and, when the sleeves incapacitate them, tilt your face up pleadingly. She gags you with the scarf, points you at the door, pushes . . . Unaware of your gratitude, you rustle forward to the world.

While the highest praise was for those who exercised 'watchful nonintervention', there was general agreement that the contribution of the editor had been a considerable one, especially felt in the excision of the superfluous. By the time they establish themselves as popular, authors are in a position to resist such pressures and less likely to find them welcome. But not always: Peter Carey describes the work of his distinguished editor, Gary Fisketjon:

> The manuscript pages come back covered with his spidery green ink, page after page, without relent. But when the final process (it took about four weeks) is over, the book feels as it felt before, just better, and I know that my friends who read the manuscript before the editing process now feel that it has, somehow, been brought into tighter, brighter life. It is invisible, but everywhere apparent . . .

Richard Ford agrees about Fisketjon:

> He questions or has comments about probably 80 per cent of the sentences. And he's not proprietary about his comments, he just wants to have things to say because he thinks – and we agree – as often as I can be brought back to reconsider a sentence, the more likely I am to write a good sentence.

Fisketjon in turn likes to quote Maxwell Perkins: 'Don't ever get to feeling important about yourself, because an editor at most releases energy. He creates nothing.' In this conception the editor is more like a coach than a collaborator, explaining to the author what still needs to be done.[37] While in some cases an editor's work will erase traces of the agency of the executive author, in others it may motivate revisions that intensify them.

Obviously to separate out the contributions of a reviser is one of the most dificult tasks for attribution studies. This is particularly so when the work being revised is itself collaborative. Among the Renaissance dramatists Philip Massinger is notable as an exceptionally thorough reviser who, as well as imposing his own dramatic style on that of his predecessors, would write new text out in full rather than merely marking up the original. Since his personal habits of spelling and presentation are very well documented, and those of Fletcher the dramatist who was his principal victim are likewise quite distinctive, it is usually possible to separate the work of the two. But Fletcher during his lifetime worked frequently with collaborators who included Massinger. How are we to untangle the agencies at work in a play written by these two which was further revised after Fletcher's death by Massinger? Another kind of challenge is to look back through time from a much-revised later version for traces of a lost original. Shakespeare and Fletcher's *Cardenio*, which survives only in a brutal eighteenth-century rewriting by Lewis Theobald as *Double Falsehood; or, the Distrest Lovers* (1728), has been much sieved for tarnished particles of Shakespearean gold.

CONCLUSION

This broad separating out of phases given in this chapter falls considerably short of giving a complete muster roll of authorial functions but will suggest some of the varieties of individual agency likely to be involved in the composition of a piece of published writing. It is necessary to repeat that no single such breaking down of authorship into separate operations would hold for all times, places, genres and authors; moreover, from time to time we really will encounter an author who works in a cork-lined room, has perfect handwriting, and never revises. But the processes responsible for the final form of the majority of works are more complex and on occasions utterly baffling. The attributionist who sees furthest is the one with the richest sense of the possibilities in the given case.

CHAPTER FOUR

External evidence

Attribution studies distinguishes conventionally between internal and external evidence. Broadly, internal evidence is that from the work itself and external evidence that from the social world within which the work is created, promulgated and read; but there will always be overlap. Often one kind of evidence only acquires meaning by reference to the other. (Ephim Fogel proposed the use of 'internal-external evidence' for such cases, but that seems excessive for what is simply a distinction of convenience.[1]) External evidence as treated here covers the following kinds:

(1) Contemporary attributions contained in incipits, explicits, titles, and from documents purporting to impart information about the circumstances of composition – especially diaries, correspondence, publishers' records, and records of legal proceedings;
(2) Biographical evidence, which would include information about a putative author's allegiances, whereabouts, dates, personal ties, and political and religious affiliations;
(3) The history of earlier attributions of the work and the circumstances under which they were made.

Internal evidence, to be considered in the course of the next three chapters, covers

(1) Stylistic evidence;
(2) Self-reference and self-presentation within the work;
(3) Evidence from the themes, ideas, beliefs and conceptions of genre manifested in the work.

The second class of external evidence and the third of internal will inevitably overlap. The distinction in any given argument depends on whether the researcher is working inward from the context or outward from the detail of the text.

External evidence allows us to locate the work's genesis in its time, its place, its culture, its immediate environment and, if we are exceptionally lucky, at a particular desk in a particular room. The best current account of the scholarly practices involved in historical contextualisation is that given by Robert D. Hume in *Reconstructing Contexts: The Aims and Principles of Archaeo-Historicism*.[2] Particularly pertinent is his section headed 'The Constructedness of Contexts' (pp. 137–41), which builds on a similar discussion in David Perkins's *Is Literary History Possible?* (1992). Hume, that most meticulous of documentary scholars, has no wish to relativise the past: his point is rather that in order to use it we have to create it, working as conscientiously as we can from its surviving documentary traces and never deceiving ourselves about the '*radical selectivity* of what we do':

> To imagine or pretend that the contexts we employ for interpretive purposes are the real thing is perfectly insane. The past is gone; we cannot conjure it up and use it as though it were a present and accessible reality. However carefully we reconstruct a context – and validate it as a legitimate representation of the past as best we can conceive it – the fact remains that it is a construction. Assembling a context is at least as radical an act as textual interpretation – indeed I would say far more so, since any reader can go to the text, point to a line or a passage, and start arguing. Objecting to a context presents far greater complexities: one must identify gaps and absences, and try to comprehend what often turn out to be unstated principles of selection or assembly. Criticism is full of blandly authoritative assertions about Renaissance this or neoclassical that. 'The Victorian reader believed . . . '. Who made these rules? Who justifies them? (p. 138)

The historical context (whether it is that of ancient Rome or last week) is something we build in order to perform a particular kind of reading: in the attributionist's case this is the reading of an absent signifier in the form of an authorial name or names. The context derives whatever 'reality' it may possess from its capacity to fulfil that need, its function being instrumental or heuristic. Hume proposes commonsense principles for constructing contexts:

> (1) avoid a priori assumptions; (2) eschew single viewpoint and uniformitarianism; (3) stick to a specific site and a narrow time range; (4) expect to have to take change into account if covering more than a very few years; (5) cite primary documents as your evidence and explain principles of selection and exclusion; (6) always remember that any context is a constructed hypothesis. (p. 71)

When the task of contextualisation is done badly, we find that scholarship has been replaced by a form of fiction in which this or that candidate is awarded the role of hero and the golden fleece is the prize of whole or part authorship of given texts.

The great bibliographical scholar D. F. McKenzie pointed to exactly this kind of danger in his classic paper 'Printers of the mind'. His subject was the way in which visually evident symmetries in printed books of the early modern period had been made the basis of ingenious accounts of the day-to-day operation of the printing shops that produced them, which were then used as the basis for editorial decisions. By returning to the actual records of industry practice he was able to demonstrate not only that these speculative contexts were entirely incorrect, but that the real work patterns were 'of such an unpredictable complexity, even for such a small printing shop, that no amount of inference from what we think of as bibliographical evidence could ever have led to their reconstruction'.[3] The difference, which is as important for attribution studies as for the history of the book, is one between a valid context constructed from an exhaustive but always sceptical study of the external evidence and an invalid one constructed by treating certain kinds of internal evidence as if they were external. There may well be situations in which evidence of any kind is in such short supply that there is no option but to proceed in this circular way – first using Homer to construct archaic Greece and then our construction of archaic Greece to explain Homer – but this is a desperate strategy.

What used to be hard to acknowledge but is now generally recognised is that even rigorously conducted contextual scholarship still calls for the exercise of imagination culminating in an act of personal judgement. What is less often acknowledged is that this applies as much to the users of quantitative methods as it does to those who reason in a forensic way. A table of stylistic ratios is in the end just another way of figuring a name – a metonymy or perhaps a metaphor (a matter considered in Chapter twelve). It is composed from the textual detritus of the past and must return to history through the act of asserting an attribution. It is an illusion to believe that it has ever become decontextualised.

EXTERNAL VERSUS INTERNAL

Until recent times external evidence has usually been granted a higher status than internal evidence. Samuel Schoenbaum insisted in 1960 that 'External evidence can and often does provide incontestable proof; internal evidence can only support hypotheses or corroborate external evidence.'[4] Arthur Sherbo's attempt to challenge this view was universally frowned upon at the time. These ideas are further pursued in Schoenbaum's *Internal Evidence and Elizabethan Dramatic Authorship* (1966), which takes a wicked delight in exposing some of the wilder confusions that had arisen from an overfanciful use of internal evidence. His dismissal of 'a host of articles (all on single plays)' from the early decades of the twentieth century is performed with the annoyed weariness of one who has had to search through too many mullock heaps for too few grains of gold:

> The metrical tables, the word-lists, the impressionistic comments on theme, character, and plot, the final brandishing of the parallels – all designed to create a 'cumulative impression' – were to constitute a durable formula. (*IE*, p. 68)

What was principally objected to here was a naive Baconism which held that an accumulation of individually unpersuasive evidence would somehow prove conclusive through its sheer bulk. Schoenbaum's ingrained scepticism led him to question a number of attributions now generally accepted; but he was perfectly correct about the unjustified dogmatism that characterised many arguments for the attributions of English Renaissance plays by the scholars castigated by Greg as 'parallelographers'. 'It is difficult to see', Schoenbaum concludes, 'why a great heap of rubbish should possess any more value than a small pile of the same rubbish.' (*IE*, p. 197)

Schoenbaum's book appeared at the peak of a reaction in favour of external evidence against the impressionistic use of internal evidence. Today the boot is on the other foot, with some of the more fervent champions of stylometry (an internal method, albeit quantitative and the reverse of impressionistic) routinely citing probabilities of millions to one that theirs is the right answer. There are grave problems, to be considered elsewhere, with such claims; but certainly the balance of confidence has shifted back in favour of the internal. Stylometric studies regularly appear that pay no attention at all to external evidence, as if it was somehow of no significance, or do so only in a perfunctory manner: it may even be dismissed for being unquantifiable. None of this matters when solid evidence of both kinds points to the same result; but when there is conflict between them we have to judge which of the two is more persuasive or else deliver an open verdict. This must depend entirely on the quality and persuasiveness of the research presented. Neither kind should be given priority by fiat.

NAMING THE AUTHOR

The most common reason for believing that a particular author wrote a particular work is that someone presumed to have first-hand knowledge tells us so. This telling usually takes the form of an ascription on a title-page or in an incipit, explicit or colophon, or in the item, title or contents-list of an anthologised piece. It may be supported by legal and book-trade records. There may be direct corroborating evidence in correspondence and personal recollections of the period of composition, such as Coleridge's famous story of the composition of 'Kubla Khan' being interrupted by a person from Porlock (the point is not whether the incident ever happened but that it constitutes a claim by Coleridge to the authorship of the poem). If we can confirm a title-page ascription from other evidence, we have satisfied the first requirement of attribution studies; however, we must be careful that the name is attached to the right bearer of it. *The Long Parliament Revived* (1661), which is attributed on its title-page to Thomas Philips, is credited in the Wing *Short-title Catalogue* and most library catalogues to Sir William Drake; however, Sir William's only connection with it was that he sat in the parliament to which a merchant, also named William Drake, confessed that he was the true author.[5]

Quite often a work comes down to us with a pseudonym or no name at all: these cases are the most common concern of the attributionist. The Gawain-poet (if there ever was one rather than several) remains just the Gawain-poet and we are not entirely sure about B. Traven, despite the existence of a considerable 'search for Traven' literature.[6] On encountering a problem of this kind our first port of call for writing in English may well be Halkett and Laing along with more specialised dictionaries of anonymous and pseudonymous writings; however, we must remember that the identifications found in dictionaries of pseudonyms are not for the most part based on research but simply taken over from other sources, particularly library catalogues. (Library cataloguers are the hoplites or foot-soldiers of attribution studies.) So as a next step we should go directly to the standard scholarly bibliographies and the on-line catalogues of the world's great libraries to see what they have to say about the text concerned.

Yet, dictionaries of pseudonyms and library catalogues are mainly concerned with books, whereas, from the seventeenth century onward, many of the most pressing cases of unknown or disputed authorship are found in newspapers, periodicals and evanescent pamphlets. The greater part of surviving English-language journalism even as late as the 1960s was either anonymous or pseudonymous. There will sometimes be in-house records identifying authors. In 1998 the *Times Literary Supplement* released an on-line archive of the authors of its many decades of anonymous reviews, a decision that was seen as unprincipled by those whose cover had been blown, but was otherwise welcomed. Guessing the real authors of these reviews had once been a favourite parlour game, now replaced by guessing the identities of anonymous referees for book and journal submissions and grant applications.[7] The *Wellesley Index to Victorian Periodicals* identifies many contributors to the quarterly and monthly journals it covers by drawing on such sources as payment ledgers, marked-up file copies and editorial correspondence.

This makes the task of the attributionist much easier than it was when Pierre Danchin, whose monumental edition of the prologues and epilogues of English plays from 1660 to 1800 brings forward many fascinating authorship problems, worked during and after the Second World War on the Catholic poet, Francis Thompson (d. 1907). It was then believed that Thompson had written little during the last decade of his life; but Danchin was able to attribute a large number of articles to him, partly on external and partly on internal evidence. It was known that Thompson had contributed to the *Athenaeum* and, in a study of that magazine by Leslie Marchand, Danchin found a reference to an annotated file of the magazine held in the offices of the *New Statesman*, with which the *Athenaeum* had later merged. Here is his description of what followed:

> From Leeds, where I had been sent by the British Council, I then went to London, to see the editor of *The New Statesman and Nation*. He first told me he had no knowledge of the existence of this file; but then someone mentioned a series of volumes kept in the basement, after their return from storage outside London during the Blitz. They then told me they would look and tell me if I was right. I returned to Leeds, very pessimistic about the outcome of my visit. But, a few days later, the editor wrote that I was right: they had indeed an annotated file of *The Athenaeum*, but could not undertake the 'enormous task' of checking the articles in which I was interested; I was welcome to come and do it myself. I returned to London, the 'enormous task' took me a couple of hours; the file was annotated with the name of the writer of each article, and, occasionally, with the amount paid him (interestingly, Francis Thompson was particularly badly paid). Checking the articles I had retained as possibly by Thompson, I found that I had been right in all but two cases, and this enabled me to improve and perfect my method.[8]

Danchin passed on his findings to Terence Connolly, the leading Thompson scholar at the time, who published them without acknowledgement. In some cases similar evidence also exists for daily newspapers, and can be tracked down, but an enormous amount has been lost.

One much-discussed body of newspaper contributions is the articles submitted by Coleridge to the *Morning Post* and its evening counterpart the *Courier* between 1798 and 1818. Most of the fine detail of these attributions has been determined by internal evidence (and will be discussed under that heading); but external evidence existed in the form of Coleridge's and others' acknowledgement of his involvement, the sporadic appearances of pseudonyms, place names or initials, and a file of clippings which survived long enough to be used by his daughter Sara in preparing her own edition of the material in 1850. The names of the other principal writers involved in the papers are also known and the likelihood of Coleridge's authorship of certain pieces can be tested against knowledge of his whereabouts at the time. So, in 1802 he sent a number of contributions from Keswick, including three reports of a local bigamy scandal, but had left by the time a fourth report was sent.[9] One would expect his work to be identifiable from its attitudes; but David Erdman, the modern editor of this material, warns 'it is my own impression that, for the whole period of his writing for the *Morning Post*, the opinions of Coleridge are the opinions of the newspaper – and vice versa'. In the case of the *Courier*, however, where he was allowed more independence, it may happen that 'the clue to Coleridgean authorship or interference is a *difference* of opinion'.[10]

Coleridge belonged to a tradition of high-profile metropolitan journalism in which information about contributors had a fair chance of being preserved. Provincial, colonial and frontier journalism were less accommodating. Between February 1871 and February 1872 a series of forty articles under the heading 'My adventures and researches in the Pacific' appeared in the *Australian Town and Country Journal* under the pseudonym 'A Master Mariner'. Alongside improbable accounts of derring-do they included much valuable information on Pacific archaeology, including a series of woodcut illustrations of the twelfth- to thirteenth-century ruins at Nan Madol on the Micronesian island of Pohnpei.[11] The series began with the archaeological articles, continued with the stories of derring-do and concluded with 'rambling reminiscences, full of diatribe against missionaries' ('Literary detection', p. 10). Fortunately the Mariner had avoided well-known islands, where by 1871 the body of printed sources was already huge, and concentrated on little-known ones where he was less likely to be contradicted. Dirk Spennemann and Jane Downing discovered that material for one account was similar to that given in Stonewater Cooper's *Coral Lands*, a book published nine years after the Master Mariner's articles but not derived from them. Cooper gave his source as memoranda by Handley Bathurst Sterndale that had appeared in the 1874 *Appendix to the Journals of the House of Representatives of New Zealand* (again later than the Master Mariner articles); these in turn proved to be based on another series of anonymous articles published in the Auckland *Daily Southern Cross* in 1873–4 which left no doubt that Sterndale was the 'Master Mariner'. Two useful points that arise from this story are the common practice among frontier journalists (and editors) of recycling material in one forum after another, and the fact that identification depended not on the discovery of sources but on working back from later recensions of the core material. The consistent difficulty of such work is that files of the relevant papers and magazines can rarely be consulted together in the same place and even then may suffer from gaps.

Letters to the editor pose a related problem. Newspapers from the eighteenth century onward often feature letters to and from regular correspondents writing under distinctive pseudonyms. So many of these were sent to the *Spectator* that they had to be published in a separate volume, Charles Lillie's *Original and genuine letters sent to the Tatler and Spectator, during the time those works were publishing. None of which have been before printed* (London, 1725). Coleridge contributed letters as well as editorial material to the *Morning Post* and *Courier*, using the pseudonyms 'Humanitas', 'ΣΤΗΣ', 'A lover of universal toleration' and 'Plato'. What Martin Battestin identifies as Fielding's contributions to the *Craftsman* are also in the form of letters. Some of the contributors to this tradition of journalism were staff writers who, in order to keep an issue alive, wrote letters in response to leaders of their own composition when no one else had bothered to do so; but there were also genuine letter writers who built up a considerable *œuvre* by writing continually, such as the celebrated 'Junius' of the late eighteenth-century *Public Advertiser*, whose identity was only confirmed in 1962.[12] Difficulty may occur when pseudonyms such as 'civicus', 'medicus' and 'pro bono publico' are used by a number of contributors or by the same contributor for different letters. Sheridan's *The Critic* (1779) introduces the character of Mr Puff, who writes letters to order under such names as 'a CONSCIENTIOUS BAKER' and 'a DETESTER OF VISIBLE BRICK-WORK' in the style of Junius.[13] Today, when daily newspapers use only a small proportion of letters received, cunning operators will use a variety of names to get published.

Journalism written under a pseudonym can often be followed through successive issues of a serial publication until internal evidence permits identification. Even without James Edward Neild's own summary of his professional career, we should have had little difficulty in picking that the author of the weekly commentary signed 'Jacques' that appeared in the *Australasian* between 1864 and 1872 was an anti-clerical, medically trained writer born in the north of England who was also a fanatical

Shakespearean but disliked opera. What might be puzzling was that these features continued to be evident in the writing of his successor 'Tahite' and in the unsigned columns that followed after 'Tahite' self-destructed on 28 December 1878 with a performative 'And now I cease to be'. Clearly, either this persona went with the job, so to speak, or the same writer was still at work (which was the actual case). In an earlier incarnation as 'Christopher Sly', Neild had become notorious enough to be the subject of a cartoon in a rival newspaper in which he was being sliced to pieces by a knight in armour who carried a banner instancing his critical crimes.[14] Any hint that a journalist is replying to criticisms or acknowledging praise should be followed up at once in the organ concerned. Journalism is nothing if not gladiatorial and fellow journalists will usually know things not revealed to the public at large.

And not only journalists! Any anonymous or pseudonymous work that gives rise to a controversy is likely to elicit replies that may reveal the identity of the original assailant. In 1674 Elkanah Settle replied to an anonymous attack on his latest hit play:

> Casting my Eye upon a Pamphlet entitled *Notes and Observations on the Empress of Morocco*; and finding no Authors name to it, I used my best indeavour to get that knowledge by my Examination of the Style, which the unkind Printer had denied me . . . And thereupon with very little Conjuration, by those three remarkable Qualities of *Railing*, *Boasting* and *Thieving* I found a *Dryden* in the Frontispiece. Then going through the Preface, I observ'd the drawing of a Fools Picture to be the design of the whole piece, and reflecting on the Painter I consider'd, that probably his Pamphlet might be like his Plays, not to be written without help. And according to expectation I discovered the Author of *Epsome-Wells* [Shadwell], and the Author of *Pandion* and *Amphigenia* [Crowne] lent their assistance.[15]

Settle claims to have identified his authors purely by style but is likely to have had additional sources of information. The attribution of the preface to Dryden is generally accepted. Crowne in the 'Epistle to the Reader' of his *Caligula* (1698) made a retroactive claim to 'above three parts of four' of the tract, which, given that Dryden, though not Shadwell, was still alive, must carry some weight. Although Settle's postscript (pp. 69–72) is attributed to Dryden by Malone, its critical position is more suggestive of Shadwell.[16] *Notes and Observations* remains an interesting mystery for being the earliest example of the 'close reading' of a dramatic text in the language.

Settle was also himself a candidate for another attribution which was plausibly resolved by a search for a response to provocation. In 1992 David Dyregrov reconsidered the evidence for the authorship of

The Fairy Queen, a 'semi-opera' of 1692 best known for Purcell's magnificent music.[17] The piece was actually an adaptation of *A Midsummer Night's Dream* but Purcell was given none of the original play to set; instead, an elaborate masque was written for the end of each act, a collectively substantial addition which is uncredited in the contemporary printings. Insofar as there was a candidate for authorship whose case was based on anything more than supposition, it was Settle, because he had written a lost Bartholomew Fair droll with the same title; but this, Dyregrov argues, was more likely to have been an anti-Catholic political satire than an adaptation of Shakespeare; and, in any case, the compiler of the 1692 *Fairy Queen* had taken his text from the fourth Shakespeare folio which was unpublished at the date of Settle's droll. Dyregrov now performed an ingenious piece of lateral thinking. *The Fairy Queen* contains what has come to be called the 'scene of the drunken poet' which was written to ridicule the dramatist Thomas Durfey. Such attacks normally led to swift revenge, and in Durfey's next play, *The Richmond Heiress*, there was an unpleasant character named Cunnington who was clearly modelled on the actor and dancer Joe Haines. Just as the Durfey-like drunken poet had been beaten on stage in *The Fairy Queen*, the same fate befalls Cunnington in *The Richmond Heiress*:

> But in addition, D'Urfey, for no very compelling dramatic reasons, has Cunnington tell Quickwit how he is arranging a masquerade ball and a 'Masque too of *Pluto*, *Orpheus*, and *Eurydice*, of my Composing, and the Musick of Mr. *Purcels*.' To this, his antagonist comments: 'Ay hang ye, you us'd to be Ingenious enough at these things' (V.iv).[18]

With this lead, Dyregrov was able to draw together additional external and internal evidence strengthening the case for Haines being the reviser/augmenter. He was also able to give a good reason why Haines might not have wanted his name associated with the hit of the season – that he was deeply in debt. Once it was known that he was expecting third-day income from a play, his creditors would have been calling for their share.

Reviews of all kinds – book, play and music – will often retail privileged information about authorship and derivation. Until Patrick Spedding's discovery of a copy of Eliza Haywood's *The History of Miss Leonora Meadowson* (1788) in the Fales Library of New York University, the existence of the work was known only from one advertisement and two short reviews.[19] One problem with theatre and music reviews arises from the practice of daily journalism from the nineteenth century onward that they should be written immediately after the performance so as to be present in the next morning's papers. This meant that they were rarely ready in time for the paper's first edition (usually printed before midnight for out-of-town distribution). In cases where the statutory deposit copy was taken from the first edition, neither the newspaper's own copies nor that of the relevant deposit library may contain the reviews: one has to search for them in the journalist's own clippings book or those of performers or theatre companies concerned – assuming these exist and are traceable. Unfavourable reviews are more likely to disappear than complimentary ones! Book reviews are fortunately less sinkable and will frequently contain evidence for the authorship of anonymous and pseudonymous works.

Much evidence for books of unknown and disputed authorship lies in book-trade records. Researchers into Renaissance and early-modern authors draw heavily on the register kept by the Stationers' Company. Entry in the register was the means by which booksellers established copyright in the works they published: it offers a date, sometimes more information than appears on the title-page and, where books are entered in groups, possible affiliations with other publications. There are also entries for books that were never published or not at the time of entry. Shakespeare's *Troilus and Cressida* was entered on 7 February 1603 but did not appear until after re-entry in 1609. Many major publishers of the nineteenth and twentieth centuries have left large archives, which are now available to scholars through such series as the Chadwyck-Healey microfilm edition 'Archives of British Publishers'. Joseph McAleer's *Passion's Fortune: The Story of Mills and Boon* draws on an archive of letters between the publisher and authors that had not been available a decade earlier when he was writing his previous study, *Popular Reading and Publishing in Britain 1914–1950*.[20] Both these books throw much incidental light on the use of pseudonyms in genre fiction.

Remember that a book may have been sent to more than one publisher before being accepted and that correspondence or a reader's report may survive in the archive of a publisher other than that responsible for bringing it forward – also that both titles and authorial names may change between submission and publication. Newspaper advertisements for new books – especially those of eighteenth-century newspapers which specify 'this day published' – are also of value, most obviously for dating but also at times for authorship and the existence of lost works.

The stage has its own records, among which are Philip Henslowe's famous diaries, which preserve so much otherwise unobtainable information about the authorship of Elizabethan plays. Working from Henslowe, William J. Lawrence established that, of 128 new plays put on by the Admiral's Men between 1597 and 1603, 70 were collaboratively written, sometimes with up to five dramatists involved.[21] An immense amount of information about authorship is contained in the records and file copies of British plays held in the Lord Chamberlain's Collection, the main body of which is now in the British Library with some eighteenth-century material in the Huntington Library's Larpent Collection. These cover the period of the Licensing Act (1737–1968); but the Lord Chamberlain and his deputy, the Master of the Revels, had already been active as censors of plays in Shakespeare's time. One book from this earlier series survived long enough for some of its material to be transcribed in the eighteenth century. Other legislatures throughout the English-speaking world maintained parallel systems of licensing and censorship. Helen Oppenheim was able to establish the transported convict Edward Geoghegan as the author of *The Hibernian Father* and seven other plays from a letter in the New South Wales colonial secretary's archive.[22]

Legal records in all their baffling multiplicity are a vital source of information. The Star Chamber of the early Stuart period heard several cases concerning the authorship of libellous poems circulated by being sung in taverns or posted up in public places. Here is an example:

> John Pilkington did in the moneth of Aprill nowe last past most malitiously frame and contrive an vntrue scandelous and most infamous Libell in wrytinge ag^{t}. Yo^{r} said Subiecte and his said wife in theis words followinge (vizt) Henrie Skipwith his wife him Wippeth, because he Married a Twanger, Hee married her a riche Whoare, and hath made her full poore, and paies her olde debtes for anger.[23]

This is as nice a nailing down of responsibility for an ephemeral piece as one could hope for: yet thousands of composers of surviving verse libels who evaded the law remain irretrievably anonymous. The book trade and the theatre both generated many legal disputes over contracts and copyrights. A court case over a debt led to the proposal that an unknown play by Thomas Middleton called *The Vyper and her Broode* could have been identical with the anonymous *The Revenger's Tragedy*.[24] Some cases, especially for treason and libel, are directly concerned with questions of authorship; in others it arises incidentally. The suspected authors of the Elizabethan Martin Marprelate tracts (1588–9) were hunted down by the authorities: one died in prison and the other was executed.

Libraries – particularly the great national libraries – sometimes hold presentation or deposit copies containing an inscription that may reveal authorship, though in recent times deposit has been the responsibility of the publisher. In other cases copies of an anonymous or pseudonymous book may have been sent to friends of the author with revealing inscriptions, or inscribed by the recipient with the author's real name. In some cases an author's own copy may survive, recognisable from corrections and revisions. However, care must be taken: I recently bought a copy of my own book *The Golden Age of Australian Opera* which had been marked up by an enthusiastic (and unfortunately anonymous) reader in ways that could easily have been mistaken for an author's revisions. The locations of individual copies from a particular edition can now be discovered fairly painlessly from on-line catalogues; but even today few libraries have their full holdings electronically recorded and in cases of serious doubt personal searches and letters of enquiry are still necessary. Tracking down authors' books and letters that remain in the possession of their descendants or of the descendants of friends and patrons will often involve consulting sale catalogues, wills, street directories and electoral registers; however, the musicologist Ralph Kirkpatrick was able to locate descendants of the composer Domenico Scarlatti (1685–1757) simply by looking in the Madrid telephone directory. There will be cases where the study of provenances of surviving copies of the first printing of an anonymous or pseudonymous book may lead us not to the author but at least to the circle of the author. The presence of a book in the auctioneer's sale catalogue of a library (or its absence therefrom) may also be indicative: one would expect the author of an anonymous work at least to have possessed a copy and others to have been presented to close friends. Of course, an author's name on a copy can be a fake added to increase its value and one has to be wary of books owned by individuals of the same name. The specialised knowledge required for research into authors' books is valuably summarised in David Pearson's *Provenance Research in Book History: A Handbook*.[25]

Evidence relating to the writing of a book may also survive in diaries, letters and biographies. Consider Samuel Johnson's story of the sale of Goldsmith's *The Vicar of Wakefield*:

> I received one morning a message from poor Goldsmith that he was in great distress, and, as it was not in his power to come to me, begging that I would come to him as soon as possible. I sent him a guinea, and promised to come to him directly. I accordingly went as soon as I was drest, and found that his landlady had arrested him for his rent, at which he was in a violent passion. I perceived that he had already changed my guinea, and had got a bottle of Madeira and a glass before him. I put the cork into the bottle, desired he would

be calm, and began to talk to him of the means by which he might be extricated. He then told me that he had a novel ready for the press, which he produced to me. I looked into it, and saw its merit; told the landlady I should soon return, and having gone to a bookseller, sold it for sixty pounds. I brought Goldsmith the money, and he discharged his rent, not without rating his landlady in a high tone for having used him so ill.[26]

Johnson's story would be strong corroborative evidence of authorship if there was any doubt in the matter, which in this case there is not. On the other hand anecdotes, especially good ones, always need to be treated with caution, as it is likely that they have been refined as performance pieces through being much repeated or that different events have become fused in the teller's memory. In the Goldsmith instance we will recognise that this is not Johnson speaking directly but Johnson as reported by Boswell, but not, unless we have special knowledge, that the financial details are wrong – Johnson only disposed of a third share in the work on his morning's excursion. What we can have more confidence in is the detail of putting the cork back into the bottle: this is one of the tangential details which stick in memory even when grander matters have grown uncertain. By this principle, originally enunciated by Peter Laslett, Thomas Percy's recollection of an earlier visit to Goldsmith is a more persuasive one:

The Doctor was writing his *Enquiry, etc.* in a wretched dirty room, in which there was but one chair, and when he, from civility, offered it to his visitant, himself was obliged to sit in the window.[27]

Here it is the visit which is the major element of the anecdote and the name of the work the circumstantial detail, reversing the cork-in-the-bottle rule. Sometimes, of course, stories are designed from the beginning to deceive. Among these are pious anecdotes of heretical writers making deathbed recantations of their profane writings, though in the case of Rochester this really does seem to have happened.

Letters, from Dryden's time onwards, preserve much information about authorship. One from Robert Southey to his uncle reveals that, with some embarrassment, he had agreed to be a paid ghost for a work that appeared in 1813 as *An exposure of the misrepresentations and calumnies in Mr. Marsh's review of Sir George Barlow's administration at Madras, by the relatives of Sir George Barlow*.[28] From the great age of personal letter writing between the late eighteenth and mid-twentieth centuries we are often able to trace both the writing and reception of works in great detail. Philip Larkin and Kingsley Amis corresponded regularly throughout most of their writing lives about work in progress, often sent work for comment – acting as each other's editors – and sometimes collaborated by post. Amis managed to lose twenty years of Larkin's letters but Larkin preserved the entire series of Amis's.[29] On 4 August 1950 in a pointed example of revisionary authorship in action, Amis gave Larkin several reasons why he should use 'unpriceable' rather than 'unprintable' in the last line of his poem 'If, My Darling'.[30] This is external evidence at its most specific and revealing.

It is important that no surviving attribution be overlooked. In claiming the satire 'An allusion to Tacitus' as possibly by Rochester, I was guided, among other evidence, by Robert Wolseley's statement that towards the end of Rochester's life he '*was inquisitive after all kind of Histories, that concern'd* England, *both ancient and modern*' and that his pen was '*usually imploy'd like the Arms of the ancient Heroes, to stop the progress of arbitrary Oppression, and beat down the Bruitishness of headstrong Will; to do his King and Countrey justice upon such publick State-Thieves, as wou'd beggar a Kingdom to enrich themselves*'.[31] No poems then regarded as canonical fitted this description with its clear evocation of the political struggles over the Exclusion Bill, whereas the 'Allusion' (not to be confused with Rochester's separate 'An allusion to Horace') was exactly of the type described. The poem survives in two contemporary MS anthologies of verse by Rochester, apparently circulated within his extended family, and eleven other contemporary sources which give no author's name. It was only after my edition was in print that I came across a single line from the poem in J. W. Ebsworth's notes to his 1881 edition of *The Roxburghe Ballads* ascribed to Wolseley himself.[32] The source of this attribution is not revealed and its significance has still to be determined. Wolseley was close to Rochester, for whom he served as a kind of literary executor. To complicate matters, another poem definitely by Rochester, 'Artemiza to Chloe', appears in one normally well-informed MS source with the rubric 'This poeme is supposed, to bee made by ye Earle of Rochester, or Mr Wolseley'.[33] The uncertainty over the 'Allusion' extends to the prose skit 'To the reader', attributed by me to Rochester on the grounds of its presence in the same two manuscripts, and which includes a shorter version of the 'Allusion'. Could both be works by a Rochester disciple which had infiltrated an apparently authoritative collection; or could Wolseley have been the compiler of that collection and merely assisted in putting the 'Allusion' into circulation from it? The vital step in solving this problem will be the discovery of Ebsworth's authority for his attribution.

By using personal, official and commercial records in combination, together with correspondence and surviving ascriptions, it is possible to create a general picture of a clandestine writing culture which can then be used to investigate the circumstances of origin of individual texts. East European *samizdat* writing of the Cold War period is still too close to us for this process of study to have proceeded very far: one can only hope that still-living survivors of that heroic culture are chronicling it for the benefit of future researchers. The anonymous and pseudonymous writings of the French Enlightenment currently engage a devoted band of attributionists publishing through the annual *La Lettre clandestine*.

PSEUDONYMS AND MOTTOS

Pseudonyms are a world in themselves. Consider this from a review by Christopher Tiffin of Juliet Flesch's bibliography of Australian romance novels:

> Take the case of Lee Pattinson who is credited with just one novel under her real name. The biographical note adds: 'Also writes as Nonie Arden, Rebecca Dee, Kerry Mitchell and Pamela Nicholls sharing some of these pseudonyms with Rena Cross.' Checking 'Nonie Arden' in the bibliography we find five novels. Under 'Rebecca Dee' we find a further five, but also a note saying that this pseudonym is shared by Rena Cross. 'Kerry Mitchell' is credited with five novels dated 1960 (one of which was reissued in 1962 under a different title), seven dated 1961, three dated 1962, and two dated 1963. However, one of the 1961 titles, we are told, was actually written by Ray Slattery. There is no listing under 'Pamela Nicholls', implying that Pattinson used this name either for magazine stories or work other than romance fiction. There is no cross reference to 'Teri Lester', but we learn from another part of the bibliography that this is the pseudonym of Lee Pattinson and Richard Wilkes Hunter who together published two romances.
>
> Backtracking to Rena Cross who is also sometimes 'Rebecca Dee', we find that this is the real name of someone who wrote as 'Rene Crane', 'Rebecca Dee', 'John Duffy', 'Christine James', 'Karen Miller' and 'Geoffrey Tolhurst', and that she 'shared some pseudonyms' with Lee Pattinson. Of these six pseudonyms, only 'Rebecca Dee' and 'Karen Miller' occur in the bibliography. 'Karen Miller' wrote eleven novels, one of which, however, is the 1961 title already listed under 'Kerry Mitchell' (= Lee Pattinson) but actually ascribed to Ray Slattery.[34]

Such transformations are characteristic of genre writing at every place and time. Tiffin notes that 'in reading through this list one is reminded how dependent we are on stable authorship in categorising books' (p. 61). Flesch subverts this assumption by alphabetising her material under pseudonyms, not actual authors (thus the difficulty in identifying the Pattinson *œuvre*); moreover, these pseudonyms are spoken of in the entries as if they are actual authors with a gender ('Only two of the five books written by Ms Lester have been published in Australia'). In many instances the game of inventing aliases for genre writing seems to have been indulged in chiefly for its own sake, as it is surely less beneficial for authors than establishing and maintaining a single popular name. Practical reasons given include the unwillingness of publishers to saturate the market with the works of a particular writer and the need to evade contractual restrictions by spreading work over a number of publishers.

Of course pseudonyms may themselves be a source of information. In the passage from the Tiffin review Rena Cross is recognisable in 'Rene Crane', 'Kerry Mitchell' in 'Karen Miller' and most of 'Teri Lester' is present in *Ri*chard Wi*l*k*es*-Hun*ter*. The nineteenth-century bibliographer of erotica, H. S. Ashbee, brought out his books under the pseudonym Pisanus Fraxi, an anagram of 'fraxinus apis' which is Latin for 'ash' (tree), 'bee'. A considerable number of modern pseudonyms are simply the author's two forenames, omitting the surname, as in Richmal Crompton [Lamburn] and Nevil Shute [Norway] (this may also be a conscious reclaiming of a maternal surname in place of the patriarchal). When a surname has to be invented certain names seem to possess a special attractiveness. In the eighteenth century aristocratic names like Stanhope and Villiers were popular. In the twentieth century Scottish names like Campbell and Hamilton have exerted a mysterious pull: pseudonymous Hamiltons include C. S. Lewis, Judith Merrill and Edward L. Stratemeyer. The most important requirement for a surname to be used professionally is that it should be odd enough to be memorable. No one would set out to make a career as a writer as John Grey or Jane Smith: to have been born L. Sprague de Camp is itself a bonus. In the early and mid-twentieth century, there was a tendency to replace central European names, especially Slavic and Jewish ones, with conventional Anglo-Celtic ones. None of Stratemeyer's many names (see below) was nearly as exotic as his real one. French-sounding names on the other hand had a vogue in romance writing. 'Daphne du Blanc' turns up incongruously in a list of eight pseudonyms used by Arthur William Groom (1898–1964). The attributionist soon develops a sense for the shape and sound of an invented name – one worked out so that it will look arresting on a book jacket.

In work produced under the factory system, pseudonyms are simply part of the product to be assigned by the publisher, not devised by the writer. Edward L. Stratemeyer (1862–1930), a prolific American writer of juvenile fiction, used or managed at least seventy pseudonyms through his Stratemeyer Syndicate. Victor Appleton was used for the 'Don Sturdy' series, Victor Appleton II for the 'Tom Swift jr.' series, Philip A. Bartlett for the 'Roy Stover Mystery' series, May Hollis Barton for the 'Barton Books for Girls' series, Charles Amory Beach for the 'Air Service Boys' series and so on through the alphabet to Clarence Young who appeared as the author of 'Jack Ranger', 'Motor Boys' and 'Racer Boys' books. Franklin W. Dixon was the collective pseudonym for the 'Hardy Boys', Carolyn Keene for Nancy Drew, and Laura Lee Hope for the Bobbsey Twins – all three still in production. It was usual for a single author (often Stratemeyer himself during his lifetime) to be in charge of each pseudonym but to draw on the assistance of 'half ghosts'.[35] Knowing these things George Orwell (alias Eric Blair) in his *Horizon* essay on 'Boys' weeklies' was perfectly within his rights to assume that 'Frank Richards' stood in the same relationship to the 'Billy Bunter' series of boys' stories and 'Bessie Bunter' series of girls' stories and was as surprised as anyone when a perfectly real Frank Richards asserted his authorship of every single word.[36] Genre fiction can in this respect be viewed as an attributionist's Garden of Eden, Amazonian rainforest or magician's hall of mirrors depending on taste. The more troubling question is whether there is any point in assigning authors to a literary product which sets out from the start to be indistinguishable. Tiffin concludes that, in the romance genre, the pseudonymous has a greater reality than the actual – a sobering thought for attributionists but not one that should bother poststructuralists unless it meant that royalties were going to the wrong address, which it rarely if ever does. The responses to this are that genre fiction has its own writers of exceptional talent whose work deserves to be tracked down and identified and that writers famous for other things have often written such pieces.

Many books used to come out under their author's initials, but not always in the right order: there is still a school who believe that Thorpe's 'Mr W. H.' in the dedication to Shakespeare's *Sonnets* is really Mr H[enry] W[riothesly]. William Camden first issued his *Brittannia* (1586) under the initials 'M. N.', being the last not the first letters of his name. Many early initials incorporate titles and honorifics: the 1735 first collected edition of Swift's works identifies him only as J.S.D.D.D.S.P.D. (Jonathan Swift, Doctor of Divinity, Dean of St Patrick's Dublin). 'Smectymnuus', the name attached to a famous seventeenth-century anti-episcopal pamphlet, was a compaction of the initials of its five authors, beginning with Stephen Marshal and ending with William Spurstow. There are also 'null initials', like A.B. and N.N. which mean nothing at all. The fact that the first pair are the initials of real people such as Aphra Behn and Alexander Brome should prompt caution about assuming their authorship of such works as 'Rebellions antidote' attributed to Behn by Janet Todd and Virginia Crompton.[37] Essential reading before any attempt is made to unriddle early-modern initials is Franklin B. Williams, jr., 'An initiation into initials'.[38] Frank Molloy has investigated the inventive use of pseudonyms and initials made by the poet Victor J. Daley (1858–1905), who disguised his primary name as 'V.J.D.', 'V. Jay', 'V.' or 'D.' but never used 'V.D.', which in his day was an abbreviation for venereal disease, and was in any case already used by his colleague Valentine Day. Both Valentine Day and Victor J. Daley were themselves pseudonyms. Daley also published as Creeve Roe, C.R., 'L'homme qui rit', Ezra Quair, Mercutio, Quixote and no doubt other names, and was in this typical of staff and freelance journalists of his day.[39]

One of the most puzzling and evocative of initials is inscribed on a rock wall in the Pilbara district of northern Australia above a crude illustration of a ship's wheel and the date 1771. The inscriber began work with a metal tool of some kind but then switched to a pounding stone. The site is close to a river bed along which he may have been journeying, presumably in the company of aborigines since he could hardly have survived in that environment without their help. There was no European settlement on the Australian continent in 1771. 'H' was most likely a shipwrecked or marooned sailor, probably from a Dutch East-Indiaman. Attribution studies are unlikely to make much further progress with this mystery.[40]

From early times until late in the nineteenth century it was common for books to appear with a motto or epigraph on the title-page. Some of these were traditional and shared by many writers; so, first books would often appear with Martial's '*i, fuge; sed poteras tutior esse domi*' (periphrastically: 'Go into the world, book, but you would have been safer staying home'). Yet in other cases an author might use a particular motto in a way that made it almost a second signature – as with the '*stat nominis umbra*' of the letters of Junius. Shakespeare's contemporary, Thomas Heywood, had two mottoes – one for his plays and prose works ('*Et prodesse solent et delectare*') and another for his pageants ('*Redeunt spectacula*'). If an anonymous work were to turn up bearing either of these mottoes, Heywood would have to be considered: conversely one would hesitate before crediting him with a work that did not. James G. McManaway used the presence of an unusual motto '*Hector adest; secumque deos in praelia ducit*' on the anonymous *Dick of Devonshire* (entered in the Stationers' Register, 1626) and the pseudonymous *The Bloody Banquet*

(1639) to suggest common authorship – possibly that of Thomas Drew or Robert Davenport.[41] On the other hand, that '*semel insanivimus omnes*' ('We've all been crazy once') occurs both on Alexander Radcliffe's book of libertine verse, *The Ramble* (1682), and a narrative poem of seduction called *Gallantry A-La-Mode* (1674) is intriguing; but closer inspection backed up by stylometric tests conducted by John Burrows does not yield any grounds for suspecting common authorship. In a case solved by Charles and Ruth Prouty the initials T.M.Q. were established as standing for George Gascoigne since they represented his regular motto '*Tam Marti quàm [Mercurio]*'.[42] There are countless small puzzles of this kind.

As with pseudonyms a motto will occasionally be an anagram of the author's name. Williams gives the example from 1614 of '*R. N. Non luco, subter Rosis* [Robertus Nicolsonus]'.[43] The present writer once employed 'Lorah D. Vole' but denies any connection with Zenobia N. Vole, the author of *Osten's Bay*. Renaissance readers seem to have relished these transformations, which play with the elasticity of the signifier in a way that is thoroughly contemporary; yet even Williams who enjoys and understands the game is only prepared to excuse mystification in cases where it was really necessary to prevent legal reprisals. We must try not to find them merely annoying.

Related to the motto are the favourite quotation and the favourite author. In previous centuries, the favourite quotation might well be helpfully misremembered from early schooling: Dryden is notorious for memorially recomposed Latin, originally imbibed from Dr Busby at Westminster School and never thereafter checked. Or it may have been looked up but from an edition with distinctive readings which differ from those of the modern Loeb and can therefore be tracked down. In earlier centuries, Shakespearean lines will often have been absorbed from performing versions with striking differences from modern scholarly ones, including Colley Cibber's rewrite of *Richard III* and Nahum Tate's of *King Lear*. Little apart from this can be learned from the favourite author if that author happens to be Horace or Shakespeare but an unusual or eccentric fondness, like the fictional Walter Shandy's for the equally fictional Slawkenbergius, might well be indicative.

CONSTRUCTING CONTEXTS

Having considered documentary sources directly related to genesis and distribution, we move into the wider contextualisation of the work, locating it as fully and as precisely as possible in its historical moment. For some studies, particularly those of authors of remote times, this will be as far as the matter can be taken. If we have located a mediaeval treatise within a particular monastery or even in the monasteries of a particular order, or a Renaissance poem or romance in the circle of a particular patron, we may well have done as much as can be done. In other cases we can employ knowledge of the context to confirm or reject assumptions about authorship. Henry Woudhuysen uses patterns in the circulation of manuscripts by Sidney to support the attribution to him of a group of three poems associated with a celebration in 1577 of Queen Elizabeth's accession day.[44] His study is exemplary for the careful way in which a bibliographical map of a writing culture is superimposed upon another of the intricate alliances forged by blood ties, politics, and religion among the Elizabethan ruling class and the points of fit carefully charted.

Such studies are most fruitful when the context is already well mapped. Shakespeare's London, Swift's and Joyce's Dublins and Woolf's Bloomsbury have all been made available to us by scholarship in a way that allows the skilled reader to recognise allegiances, antipathies and allusions. The Canterbury of the young Marlowe and the Lichfield of the young Johnson are much less familiar, even to specialists, while what Vanbrugh experienced in India or Etherege in Constantinople can only be conjectured. In dealing with twentieth-century authors we have grown used to giving a special prominence to sexual orientation as a means of self-definition and the basis of sociability; for the seventeenth and again for the nineteenth century it is no less important to be aware of the precise shading of a writer's religious belief, a field in which we are likely to be much less confident. Few of us ever gain an expert understanding of forms of knowledge that had great prestige in earlier times but now are little understood. All of us realise that to read Donne it is important to know something about alchemy, but how many readers of *Jane Eyre* pick up how deeply the novel is infiltrated by the doctrines of physiognomy and phrenology, then regarded with great seriousness?

'Walter', the still-unidentified author of the famous Victorian erotic memoir *My Secret Life*, poses particular problems of contextualisation because his world is the otherwise virtually undocumented one of prostitution and casual sex with working-class women and servants. In this respect his text is more often treated as a context for other writings, which omit all but the most indirect mentions of such things, than inspected in its own right. This huge book, which was published late in the nineteenth century in a tiny private edition with an introduction and two prefaces, is currently available in several separate paper and hardback editions.[45] The introduction claims to have been written by the publisher of the work, a friend to whom Walter had given the manuscript prior to his death. This friend, we are told, had transcribed the manuscript, omitting marginalia which identified many of the people referred to, then destroyed the original. The first preface presents itself as Walter's own introduction to his first attempt at the work, which he eventually put aside. The second preface is his introduction to the revised and extended version. In the first preface he gives us two assurances: that every account of a sexual encounter is recorded with strict accuracy, and that every reference to his family has been 'mystified' ('if I say I had ten cousins when I had but six, or that one aunt's house was in Surrey instead of Kent, or in Lancashire, it breaks the clue and cannot matter to the reader' (p. 9)). However, this does not mean that Walter has erased all biographical traces: it would be truer to say that he tempts us with the prospect of an elaborately constructed puzzle that has carefully explained rules and no shortage of clues.

> The Christian name of the servants mentioned are generally the true ones, the other names mostly false, tho phonetically resembling the true ones. Initials nearly always the true ones. . . . Streets and baudy houses named are nearly always correct. Most of the houses named are now closed or pulled down; but any middle-aged man about town would recognize them. Where a road, house, room, or garden is described, the description is exactly true, even to the situation of a tree, chair, bed, sofa, pisspot. The district is sometimes given wrongly; but it matters little whether Brompton be substituted for Hackney, or Camden Town for Walworth. Where however, owing to the incidents, it is needful, the places of amusement are given correctly. The Tower, and Argyle Rooms, for example. . . . Nor if I say I had that woman, and did this or that with her, or felt or did aught else with a man, is there a word of untruth, excepting as to the place at which the incidents occurred. But even those are mostly correctly given; this is intended to be a true history, and not a lie. (pp. 9–10)

If we were able to accept this last assurance, there would surely be enough evidence in such a lengthy work to support, if not a positive identification, at least a very narrow contextualisation.

Readers of Walter have generally been prepared to offer him this credence on the grounds of the extraordinary vividness, particularity and at the same time unexpectedness of some of his accounts of particular incidents. However, this kind of plausibility, like any other quality of style, can be contrived by a skilful writer, and it would be rash to take anything in this extraordinary memoir entirely at its face value. As an example of this vividness, consider the following from a passage describing the seduction of a dairymaid:

I stood by the cows, pulled my prick out, begged her to let me do it again, talked all the baudiness I could, . . . lifted up the cow's tail, swore if she did not let me I would put my prick up the cow. It was funny to see a woman . . . pulling vigorously at a cow's teats, whilst a man with his prick exposed was holding up a cow's tail, showing its cacked arse, and not too clean cunt. What absurdity will not a lewed man do? (p. 253)

This passage is either the record of a genuine, bizarre experience or an unusually refined art of faking such experiences. Most readers, I think, would accept the first possibility without too much trouble. In a slightly later episode Walter and his cousin Fred are staying in a vicarage, part of which is used for a girls' school. Hearing distant female voices, they open a locked door in their bedroom and find it leads to a passage which in turn leads to the wall of the school bathroom. By making apertures in the wall they are able to watch the girls taking their baths and two lesbian servants making love (pp. 326–32). This passage is more difficult to take at its face value because, while it displays the same circumstantiality, its structure is that of a conventional pornographic narrative. While one cannot say it could not have happened, it has the stamp of invention.

The solution to this problem may well be stylistic. When Walter writes about his sexual experiences he adopts the language of pornography because that is the only one available to him: he does not have a better way of describing sex than as if it were to an invisible voyeur. Often his language at these points acquires a distinct eighteenth-century quality, suggestive of *Fanny Hill*, a work he much admired and regarded as an actual memoir. This derivation probably influences the ways in which experiences are worked up as narratives, and, possibly, invented narratives added to those based on real experiences. Such passages rapidly become tedious through repetition, making *My Secret Life* one of the few books in which one skips the sex in order to get to the interesting bits. But when Walter is not directly involved in trying to arouse sexual excitement in himself or the reader he is able, drawing on diaries which were close to the events but also on a good memory, to write in a different style which is much more vivid, pictorial and apparently honest. Certainly I believe there is enough unfalsified fact in his narrative to justify a search for his identity. And even when he is carefully trying to deceive he need not always have been successful. He concedes as much himself: he would fain keep his 'outer life . . . hidden, but it is impossible' (p. 396).

Surprisingly little effort seems to have been directed towards discovering Walter's identity. Gershon Legman's implausible proposal that he was the bibliographer H. S. Ashbee is effectively exploded by Gordon

Grimley, while Grimley's hardly more plausible suggestion of William S. Potter seems to have sunk without trace.[46] The contextualisation of the incidents of Walter's narrative depends on having a reliable birth date. Grimley suggests *c*.1806 to *c*.1815, which would give a childhood overshadowed by the French wars and their aftermath and place the years during which he squandered his inherited fortune in debauchery in the late 1820s or early to mid-1830s. Yet one reference clearly suggests a much later date. In recounting his affair with Louise the sister of Camille, he says: 'The Argyle was just opened, and I took her there, she wanted me to go there often' (p. 244). This refers to the Argyle Rooms in Great Windmill Street, just north of Piccadilly Circus, the scene of many later events in the memoir. Raymond Mander and Joe Mitchenson are quite definite that this notorious place opened only in 1849.[47] After Walter has broken off with Louise, he says of himself: 'thrice to have had the clap, and yet not three-and-twenty' (p. 249). This would give him a birth date of 1826 or 1827, much later than Grimley's guess. The years during which he squandered his inheritance would then fall in the late 1840s and early 1850s. His cousin Fred's death in battle in India would have occurred during the Indian mutiny. The whore Irish Kate who died 'of the cholera which was then raging' would have done so in the epidemic of 1854 when Walter was about twenty-seven (pp. 360; 388). Yet, other evidence points to a birth date around 1823: I leave it to Walterologists to resolve the difference.

On pp. 33–5 Walter gives an account of his school, which from the reference to its having two headmasters, could possibly have been Charterhouse.[48] He was a day boy there *c*.1840. A further clue to date and perhaps identity occurs in the aftermath of a trip to Italy begun at Naples in December. Moving from Milan into France, Walter crosses Mont Cenis in a sledge and then travels in a coach to Grenoble, where he has an affair with a woman fellow-traveller. Both book into a hotel under false names. On p. 862 he tells us: 'It was a big old-fashioned hotel (the railway had then not quite reached the town), and none of the hotel-servants could speak anything but French and Italian.' According to Larousse,[49] the railway link from Lyons reached Grenoble on 1 July 1858 with the completion of the three-kilometre link from Piquepierre. The 33-kilometre link from Rives to Piquepierre had been opened on 10 July 1857. Presumably Walter's 'not quite' refers to this period of the final link. It is still midwinter ('it was dark at about five' (p. 869)), so we are probably by now in January or early February 1858. He says of himself and his soon-to-be lover that their names 'were entered from their passports at the frontier' (p. 868). If these records survive in the French or the Piedmontese archives, they should include those of Walter and a woman travelling with her five-year-old son. Of the woman, who passed under a name that appears to have been Maitland, Walter tells us that she had 'C.C.M.' marked on her linen (p. 873); however, this act of identifying a partner is so uncharacteristic that I suspect it of being a deliberate act of 'mystification' and that the real initials were different.

The point of the dating exercise is that adopting an early or a late date gives a totally different context not only to the author but to the writing. If certain events described took place in the 1840s rather than the 1830s a responsive reader will recreate them in different ways, will visualise clothing, and interpret manners and social assumptions differently, and in the end will construct a different Walter: a true dissident Victorian rather than a hangover from Regency libertinism. The work would be snatched from the Never-Never-Land of pornography into a real, complex, nineteenth-century milieu whose (mostly female) faces and voices are always threatening to burst through the glass walls of Walter's micro-world of obsession to announce that their stories are just as important as his own. It is also possible that certain individuals known to history might make the same journey. Could the Sarah Frazer whose four-year association with Walter ended in her mysterious disappearance from London while he was on a trip to Paris be the woman of the same name, and spelling of it, whose sumptuous Melbourne brothel was patronised by Queen Victoria's second son, the Duke of Edinburgh, during the royal tour of Australia of 1867–8? Finding a context for Walter is more important than simply finding a name for him because it makes possible the return of his atomistic but extraordinarily informative text to social and historical time.

The case of Walter also illustrates the unravelling of pseudonymity as an intended element of the reading experience. A more recent example is *The Stranger Inside: An Erotic Adventure*, which its title-page announces as 'Procured by Red Symons'. This is a 'round robin' novel written by ten well-known Australian authors, whose names, in alphabetical order, are given but whose individual contributions are unidentified. Symons explained the rationale of the book to its contributors as follows:

> It places the reader in the position of having to try and figure out each writer's bent. If any chapter meets glowing praise it can be yours. Should you have a grudge against any other contributor, you can write a damning chapter in their style.
>
> Simply put, it frees the writer and teases the reader.[50]

The list of contributors comprises five males (including Symons) and five females: the book is thus a test-case for how well the reader is skilled at distinguishing male writing from female, with the added possibility of gender impersonation. For at least some of its readers the element of the puzzle would be the primary one; for all it should at least be an element in response and enjoyment.[51] Problems of attribution can thus be manufactured in a spirit of play to which the intelligent reader is expected to respond. Possibly Walter intended exactly this as a way of adding interest to a narrative so inanely repetitious that he himself often questioned why he continued writing it.

The example of Walter illustrates both the difficulties and the necessity of establishing a context in Hume's sense. By the same token a failure of context to match some aspect of the writing can call an attribution into question. The indecent burlesque *Sodom* (the sources disagree on its title) was ascribed to Rochester in a printed edition surreptitiously published after his death. The case for his being the author has been most fully pursued by J. W. Johnson in an article published in 1987 and was challenged by the present author in the same journal six years later.[52] Among the issues addressed, the most important one seemed to me to be the contextual one of whether *Sodom* was to be viewed as a court satire. This has been taken for granted by most previous writers, with a number of courtiers named as the originals of characters in the burlesque; but this whole process depends on the prior assumption that the piece was the work of a courtier: viewed on their own merits these identifications make little or no sense. Rochester was a court insider (a gentleman of the bedchamber to Charles II) and his verified court satire is very particular in its references to court identities and current gossip. The absence of this kind of particularity from *Sodom* would itself raise both personal and generic doubts about Rochester's involvement in the piece. As it happens there is another confident early attribution to Christopher Fishbourne, who at the time of composition seems to have been an army officer serving in the Netherlands. The piece makes far better sense to me as a satire on courts by an outsider who had no first-hand knowledge of them. The independent survival of an obscene song by Fishbourne very much in the *Sodom* style gives a degree of support to the attribution.[53]

Securing a contextual reading will sometimes demand a choice between possible contexts both of which cannot be correct. One of the best-known lyrical poems from antiquity is the *Pervigilium Veneris*, a rhapsody to the power of procreation in the human and the natural worlds, which was written to be performed on the night before the festival of the goddess Venus.[54] It survives only in an imperfect text transmitted by the collection known as the *Anthologia Latina*. This appears to have been compiled in Roman north Africa in the early sixth century, giving us a *terminus ad quem* for the date of the poem. The *Anthologia* contains a strong representation of verse from the so-called 'African school' of Latin poets, centred on Carthage, including works written under the Vandal occupation of the fifth and sixth centuries. The poem's quantitative metre, the trochaic tetrameter catalectic, anticipates prosodic features of the accentual poetry of the Middle Ages. Stylistic similarities have been suggested with the four pastorals of Nemesianus (late third century) and the fragments of Tiberianus (mid-fourth century), both of the African school. All of this would suggest an origin in one of the numerous Roman towns of present-day Tunisia.

However, there is another possible contextualisation. The landscape of the poem is not African but Sicilian. The totally pagan view of the power of the generative principle suggests a milieu in which Christianity was not yet a serious challenge, which was certainly not the case in the Carthage and Hippo of Saint Augustine. We should note that the *Anthologia* contains a number of earlier, non-African works, and it is possible that the *Pervigilium* derives from, say, the second century, when there was an official revival of the worship of Venus. We should acknowledge that its 'mediaeval' metre had been used for centuries in popular and theatre songs and existed in demotic as well as learned forms. The *Pervigilium* is pretty certainly a text for singing, perhaps transmitted in this way up to the time of the surviving transcription. Might the poem have been written in second- or third-century Sicily rather than fourth- or fifth-century Africa and found its way across the narrow stretch of sea between the two? The choice between one and the other possible context is one that could only be made, if at all, by a classicist. Yet until it is made we can hardly proceed.

In a case such as this, where internal evidence has taken on an external function, contextual reasoning becomes so heavily speculative as to be of little value. The most we can hope to do is to invent increasingly complex scenarios and see which of them survive, whether by Popper's criterion of falsifiability or because they turn out to reveal unpredicted links and analogies. Boldness is all, but boldness that is always attended by the faithful squire Scepticism and the dwarf Incredulity. Yet, in other cases external evidence can provide information of a copiousness and specificity that would be impossible to obtain by any process of reasoning back from the textual phenomena. It can tell us, on the one hand, who was actually paid for an article in the *Westminster Review* and on the other precisely why one word rather than another appeared in the published version of a poem by Larkin. The attributionist's responsibility is to be open about the fullness and reliability of that evidence and not to try to make it appear any stronger, or weaker, than it actually is.

CHAPTER FIVE

Internal evidence

Whereas external evidence can often be obtained without looking beyond the title-page, the pursuit of internal evidence requires close attention to every word and phrase. However, it also requires some degree of reference to information outside the work, for, as David Lake has pointed out, 'without some unquestioned attributions no other attributions can be questioned'.[1] By an extension of this observation, evidence from, say, the opinions expressed in a work only becomes operative when there is an author or authors who might have held these opinions. If internal evidence exists in a pure form it can only be in those cases when the common authorship is established of two anonymous works. Arthur Sherbo divided up internal evidence between *style* and *ideas*, with style also embracing 'range and density of learning and allusions, and parallels of various kinds with known works by the particular writer in question'.[2] Style in the narrower sense will be considered in Chapters six and eight; this chapter will concern itself with the other elements instanced by Sherbo, along with decorum and aesthetic preference.

When Sherbo delivered his paper in 1958 there was still something suspect about the claim that questions of attribution could be determined by internal evidence alone. The generally hostile response to his position in the Erdman and Fogel volume in which it appeared and in Schoenbaum's *Internal Evidence and Elizabethan Dramatic Authorship* arose from fear that he was advocating a return to the bad old days of uncritical parallel-hunting which had discredited much early research into the authorship of English Renaissance plays. But the fact that a technique is badly applied in one case does not mean it may not be well applied elsewhere, as in Erdman's chapter on Coleridge's contributions to the *Morning Post* in his own collection. We can see now that Sherbo's argument was a prophetic one – prefiguring the new emphasis to be placed on internal evidence through the application of stylometric methods and the ability of the computer to search enormous databases of text for similarities in expression and ideas. At the time of writing we seem to be experiencing a second reaction in favour of external evidence, exemplified in the work of Furbank and Owens on Defoe.

IDEAS AND ETHOS

Discussing ideas, Sherbo entered a caution which is particularly important for the eighteenth-century texts that were his main concern:

> It is obvious that the ideas expressed in a given piece must be consonant with those of the putative author, unless a very convincing explanation for the absence, or seeming absence, of such consonance can be advanced. Sometimes, we all realize, the ideas expressed are in direct and deliberate conflict with the known views of the author in question; we generally call this irony.[3]

Irony apart, 'ideas' may represent deeply held beliefs, casual suppositions, dandyish intellectual poses, or outright fraud. Ideas propounded with some conviction over a long period are the most useful for investigating authorship: one would not expect the Laudian George Herbert to argue the Puritan position that sermons were more important than sacraments. Yet, an author might still become caught up in some transient enthusiasm or fall under the influence of some persuasive advocate of a new cause, only to move on to fresh views or revert to old ones. An idea must also have some degree of complexity if it is to offer grounds for an attribution: a conviction that the moon is made of green cheese is not as indicative as an understanding of the theory of the tides. The co-presence of two or more unrelated ideas gives each an enhanced force as indicators of common authorship. Because both belong to the same field of study, knowledge of the theory of the tides and planetary astronomy would not be as impressive as knowledge of the theory of tides *and* the microbiology of cheese-making. Only a scientific polymath or a high-school science teacher would be likely to combine such disparate kinds of expertise.

In a well-regulated mind an idea may be part of a coherent world-view which can be explored element by element. The Shakespearean ideas of 'degree' as explained by Ulysses in *Troilus and Cressida* and of 'honour' as it is described by Falstaff in *Henry IV, Part I* each require a fairly lengthy speech for their articulation and lead on seamlessly to related passages in other Shakespearean plays. However, not all minds are that well regulated. Some authors are connoisseurs or even gourmands of unusual ideas. In this class we might put Robert and Richard Burton, both the Samuel Butlers, Laurence Sterne and Aldous Huxley. Sterne mined *Chambers's Encyclopaedia* for exotic learning, while Huxley took a complete India paper edition of the *Britannica* with him on an alpine holiday. The consistencies in the world-views of these two last-named writers have to be sought in their characteristic ways of deploying what by normal standards would count as a wild profusion of information and ideas.

Ideas may be either derivative or original without prejudice to their status as markers of authorship. Derivative ideas fall under the scholarly rubric of 'influences' for which there is an enormous expert literature, albeit one that has to be used with caution. Scholars are prone to credit writers with much wider expert reading than they ever performed. As has often been pointed out, if Shakespeare had read all the books claimed to have influenced him, he would never have had time to write a word of his own. He probably picked up many of his ideas from conversation. If he needed legal knowledge it was easier to extract this from Inns-of-Court drinkers in the Devil Tavern than to search volumes of precedents. Knowledge of a writer's 'range and density of learning' can be sought from letters, diaries and recorded conversations, or the catalogue of a personal library, if one survives. However, beliefs that were commonplaces of the age, or even widely held in particular cultural sub-groups, cannot be allowed to count for much. Ideas freely available from well-known writers of the past must also be treated carefully: it is a frequent occurrence for different readers to be struck by the same passages in Homer, Dante, Milton or Foucault.

It is important when we make claims for the singularity of ideas that we understand the devious ways by which knowledge can come to be shared by select groups of contemporaries. Arcane information acquired from a single schoolmaster (consider the roll-call of writers taught by Dr Busby during his long career at Westminster School) or at a particular community of the learned, such as a university college, may be the possession of a group rather than an individual. Anglophone culture has been rich in circles, clubs and movements, some of them famous, others virtually unknown, but all leaving their distinct heritage of exclusively shared ideas.[4] We all know of Bloomsbury and the Algonquin round table but it is only recently that the lasting influence of the seventeenth-century circles of Lucius Cary, Viscount Falkland and Samuel Hartlib has been fully documented. The eighteenth-century coffee-house was a circulation point for news while at the same time often serving as a club for the like-minded, both receiving and engendering new ideas. The masonic lodge played an important role in disseminating the ideas of the Enlightenment. Long-established 'secret societies' still thrive at some older British and North American universities. At my own university, a great deal of information is exchanged between academics and students who regularly use a particular rail service. In the sixteenth and seventeenth centuries a substantial element of intellectual life was kept up through the communication of short manuscript treatises between geographically dispersed enthusiasts, projectors and believers. Moving without the intervention of the press, these semi-visible, 'reserved' writings made an enormous contribution to the transmission of ideas in their time: their modern equivalent would be new knowledge circulating between intercontinental groups of internet users.[5] Through all of these not immediately evident mechanisms, ideas that appear characteristic of an individual may well prove to be common to a group of associates.

As an example of a hermetic writing community we might take the London music critics between the 1840s and the 1870s, when the profession was dominated by the *Times*'s larger-than-life pundit, James William Davison. After each concert, all the critics, with the exception of one 'ladylike' dissenter, would gather in a front room of the Albion Tavern, close to Drury Lane. Here they would discuss the night's performance, write their copy (which would be despatched by messenger to their respective journals) and then drink together into the early hours of the morning. How many 'ideas' about works and composers were passed around during those sessions, later to appear in one or another review?[6] In the early Stuart period a wide, politically active, community of antiquarians, lawyers and writers – including some who were all three – was created through their use of Sir Robert Cotton's splendid collection of mediaeval manuscripts and state papers. At the heart of the group were the members of the Society of Antiquaries, whose deliberations were circulated in manuscript essays that did not reach the press until 1720. It would be a brave attributionist who found an 'idea' to be characteristic of any single member of this tightly-knit group. By comparison Dr Johnson's late eighteenth-century club lies open to history through the record of its interactions given by Boswell and other partakers. These examples caution us against a too easy use of the striking idea as a marker of a single author.

How do we go about comparing ideas in an anonymous work with those of a known author? An illuminating test case is that of the 'hand D' passages in the manuscript of *Sir Thomas More* (BL MS Harleian 7368). The original play was probably written in the early 1590s as a collaboration between Anthony Munday and Henry Chettle. Because of its subject matter, the Master of the Revels refused to permit it to be performed at the time; however, various 'additions' were subsequently made, the hands of which have been identified as those of an anonymous theatre scribe (hand C), of Thomas Dekker (hand E) and of Shakespeare (hand D).[7] The three hand-D pages, dated by Wells and Taylor to 1603–6, represent an authorial draft with corrections and revisions.[8] One of hand C's passages has also been attributed to Shakespeare. Palaeographic comparisons do not contradict the hypothesis that hand D is Shakespeare's but are limited by the fact that the only ascertained examples are six signatures and the two words 'by me'. No assurance of identity could be given on this slim basis. Spelling evidence (particularly the rare 'scilens') is again suggestive but not conclusive. The language of the scenes contains many parallels with other works by Shakespeare but also, as we would expect, with those of other dramatists, including Heywood.

A justly admired analysis of the ideas of the passage was given by R. W. Chambers in his essay 'Shakespeare and the play of *More*' which appeared in its fullest form in *Man's Unconquerable Mind*.[9] Chambers deprecates verbal parallels, pointing out that 'Common Elizabethan phrases have too often been claimed as proofs of two authors being the same man' (p. 226). Instead he argues from what he calls 'combinations' but that we might think of as sequences of topics in the development of an argument. Several of these are isolated and their common elements analysed. In *More* and the Jack Cade scenes of *Henry VI, Part II* he finds a parallel sequence which traverses (a) the entrance of an orator already talking, (b) 'the enumeration of things which go to make up the painful budgets of the poor, with false economics based on the *halfpenny loaf*', (c) logic-chopping based on the otherwise unknown form 'argo' for 'ergo', (d) the presentation of ridiculous reasons for rioting, (e) 'absurd statements about the corruption spread by such innovations', and (f) a sudden deviation into savagery (p. 218). In Ulysses' speech from *Troilus and Cressida*

> Shakespeare, as Raleigh says, 'extols government with a fervour that suggests a real and ever-present fear of the breaking of the flood-gates'. But my point is that this fervour, in itself highly characteristic, is expressed both in *Sir Thomas More* and in *Troilus and Cressida* by a quite individual succession of thoughts: *(a)* Degree neglected, *(b)* the flood surging over its banks, *(c)* the doing to death of the aged or the babes, *(d)* cannibal monsters. It is this linking of the thought that matters. The wording is not the same, nor have we any reason to demand that it should be the same. (p. 226)

However, in *Coriolanus* there is a verbal echo linked to one of these constituent ideas:

> It has been pointed out how frequent in Shakespeare, as illustrating insubordination or rebellion in men, is the image of waters breaking their bounds and overbearing everything. The comparison of Laertes, overbearing the officers of Claudius, to 'the ocean overpeering of his list' will occur to the reader. But both in *Coriolanus* and in D's 'three pages' this parallel in thought is closely associated with a verbal echo.
>
> Cominius leads Coriolanus away with the words
>
> Will you hence
> Before the tag return? Whose rage doth rend
> Like interrupted waters, and o'erbear
> What they are used to bear.
>
> Menenius remains to intercede for 'the consul Coriolanus':
>
> BRUTUS He consul!
> CITIZENS *No, No, No, No, No.*
>
> In the 'three pages' Surrey provokes the mob by a jeer entirely in the manner of Coriolanus himself. The mob shout him down:
>
> ALL We'll not hear my lord of Surrey:
> *No, No, No, No, No.*
> MORE Whiles they are o'er the bank of their obedience
> Thus will they bear down all things. (pp. 226–7)

The cumulative effect of these and other combinations is highly persuasive even when their individual elements may be shared with other writers. While it is conceivable that the *Henry VI* passage had been used for an elaborate kind of plagiarism which traced its original by topics not words, this could hardly apply to works yet to be written. A closely related technique traces the patterns of association involved in image clusters. Chambers drew on Caroline Spurgeon's pioneering work in this field, which was later developed from a psychoanalytic perspective by Edward A. Armstrong and has recently been reviewed from that of cognitive science in Mary Crane's *Shakespeare's Brain*, a work of great interest for attribution studies.[10]

A version of Chambers's method of combinations is given by Richard Filloy in a discussion of John Selden's *Table-talk*.[11] Selden's vast erudition and opposition to the personal rule of Charles I made him a cultural hero to the Whigs of Charles II's reign, among whom *Table-talk* circulated in manuscript for some time before it was published in 1689, thirty-five years after the author's death. But are we entitled to speak of Selden as its author? The work is a compilation by his secretary Richard Milward of things *spoken* by Selden. The form in which these were transcribed and their selection is the work of Milward, as is their arrangement under alphabetically arranged subject headings. The initial act of scribal publication appears to have been the presentation of a copy to each of its four dedicatees, all distinguished legal men and friends of Selden. This dedication is also a claim for authenticity: the four concerned may be presumed to have had a good knowledge of what was said around the eponymous table; nonetheless, Filloy correctly considered it necessary to verify the matter by comparing the opinions expressed (usually with great frankness) in the *Table-talk* with those of Selden's voluminous published works.

Filloy begins with some unexceptionable moves. Testing for common ideas rests on the assumption that 'like effects are produced by like causes' (p. 42); yet it is not enough that there are 'large similarities' between the matters which concerned Selden in real life and those considered in *Table-talk*: these will be shared with other contemporaries. What carries weight is the *treatment* of the topic, particularly a pattern of precept in one text mirrored by example in another, and the common use of rhetorical inventions that take us from the same starting point to the same end, albeit by different routes. Filloy's example of this second mode of similarity is two passages on the right of presbyteries to excommunicate, the first from a report of a speech delivered by Selden in parliament in 1645 and the second from *Table-talk.*

> No man is kept from the Sacrament, *eo nomine*, because he is guilty of any sin, by the constitution of the Reformed Churches, or because he hath not made satisfaction. Every man is a sinner; the difference is only that one is a sinner in private, the other in public; the one is as much against God as the other.
>
> * * *
>
> Christ suffered Judas to take the Communion. Those Ministers that keep their Parishioners from it, because they will not do as they will have them, revenge, rather than reform. No Man can tell whether I am fit to receive the Sacrament; for though I were fit the day before, when he examined me, at least appeared so to him, yet how can he tell, what sin I have committed that night, or the next morning, or what impious Atheistical thoughts I may have about me, when I am approaching the very Table? (p. 44)

Mere interest in this topic is not a marker of authorship, as it was a much contested one at the time. The possession of a strongly partisan view on the matter is better evidence, especially since it is one opposed equally to Laudian Anglicanism and the Puritanism of the Assembly of Divines. Both passages base their argument on the Calvinist dogma of the universal depravity of mankind but turn it by an ingenious twist into a confutation of those clergy who would stand in moral judgement on their parishioners. The second passage develops the idea of the first so as to make it even more subversive of the authority of the clergy and, in doing so, allows us to discover this subversion, in a way not immediately apparent, in the second sentence of the first passage. Taken together, the passages betray a profound Erastianism (the doctrine of the subordination of the ecclesiastical to the civil power) which neither by itself fully reveals. Both the ideological presupposition and the devious way in which it is deployed suggest common authorship.

While the evidence of ideas, if applied with the cautions just suggested, can certainly be used for positive identification, its real value lies in excluding candidates for authorship. Unless it is some kind of spoof or a piece of paid journalism, a work espousing predestination could not have been the work of an Arminian; one maintaining a uniformitarian view of the development of the natural world could not have been the work of a catastrophist; contagionist views on the spread of disease could not have been advocated by a miasmatist; a work sympathetic to the use of protective tariffs to encourage the growth of national industries could not be the work of an economic rationalist; a work espousing the sanctity of the patriarchal family is not the work of a radical feminist. Often it takes only a phrase or two to derail an attribution; on other occasions it might well be done by the absence of the expected. Most present-day works of reference give the pious Zachary Mayne (1631–94) as the author of the anonymous *Two Dissertations concerning Sense and the Imagination* (1728), but the attribution goes back no further than Robert Watt's *Bibliotheca Britannica* (1824). Tim Milnes rejects it on the grounds that Mayne's published works 'are notably free from any trace of the language of the new philosophy which saturates the *Two Dissertations*' and that 'the Bible is barely mentioned throughout the *Two Dissertations*'.[12]

Evidence from an author's reading can be particularly telling for earlier periods when books were not nearly as common as they had become a century or so after the invention of printing. R. W. Chambers produced an ingenious argument for the three texts of *Piers Plowman* being the work of the same author by analysing the quotations they contain from one part of the New Testament, the epistles, which contain a total of 121 chapters. The widest range of quotations is found in the B text which draws on twenty-two chapters. The nine quotations from the A text and eight out of the nine in the additions to the C text are all from within the same twenty-two chapters.[13] In Chaucer, by contrast, of seventy quotations from the epistles only twenty-six come from those twenty-two chapters.

PROFILING THE AUTHOR

Analyses of the kind proposed in the earlier sections can be used for a process similar to the profiling of the perpetrators of crimes or the preparation of personality inventories by psychologists. In establishing an attribution, profiles will be necessary for both the author of the anonymous or pseudonymous work and the principal suspect or suspects. Ideally that of the author and those of the suspects should be compiled by different researchers so as to remove any temptation to cook the books. Such a profile will extend beyond ethos to consider all aspects of the text which have any bearing on personality, including singularities of style. The method naturally works best with the more personal kinds of writing: one would have to proceed with great caution in attempting to profile a dramatist through his or her characters (which has not stopped many attempts). Such a matching of profiles would not establish the matter on its own but would be a useful adjunct to other arguments.

In mediaeval studies such a method is often the only kind of attribution that can be attempted. We can profile the Gawain-poet (or poets) but not identify him (or them).[14] William Langland's name is given to us as the author of *Piers Plowman*, but, apart from a few sketchy details, what we know of him is derived from his poem. Much critical writing is in effect a form of profiling: the critic attempts to define the particular sensibility or world-view of the author and to distinguish it from that of other authors. Critical analyses can be used, with proper caution, in building our sense of an author's ethos and personality but only when there is agreement between critics working from different positions, since the critic's profile has a strong tendency to be a displaced self-portrait. It goes without saying that the reader needs to be convinced that the affinities proposed are really individual. One would expect two Augustinian friars of the fifteenth century or two eighteenth-century French philosophers to show similarities in self-presentation as well as knowledge. We must also be aware of the phenomenon of authors' close modelling of themselves on a revered elder or predecessor. Lastly, we must never forget that the 'author in the work' is always a textual performance.

SELF ALLUSION

Works which include extensive descriptions of the writer's own experiences should be unproblematical – exceptions are when the author is a person of exceptional obscurity or in cases of deliberate falsification in order to prevent identification or to deflect responsibility for the text to another. When the work is of a more impersonal kind, conscious or unconscious self-reference will frequently give pointers.

To begin with an obvious case. Consider the following passage in an anonymous newspaper review of 1872 of a performance of Falconer's *Snare*, which included a morgue scene:

> A morgue, to be sure, is not a cheerful place to be in; but the writer of this chronicle has seen some very striking episodes happen in a morgue. Not many months ago he saw a ruddy-faced man turn green, on being confronted with the body of a beautiful girl whom there is every moral certainty he murdered. The law exculpated this man, but the helpless terror he showed when he saw the corpse of the woman he had loved and killed, was something never to be forgotten. Still later this chronicler saw a beautiful girl brought to the wretched shed which until lately did duty for a morgue in this city, to identify a body supposed to be that of her father. It *was* her father, and the piteous wail of anguish that poor girl gave utterance to when she saw the disfigured face of her parent still rings in his ears. You may probably remember the swamp murder about two years ago. It was full of mystery, and the ghastly social surroundings which distinguished it made altogether a dreadful drama of fearful particulars. The morgue was the centre of all the action in that murder. Dozens of persons were brought by the police, to identify the body of the poor creature who had been strangled at the back of the barracks, and the varying emotions manifested by these people, constituted so many terrible pictures of a state of existence which only now and then shows itself above the surface of the dark pitchy stream which courses through the brightest parts of civilisation.[15]

Here, again, the distinction between the 'internal' and the 'external' is a shaky one. The information that the drama critic James Edward Neild was also a forensic pathologist responsible for autopsies on suspicious deaths comes from outside the text. (He is particularly hard on implausible stage murders, sometimes even to the extent of explaining how they could have been done better.)

Of a more subtle kind are the examples of self-reference in Martin Battestin's assessment of the *Craftsman* essays which he ascribes to Henry Fielding.[16] Here the case is more difficult, since Fielding's association with the journal is only a plausible supposition. Both Fielding and the writer of *Craftsman* no. 403 were familiar with boxing and fencing matches held at Figg's amphitheatre, while the writer of no. 644 had eyewitness information from a 'friend' about events in Jamaica which had involved one of Fielding's uncles. Some of Battestin's ascriptions to Fielding are plausible, others less so; but the weakness of the method is that each is relevant only to the essay in which it occurs. The 'Jamaican' allusion cannot be admitted as evidence for the 'boxing' essay or vice versa.

PARALLELS

Of all the evidence brought in the case of *The Revenger's Tragedy*, none impresses as forcefully as the parallel noted by R. H. Barker between a speech by Vindice in that play and one by Follywit in Middleton's *A Mad World My Masters*.

> But I haue found it;
> Twill hold, tis sure, thankes, thankes to any spirit,
> That mingled it mongst my inuentions....
> Nay doubt not tis in graine, I warrant it hold collour.
>
> * * *
>
> Peace, tis mine owne yfaith, I haa'te ...
> Thankes, thankes to any spirit,
> That mingled it mongst my inuentions....
> And thou shalt see't quickly yfaith; nay tis in graine,
> I warrant it hold colour.[17]

Common authorship is not the only possible explanation of this striking parallel, but taken together with all the other evidence supporting Middleton's participation it becomes the most likely. On the other hand the mass of trivial and approximate resemblances accepted by an earlier generation of Elizabethan scholars have long been recognised as possessing little evidential value. Battestin defends the inclusion of trivial parallels on the grounds of a principle enunciated by James Earle Dease that 'the probability of Fielding's authorship of a given anonymous essay increases in proportion to the number of close correspondences (whether commonplaces or otherwise) between that essay and his known writings'.[18] But no accumulation of parallels in idiom or vocabulary between the newly ascribed essays and Fielding's known writings can prove anything at all about authorship unless it is also shown that the locutions were *not* part of the general current resources of Augustan literary English.

Simple, commonsense principles for the citing of parallels in studies of Elizabethan drama, which apply equally well to other fields, were enunciated as long ago as 1932 by Muriel St Clare Byrne.[19] They were quoted with approval by Schoenbaum,[20] and are given again here with interpolated comment.

(1) Parallels may be susceptible of at least three explanations: (a) *unsuspected identity of authorship,* (b) *plagiarism, either deliberate or unconscious,* (c) *coincidence;*

To this list should be added indebtedness to a common original falling short of plagiarism. In the high classical literature of the eighteenth century many similarities between writers arise from common imitation of a Greek or Latin source. Roger Lonsdale's Annotated English Poets edition of Gray, Collins and Goldsmith shows this process in action through the editor's exceptionally meticulous hunting down of ancient models.[21]

(2) Quality *is all-important, and parallels demand very careful grading – e.g. mere verbal parallelism is of almost no value in comparison with parallelism of thought coupled with some verbal parallelism;*

Verbal parallelism and parallelism of thought can both arise coincidentally or from a common influence. The combination of the two is certainly stronger but even that can be deceptive.

(3) mere accumulation of ungraded parallels does not prove anything;

When Byrne wrote, the accumulation of parallels was a labour-intensive business which depended on incessant reading of the works concerned. Today a phrase can be pursued almost instantaneously through the magnificent on-line LION archive, which covers all fields of English and American drama and of authored volumes of poetry up to 1900, and in many cases beyond, and is rapidly extending into prose. Greatly welcome though this is, it is noteworthy that a whole genre of 'leonine' scholarship has arisen in which a claim is buttressed by a huge list of extracted quotations without any thought being given as to whether the (frequently obscure) source could possibly have been of interest to or even accessible to the writer concerned, while the glaringly obvious model is overlooked. Now that the capacity to multiply parallels – most of which will be misleading – is almost unlimited, intelligent selectivity has never been more important.

(4) in accumulating parallels for the sake of cumulative effect we may logically proceed from the known to the collaborate, or from the known to the anonymous play, but not from the collaborate to the anonymous;

The problem of collaboration was the central one addressed in Byrne's paper. The key point here is that wording in a collaborative work belongs to no one unless the division of labour has been conclusively demarcated. Schoenbaum proposes the additional rule: '*Parallels from plays of uncertain or contested authorship prove nothing.*'

(5) in order to express ourselves as certain of attributions we must prove exhaustively that we cannot parallel words, images, and phrases as a body from other acknowledged plays of the period; in other words, the negative check must always be applied.

Here LION, Gutenberg and similar electronic archives come into their own, since as well as providing illusory parallels they also assist mightily in shooting down those which arise from the common parlance of the time. Once we have encountered an unusual expression in the writings of three or four different authors it ceases to have any value for attribution.[22] What we are looking for is occurrences restricted to two sources only: one the anonymous work and the other a signed one! Even that might not be final: if the two authorial corpora are both large enough, chance alone would dictate that they should contain a few exclusive parallels.

GENRE, DECORUM AND AESTHETIC PREFERENCE

Since all writing is generic, we must now consider how the handling of received forms can support or refute claims to common authorship. Genre comes attended by rules and techniques which can be analysed and compared, and some of the most powerful arguments for and against attribution have been of this kind. Of course there will always be parodies and travesties in which a writer disobeys rules which are usually observed with care – Mozart's 'A Musical Joke' with its consecutive fifths and octaves, mistransposed horn parts and deliberately maladroit 'rosalia' is one example. Such works can usually be recognised for what they are: what is likely to be misleading is when one writer tries out another's style experimentally. There will also be iconoclastic works in which a writer deliberately and unparodistically sets out to break rules, or abandons one style for a wholly different one.

Management of form, which is one aspect of genre, is rarely stable over a whole career. One paradigm frequently invoked is that by which a writer begins as an apprentice, slowly learning the rules and routines of a particular genre, advances to mastery, moves further still to establish a distinctive version of the inherited form – making it a vehicle for personal insights – and then in a transcendental 'last stage' moves past all rules into a transparent simplicity. Shakespeare's last plays and Beethoven's final string quartets are both frequently written about in these terms. However, having given these examples, one needs at once to qualify them. In Shakespeare's case the masterly compression of *The Tempest* is contradicted by the sprawling fecundity of *A Winter's Tale*; in Beethoven's the luminous simplicity of the op. 135 quartet sits side-by-side with the grandiose intricacy of the op. 133. The most we can say is that at the end of their careers both creators were radically innovative. For beginnings, on the other hand, there is some truth to the paradigm. All writers, musicians and artists have to address the styles and models of their time before they can progress beyond them: it is given to very few to strike out at once in a completely individual way. In some cases (consider Hardy as a novelist or Blake as a poet) what are initially infelicities in handling the reigning techniques develop into a form of originality; in other cases it is a question of a growing fluency in the use of received forms. The point in an historical phase at which a career falls will be important. For some writers the learning stage will take place in a milieu rich in experimentation and revolutionary possibilities. Here we may expect to find Bloomian strong misreadings of the parent and the trialling of a number of styles. For others learning will occur within an assured tradition in which forebears are to be revered and copied.

When looking at individual authors it is necessary to distinguish those elements that remain stable over a lifetime from those that evolve, the first kind being the valuable ones for attribution as such, and the second kind important for dating. In considering Byron's handling of the nine-line Spenserian stanza, we would need to compare his practice with that of forerunners like Spenser himself and Thompson and contemporaries such as Keats and Shelley; but we would also have to recognise that aspects of Byron's practice varied considerably even within a single work, *Childe Harold*, published between 1812 and 1818. An analysis by Harold Stein of precisely this topic reached the following conclusions:

1. The metrical construction in the first two cantos is very rigid, the stanzas are self-contained, there is normally a sharp break after the fourth line, and, most important, *Byron is really writing in couplets*. The thought is usually expressed in two lines, and the even lines are, therefore, comparatively end-stopped.
2. The second canto shows a slightly greater metrical freedom than the first.
3. The third canto has lost the rigidity of the first two, *and the bondage to the couplet is broken*.
4. The fourth canto shows a further advance in run-on lines within each stanza, and besides, *an abrupt and complete emancipation from the closed stanza*.

This analysis is supported by tables which show the average number of run-on lines per stanza rising from 1.2 in Canto one to 3.66 in Canto four and the average number of run-on stanzas from one in forty-one to one in five.[23] Such variations would have to be allowed for before comparisons with other poets were undertaken, and those poets' own usage checked for stability. Stein does not ask what aspects remained both stable and characteristically Byronic or why he should suddenly have abandoned the stanza for *ottava rima*.

There is a huge critical literature dealing with individual authors' handling of genre. Sometimes they produced their own commentary on the topic, as in Dryden's prologues, epilogues and prefaces and Henry James's prefaces to the New York edition of his novels. Alarm bells should ring when a proposed attribution breaks a writer's own publicly declared rule. Much can be learned about changing understandings of genre from textual revisions. Yeats transformed himself from a symbolist to a modernist poet, regularly altering early work to accommodate it to each new phase of his self-remaking. Pope, under the direction of Warburton, restructured his four Moral Essays so as to make the development of the argument more formal and less essay-like. We will all be aware of painters who began in the 1960s as abstract impressionists but by the 1980s had moved on to a version of the figurative, or composers who made the same kind of transition from atonal serialism to minimalism or to a version of tonality. Such alterations through revealing new conceptions of genre help to clarify the nature of the old. Attributional arguments work best with writers whose conception of genre remains stable over a professional lifetime, or who have only one or two clearly signalled developments within an overarching consistency.

AESTHETIC JUDGEMENTS

In considering George de Forrest Lord's arguments for Marvell's authorship of the second and third 'Advices to a painter', Ephim Fogel pointed to ways in which he saw the poems as being inferior to the 'Last instructions', which he accepts as by Marvell:

> I find this kind of originality, close-knit imaginative unity, fine proportioning of parts, continuous drive and relevance, and sharpness of diction and imagery in such Marvellian poems in couplets as 'Tom May's Death,' 'The Character of Holland,' 'The First Anniversary,' 'On the Victory by Blake,' and 'Upon the Death of Cromwell.' I do not find these qualities in 'The Second Advice.'[24]

This is a valid argument: Marvell is a good writer; therefore he cannot be the author of the 'Second advice', which in Fogel's view is a bad or at best a mediocre poem. Any attempt at rebuttal has to find ways of showing that it is a good poem. It can be argued that good writers can sometimes write badly; but this happens less often than is claimed. Professional craftspersons or performers who have achieved excellence will work from a platform of habitual accomplishment from which ascent is possible but descent is unlikely. They may write badly by their own standards but they will not write amateurishly or incompetently. (This is one reason for looking with scepticism at the claims for Shakespearean authorship of 'A funeral elegy in memory of the late virtuous William Peter', which even its supporters agree is an amateurish piece of writing.[25]) H. A. Mason in examining a Wyatt dubium 'I se my playnt with open eyrs', after noting that two pairs of rhyme words recur in authentic poems, concludes that it 'sounds to me more like an echo than a genuine Wyatt poem'.[26] Coming from a scholar totally saturated in the writing of Wyatt and his period this has to be respected even if we cannot quite identify, any more than Mason himself, the elements which gave rise to this holistic perception; nor, on the other hand, would we wish to claim finality for it. To omit qualitative judgement of this kind from attribution studies is to omit the very qualities that make us read the verse of Marvell with an attention and delight that does not attend our reading of the verse of, say, Richard Flecknoe or Elkanah Settle, and are one of our main reasons for being interested in attribution in the first place. No quantitative test can ever tell us that a particular piece of writing is aesthetically good or bad; and yet, as alert and experienced readers, this is the first and most pressing judgement we make about it.

So literary quality is a genuine attribute of writing and one that can be recognised. As such it will be one of the criteria drawn on in conferring or denying attribution. The problem lies in how it is to be established, a matter that comes under the philosophical problem of testimony.[27] Fogel's method is comparative: a number of qualities he perceives to be present in examples of Marvell's authentic verse using the same metrical form are perceived to be absent from the 'Second advice'. If other experienced scholarly readers were to arrive independently at the same judgement, the matter would be settled by general agreement. Unfortunately, this is not always the case. Take 'On the victory by Blake', one of the comparative texts cited by Fogel. In 1995 Elsie Duncan-Jones reported the discovery of a new manuscript of the poem which was signed at the end with the letters 'R. F.' and dated 'July 9 <16>57'. 'R. F.' is so far unidentified: Duncan-Jones relinquishes with obvious reluctance the possibility that he might be the despised Flecknoe. In proposing that the poem be removed from the Marvell canon, she did not have to look far for critical opinions that were directly opposed to Fogel's:

> This may, I hope, turn the scales against the notion that this often crude and markedly unskilful poem must be ascribed to Marvell. In the centuries during which the poem has been before the public I cannot find that any editor or biographer of Marvell has expressed admiration of it, except the adoring and often uncritical Grosart . . . Augustine Birrell in his book on Marvell in the English Men of Letters series found the lines 'not worthy of so glorious an occasion'. Pierre Legouis in his *André Marvell* objected to the trifling conceits, the gross flattery of Cromwell, the unrelenting denigration of Spain. Much later, in his revision (1971) of Margoliouth's edition Legouis remarked that if 'Blake's victory' were banished from the canon it would be no loss to Marvell's reputation, 'literary or moral'. . . . Annabel Patterson . . . boldly calls the poem 'a piece of unquestioning and uninteresting propaganda'.[28]

An attendant piece of evidence was that the poem had been excised from the important Bodley copy of Marvell's *Miscellany Poems* (MS Eng. poet. d 49) which contains extensive manuscript additions and corrections by a member of the poet's circle. The much more accomplished 'Tom May's death', cited by Fogel, is also deleted from the Bodley volume, and is doubted by some Marvell scholars. Literary evaluations are established by consensus, which in turn rests on and may be challenged by argued demonstration. Such demonstrations are always time-bound and as such will often be strongly ideological, but when unanimous have to be allowed weight as a collective validation of discrete individual judgements. Duncan-Jones's claim is that such a consensus about the inferiority of 'Blake's victory' has existed for well over a century. When Fogel argued that the 'Second advice' fell below Marvell's high standards of poetic craftsmanship, while accepting that the inferior and, as we now realise, unauthentic 'Blake's victory' reached those standards, he called into question his own qualification to make such a judgement.

And there is the rub. Consensus of the kind required is far from universal in criticism; violent dissent is not unknown; and in many cases the target texts inhabit a middle ground that arouses neither strong approval or disapproval. Only in the first of these three cases can the criterion of literary value be used with assurance. In a general sense such distinctions are genuine – if they were not there would be no commonly held judgements of excellence in this or any other aspect of human experience – but in particular cases few claims are immune from contention.

In 1902 a manuscript of the *Paradoxe sur le comédien*, previously attributed to Diderot, was discovered in the handwriting of his disciple Jacques-André Naigeon. This contained many revisions and additions written partly between the lines and partly in the margins, and gave every appearance of being an authorial manuscript. Although drawing undisguisedly on an earlier work by Diderot, it was republished by Ernest Dupuy as a work by Naigeon. The questioning of the attribution led to a questioning of the value of the work. André Morize includes among the parties to the debate

> those who, in spite of the general admiration aroused for nearly a century by the *Paradoxe*, affirm that they always have thought 'something was the matter with it'. Larroumet recalls that quite a while before he spoke disparagingly of its artistic worth. Another says:
>
> > This celebrated work bristles with inaccuracies, improprieties, incoherences, which strike me only now that they have been pointed out to me. But, in truth, I have always considered it diffuse, tedious, overrated, and, to be frank, I am thankful that I shall no longer have to blush for my lukewarmness.
>
> All these writers accept Dupuy's theory with satisfaction and do not hesitate to cross the *Paradoxe* off the list of Diderot's works.[29]

Another group stuck doggedly by its original admiration. It included Emile Faguet who divided his defence of Diderot's authorship into arguments from fact and arguments from taste. Faguet accepted the arguments from fact as inconclusive or favouring Naigeon and turned to taste to resolve the matter. His argument from taste was the same one as Fogel applied to the 'Second advice', except that in this case there were only two candidates: Diderot and Naigeon. The poor standard of Naigeon's unaided works convinced Faguet that he would have been totally incapable of creating the original parts of the *Paradoxe*. He conceded he could not solve the problem of the manuscript but regarded it as insignificant besides the disparity in quality between the two writers. In retrospect one can only applaud Faguet's perspicacity; and yet the fact remains that other experienced and well-qualified scholars took the opposite view. It is true that Faguet's sense of the aesthetic worth of the piece led him to undertake a stylistic analysis that many scholars and readers of his time presumably found convincing; but the central problem – that of the manuscript – only found an acceptable solution after the textual work of Bédier (discussed in Chapter nine below).

To gain a contemporary purchase on this affair let us assume that some decades after the death of Michel Foucault a work was published under his name from a typescript found in a hotel in Algeria where he was known to have stayed; that it was well reviewed and set for reading by undergraduates; then some decades later still a second version surfaced among the papers of some lesser-known theorist from the Foucault circle showing the same apparent signs of authorship as the manuscript of the *Paradoxe*. The matter might not be so serious to us as it was to the guardians of the French canon in 1902 but it would matter in the sense that the exposure of the work as by another author would put into question the whole nature of our understanding of Foucault and his ideas – suggesting that we had only read him in a superficial and unquestioning way. The matter would be one we would want to see resolved. Until it was, we would probably quietly drop the work from reading lists and cease to quote it. When its authenticity was validated we would be delighted because it restored our faith in ourselves as discriminating readers, which is to say readers of texts not reputations.

The subject of internal evidence now passes over into that of stylistic evidence which will be the subject of the next chapter.

CHAPTER SIX

Stylistic evidence

Personal style is an extraordinary thing that exhibits itself in a great variety of ways besides writing. Considered as expression, it begins with the infant's first cry, identifying itself as a new and particular individual and distinguishing itself, at least to its mother and close family, from all other newly-born infants – an act both of self-expression and self-definition! The new individualist linguistics of Barbara Johnstone holds language to be 'just as crucially self-expressive as it is referential or relationship-affirming, poetic or rhetorical':

> As it does the other things it does – refer to situations in the world, affirm people's connectedness, comment on itself, claim assent and adherence – talk always also shows who speakers take themselves to be, how they align themselves with others and how they differentiate themselves from others. All talk displays its speaker's individual voice. This is necessary because self-expression is necessary: no matter how much a society may value conformity or define people in relationship to others, individuals must on some level express individuated selves.[1]

The difficulty for attribution studies lies in finding a way to conceptualise this linguistic individuation in such a way that it can be directly modelled and tested.

From the complementary viewpoint of recognition, a sense of individuality derives from the same infant's urgent need to distinguish the mother from other women, family members from others of the community, and members of the community from strangers. Long before the acquisition of speech, networks in our brains are devoted to processing sensory messages which establish the identities of other human beings. Our recognition of literary style is a distant outcome of that primitive awareness, enriched by skills we have developed in making other important discriminations: the edible from the inedible, the safe from the dangerous, sincerity from insincerity, the true from the false. Individuals in whom these skills are imperfectly developed lurch through life, and through scholarship, doing endless harm to themselves and others.

Such discriminatory skills, as well as remaining essential for survival, will also be enhanced and celebrated in art and ritual. Members of hunter-gatherer societies develop astonishing abilities to recognise the traces left by the movement of animals and to track them over long periods. Minute signs apprehended through each of the senses are integrated into a way of reading the environment which is totally baffling to urban visitors, who will starve to death in an environment that would keep a nomad in luxurious plenty. Hence arises a culture of performances through which the nomads celebrate their response to the natural world. Yet those urban visitors have a special competence in decoding the messages of their own environments (e.g. crossing Broadway without being run over) and have generated their own ways of celebrating that competence (e.g. enjoying Broadway musicals).

Many of these competences are only dimly recognised by those who possess them. When carpets were laid in the corridor outside my office, I discovered that I had lost a way of reading this environment of which I had never consciously been aware. For years I had been subliminally processing the sound of approaching footsteps and building expectations on the basis of these, even to the point of identifying visitors before they appeared. Like a great deal of mental processing, such peripheral perceptions only come to conscious attention when the mind judges that they are of urgent relevance; moreover, in most practical cases they will not let us down. But from time to time we may not be sure whether the face in the passing crowd, the footstep in the (uncarpeted) hall, the sound of a distant car is really that which our immediate response suggests. The experience will be of a brief moment of arousal or preliminary recognition followed by puzzlement, or a fear that we have been mistaken, and a rechecking of the memory, which seems to have the power of rearticulating itself despite our not having consciously attended to it. And on some occasions, owing either to a failure of the delicate recognition mechanism or the action of a predisposition so strong that it overwhelms the instinctual process, we will be in error. Add to this that it is sometimes difficult to perform consciously in an artificial environment what we are perfectly able to perform on the fringes of consciousness when immersed in the current of experience. It is to deal with such situations in language that stylistics, in the sense of a systematic examination of the characteristic physical features of a message, becomes necessary in order to test the intuitions of the witness.

It will also be obvious that such apprehensions work best when the target has strong individual characteristics, rather than subtle inflections around a norm. Donald Foster's identification of Joe Klein as the author of *Primary Colors* and Tom Hawkins as 'Wanda Tinasky' was assisted by both being eccentric stylists.[2] Joseph W. Reed writes of John O'Hara: 'His prose style is unmistakably his: it is possible to stare at a page of his prose in *The New Yorker*, as one might stare at a page of Thomas Carlyle's prose in *The Edinburgh Review*, and know at once it is his. His prose lends support to the assertion that style is metabolic.'[3] Writing does not have to be good to have this effect – the style of such celebrated bad writers as William McGonagall and Amanda McKittrick Ros is among the most singular in the language. All that is required is that it should be bad in a distinctive way. This kind of intuitive recognition may well be highly effective for stylists as singular as O'Hara and Carlyle and readers as sensitive as Reed when the page concerned appears in journals with which the writers had a recorded connection. But experience shows that it is also easy to be wrong.

One immediate problem is that the successful original stylist is likely to have imitators who deliberately copy those same features that gave rise to distinctiveness. As it happens, both the *New Yorker* and the *Edinburgh Review* were known for a particular house-style which contributors were encouraged to imitate. Imitation Carlyles (or Macaulays – a much larger tribe) and O'Haras are not always as easy to distinguish from the originals as Reed implies. Contributors of unsolicited stories to *Black Mask* in the 1930s were likely as not to receive a form letter conveying the message 'rewrite so it's more like Hammett'. One would need very refined antennae to make an intuitive identification of individual authorial styles from pseudonymous, highly derivative category fiction either then or now. If one did so it would be more likely to be from some attendant personal idiosyncrasy than any holistic assessment of style. In cases where the writing is conventional or impersonal it is only by a minute examination of expression that we will be able to determine authorship.

STYLISTICS AND ATTRIBUTION

While the advent of statistical, computer-based stylometry (discussed in Chapter eight) has enormously improved our ability to discriminate on quantitative grounds between the language of individual writers, older methods still have validity if properly applied and will continue to be the principal means by which problems are identified as deserving closer study. In many cases stylistic reasoning can be perfectly persuasive without any resort to statistical processing, while, viewing the matter the other way round, numbers and ratios can never be fully persuasive when we have no understanding of what elements in the language of the text have given rise to them. Such investigations can proceed either negatively or positively. The first way is obviously the simpler: if we can show that some particular aspect of the text is wholly uncharacteristic of the author concerned, the case may be dismissed out of hand. Arthur Sherbo in rejecting the attribution to Samuel Johnson of the Preface to Hampton's *Polybius* points out that it uses '*the former*' and '*the latter*' of which Johnson had on two occasions expressed a strong dislike, remarking on one of them: 'As long as you have the use of your tongue and your pen, never, sir, be reduced to that shift.'[4] In working from positives, unless we are lucky enough to have detected a singular and unobtrusive habit of expression, it is only by recognising a number of characteristic features of style present *in combination* that we can have any kind of security in a judgement.

The literature of religious controversy of the later seventeenth century offers scope for the application of both procedures. Although Charles II had regained the throne in 1660 with the aid of the Presbyterians, he soon turned against them and those members of the former Puritan alliance who had come to a partial accommodation with the re-established Church of England. Under the Act of Uniformity of 1662 all clergy who would not agree to use the Anglican prayer book were ejected from their livings and became 'Non-conformists', liable under further legislation to various kinds of legal persecution. As a result of this great division of the nation, political controversy for the remainder of the century was always closely involved with religious questions. In order to avoid persecution, much of this controversial printed material had to be either anonymous or pseudonymous; Andrew Marvell was one sympathiser with the Nonconformists who was under suspicion of seditious writing. When William, Lord Russell was executed for treason in 1683 his 'dying speech', which was on the streets in a matter of hours, became an influential piece of Whig polemic. It was assumed partly on stylistic and partly on circumstantial grounds that Gilbert Burnet had either written it or assisted in its writing and he was soon on his way into exile in Holland to escape a worse fate.

Whether a pamphlet of this period is written from an Anglican or a Non-conformist viewpoint or is the work of an undecided 'trimmer' is usually easy enough to determine from content, and yet there were also clearly recognised forms of phraseology that were characteristic of each party. Some Non-conformist examples are listed by the 'loyal' writer, Roger L'Estrange, writing in 1680. His actual point is the more searching one that such phrases were not only characteristic of his opponents but had a particular cultic meaning which did not apply when the same terms were used by orthodox writers:

> Mr *Baxters* Works will be as good as a *Non-conformists Dictionary* to us: and assist the World toward the Understanding of the *Holy Dialect*, in a Wonderful manner. For the *Purity of the Gospel*; the *ways of Christ*: the *Ordinances of the Lord*; the *Power of Godlynesse*; the *Foundations of Faith*; the *Holy Discipline*: A *Blessed Reformation*, &c. These are *Words*, and *Expressions*, that signify quite another thing to *Them*, then they do to *Us*. *Faithful Pastors; Laborious Ministers; Heavenly Guides; Zealous Protestants*; The *Upright in the Land: Humble Petitioners; Just Priviledges; Higher Powers; Glorious Kings*; Holy *Covenanting unto the Lord*, &c. This is not to be taken now, as the *Language Currant* of the *Nation*, but only as a Privy *Cypher* of *Intelligence* betwixt Themselves, and the *Cant*, or *Jargon* of the *Party*. Nay, they fly from us in their *Speech*, their *Manners*, their *Meaning*, as well as in their *Profession*.[5]

L'Estrange has identified the Presbyterians as what we would call a discourse community and wishes to demonstrate that they differ from Anglicans (accepted by him as the norm rather than just another such community) not only by the content of their writing but by a fundamental difference in their habitual lexicon. To identify a piece of writing as emanating from a particular discourse community may be an important part of the process of establishing an attribution. Erasmus, for example, identifies his Jerome-forger as a member of the Augustinian order, and could no doubt have distinguished writers from the other major Catholic orders, much as L'Estrange, if put to it, could probably have distinguished a tract written by a Quaker from one written by an Independent or an Anabaptist, irrespective of its specific doctrinal content. In the pamphlet wars of the Restoration, the same kind of thing could be done from the other side, as by Marvell in his systematic demolition of the future bishop, Samuel Parker, in the two parts of *The Rehearsal Transpos'd*, which includes similar analysis of the specialised meanings given by high-church Anglicans to commonly used words. These were battles over ways of using language as much as over theology.[6]

It is not a hard thing then to distinguish a Non-conformist from a Conformist, providing there is no conscious deception in the case, and between writers from the major traditions of non-conformism. But how are we to progress beyond this? Non-conformists are often held to have deliberately cultivated a 'plain' style, but within this there were many distinctions. N. H. Keeble gives a summary description of some of these:

> No single epithet could encompass Howe's own inelegancy, Bate's fluency, Penn's poised and often aphoristically pointed lucidity, Baxter's unpretentious and direct urgency, Owen's ponderous comprehensiveness, Fox's visionary fervour and admonitory trenchancy, or the shifting registers of Bunyan's prose, colloquial, biblical, theological, personal, narrative; nor do any of these phrases adequately represent the variety within the writings of any one individual.[7]

Keeble could no doubt have expressed these broad distinctions in a more particular way had that been the task before him. The challenge for attributional stylistics would be to frame a description so precise as to allow someone who was not a specialist in the literature to distinguish the particular writer from co-religionists and imitators.

L'Estrange's own prose illustrates some of the ways in which such an analysis could be taken further. Wing's *Short Title Catalogue* attributes 130 items to him, but his devious life as both propagandist and censor for Charles II and James II almost certainly gave rise to more, including rewritings of other authors' work submitted to him for licensing. He is a good case to study since most of his acknowledged work was published by his trusted associates Henry and Joanna Brome. For many years he had an office directly above their bookshop from which he could monitor the production of his texts. Here is a brief description of his manner, given by an eighteenth-century political writer, Thomas Gordon. L'Estrange's writings

> . . . are full of technical terms, of phrases picked up in the street from apprentices and porters, and nothing can be more low and nauseous. His sentences, besides their grossness, are lively nothings, which can never be translated (the only way to try language) and will hardly bear repetition: *between hawk and buzzard*: *clawed him with kindness*: *alert and friskie*: *guzzling down tipple*: *would not keep touch*: *a queer putt*; *lay cursed hard upon their gizzard*: *cramm his gut*; *conceited noddy*: *old chuff*: and the like, are some of SIR ROGER's choice flowers.[8]

This is part of a literary-political put-down, and would not tell us much about L'Estrange if we were not well acquainted with his work already. But it would give us some general sense of his manner. He uses colloquial phrases and demotic syntax. His images are hard to translate. He is a lively, opinionated writer. If we were to run across a passage by Halifax or Sir Thomas Browne we would probably guess even from such a slim account that this was not L'Estrange.

Here is the beginning of a much fuller account from James Sutherland's *English Literature of the Late Seventeenth Century*:

> His historical importance in helping to establish that conversational type of prose which became widespread during the Restoration period can hardly be overestimated; he is always and immediately intelligible, and his idiom is that of the tavern and the market-place mixed with the fashionable slang of the day, appealing not to gentlemen and scholars but to men of affairs, to shopkeepers and artisans. His prose abounds with homely words and phrases – 'one egg is not liker [*sic*] another'; 'This is only crying Whore first'; 'to turn up trump'; 'to go thorough-stich'; ''tis early days yet', and so on. He is an adept at putting a situation in a vigorous metaphor: when Halifax . . . suggested that James II's Declaration of Indulgence must be viewed with suspicion, the loyal L'Estrange leapt to the King's defence with 'A Man helps his friend up the Ladder; and has his Teeth Dash'd out for his Pains'. He continually addresses his reader-listener with a 'Well!', or 'You cannot but take notice . . . ', or '"But what", ye'll say . . . '; and he puts him at his ease with a frequent use of colloquial contractions such as 'on't', 'to't', 'e'en', etc. He breaks off from time to time to tell a story, and that gives him the chance to introduce a snatch of racy dialogue. . . . He was perhaps at his best when he employed his favourite dialogue form . . . But everywhere in his political writing we find the same sense of urgency, the same air of righteous indignation, and the colloquial syntax that goes with it.[9]

Sutherland, like Gordon, is particularly struck by L'Estrange's vivid colloquial phrases. One might begin by systematically collecting these over a range of works, and then looking for the same phrases in a control group of texts by other Royalist controversialists. We would expect to discover a number which were either unique to L'Estrange or used by him much more frequently than by the control group. We would also test, as was suggested earlier, for the incidence of high-scoring phrases in combination, since an imitator might well pick up a particular isolated phrase. For the drama and poetry of his time such a search would be possible, as virtually all of the former and a high proportion of the latter is electronically searchable on the LION archive; but relatively little polemic and devotional prose of the late seventeenth century, or any other period, is so far available in electronic form – far too little, probably, for us to be able to establish particular locutions as singular to a particular author. Donald W. Foster in his application of the same technique to Shakespeare is better served by the databases at his disposal.

The method of identifying an author through characteristic words and phrases is, of course, only one of several available, and would need to be supplemented by comparisons of tone, accidence and syntax (to look no further) and close attention to fine shades of ideology. It is mentioned here simply as one of particular value for the field of politico-religious debate occupied by L'Estrange and his Puritan opponents and for analogous traditions in other times and cultures, such as that of the French *Mazarinades*.[10]

SYNONYMS

Discrimination based on preference among synonyms has been particularly favoured in studies of collaboration in pre-1642 drama. It is most effective when applied to situations where the preference is least likely to have been overwritten by transcribers or compositors, i.e. in holograph materials or where there was close contact between the writer and a scribe or printer. In Rochester's holograph letters (about 10,000 words of text) there is a strong preference for 'upon' over 'on' but this does not extend to his verse: writing in metre seems to have reversed the preference. This particular discriminant is also useful with Shakespeare and was one of the main clues for the identification of Philip Francis as Junius and for unravelling the authorship of the disputed *Federalist* papers. Such preferences are most persuasive when used as negative evidence to reject attributions or in choosing between two or three known candidates when there is no possibility of dark horses. One begins by compiling a list of doublets and establishing the ratios they exhibit in the writings of the assumed author and the control texts. Some obvious candidates are listed below. It will be seen that some only apply to particular periods of the language while others are timeless.

among/amongst, actually/in fact/of course, although/though, and/also, and so on/etcetera, around/round, ate/eat (as preterite), because/since, beyond/outside, commonly/usually, each other/one another, everybody/everyone, farther/further, fewer/less (with regard to the number of items), hardly/scarcely, has/hath, inside/within, inward/inwards, like/such as, merely/simply, nobody/no one, no doubt/undoubtedly/doubtless, on/upon, outside/without, outward/outwards, particularly/specially, since/because, somebody/someone, till/until, 'tis/it's, that/which (as relatives), toward/towards, whatever/whatsoever, while/whilst.[11]

The choice between 'thou' and 'ye/you' is a rule-determined one but that between 'ye' and 'you' is a personal matter. In comparing the preferencest of Fletcher and Massinger in their unaided plays, Cyrus Hoy establishes an overwhelming preference for 'ye' over 'you' on Fletcher's part and exactly the reverse on that of Massinger, who in response shows a greater fondness for 'hath' over 'has' and 'them' over ''em'. This provides a good starting point for the examination of their respective shares in their collaborative plays though one that becomes less effective when we encounter passages apparently by Fletcher transcribed by Massinger.[12] Fielding's anachronistic preference for 'hath' over 'has' has often been noticed.

From the eighteenth century onwards we have dictionaries of synonyms which explain how words of similar meaning were distinguished in usage at the time of compilation. An example of particular interest because of the hostile reactions it provoked from male critics such as Horace Walpole and William Gifford was Hester Lynch Piozzi's *British Synonyms; or, an attempt at regulating the choice of words in familiar conversation.*[13] Although remembered as the friend and memoirist of Johnson, Piozzi made an effort in this work to free herself from the Johnsonian tradition of prescribing how 'to write with propriety' in order to record the actual practice of educated spoken English (i. ii). Her method was to demonstrate either by definition or example how a careful speaker would distinguish within groups such as 'close, covetous, avaricious, stingy, parsimonious, near, niggardly, penurious'. In cases where there was no agreed difference in meaning or register, a consistent choice of one over another would be a personal one likely to show as an authorship marker.

At all periods of the English language there has been a very large class of synonyms and near-synonyms in which one element is of French or Latin derivation and the other Anglo-Saxon, typified by alter/change, ascend/go up (transitive), ascend/rise (intransitive), commence/begin, seat/chair, sense/meaning/thought etc. Frederick Erastus Pierce used the 'three-syllable Latin word-test' as a means of distinguishing between Webster and Dekker, though his carrying through of this idea is ridiculed by Schoenbaum.[14] Significant differences might be found in checking for ratios between words of English, French, Greek and Latin derivation used by particular authors. While statistics of average word length may well reflect this in a very general way, greater etymological specificity would permit more precise kinds of discrimination. In some cases doublets represent different stages in a process of linguistic change. Today the distinction between 'less' for quantity and 'fewer' for number is a matter of taste, little heard in colloquial speech but still observed in some formal writing: in a century's time the first will probably have replaced the second even with careful writers. We should also take note of the many regional variations in grammar and vocabulary which have been intensively studied by philologists and dialecticians. Linguistic maps exist for the Middle English period showing the geographical boundaries between various dialectal forms at given historical stages. Television, cinema and radio, by broadening our exposure to world varieties of regional spoken English, have enhanced our capacity to determine a speaker's place of origin; however, being able to do this from speech does not mean we would be able to do so from writing, especially formal writing for publication, which is a grapholect not a dialect.

A preponderance of one member of a doublet over the other at an early period of an author's life may not survive into later works. Ellegård instances Philip Francis's changes in preference from 'upon' to 'on' and 'until' to 'till' which are dateable to the mid-1770s after the composition of the Junius letters.[15] There is also an influence of register, with Francis preferring the longer alternatives in his more formal writings. Most living writers born before 1950 will have passed through a conscious process of eliminating gender-specific terms from general statements, especially the use of singular 'he' in a universal sense. Their choice of how to accomplish this particular change – whether by substituting universal 'she' or 'he or she', putting such statements into the plural, using portmanteau 's/he' or adopting singular 'they' – may itself be evidence for authorship or non-authorship. Writers may prefer one favoured word for texts designed to be read silently and another for texts to be read aloud. Words such as 'literary' in the phrase 'literary theory' and 'particularly', which repeat the same element, are more often mispronounced and miswritten than those whose constituents are more heterogeneous. A public speaker aware of this might substitute 'critical' for the first and 'specially' for the second.[16]

Studying the transmissional variants of a widely copied or reprinted work as given in the textual notes to a scholarly edition will quickly suggest a wider range of equivalent forms to be tested, since such lists identify alternatives that were current at that particular period. Even looking at one's own mistranscriptions can be instructive. It is common for a word towards the end of a phrase, because it has been held in memory longer, to be replaced by another of equivalent appearance or meaning that is more habitual to the transcriber. Another clue to culturally available near-equivalents is the practice in drafting of offering two alternatives linked by 'and', e.g. 'type and class', then in revision removing the one seen as less exact. Another writer might make the choice differently. Through this and other kinds of information a list of doublets appropriate to the problem under investigation can be assembled, and authorial preferences established.

RARE AND UNUSUAL WORDS

Another clue to authorship is rare and unusual vocabulary. Among the evidence used by Donald W. Foster to nail the author of *Primary Colors* was the word 'tarmac-hopping', applied to politicians who move rapidly from one airport to another. Foster relies heavily on this technique in his contentious attribution of 'A funeral elegy in memory of the late virtuous William Peter' to Shakespeare (discussed in Chapter eight). In identifying Coleridge's contributions to the *Morning Post* David Erdman was alerted by such words as 'sequaciousness', 'weather-wisdom', 'fugacious', 'unadding' and 'humanness'. The last of these was 'a word he uses in 1806 in a letter as a conscious coinage, which is cited in *OED* from a letter of his of 1802, and which appears in italics in one of the newly attributed essays of 1800 on Washington'.[17] In one case the unusual expression 'accommodation ladder' led to a manuscript notebook in which it had been jotted down and then to a loose scrap of paper where it recurred in what proved to be some rough notes for the article in question.[18] With this last finding, irrefutable external evidence was added to indicative stylistic evidence. The problem with vocabulary is always one of *how* rare and how unusual. It is mortifying to have claimed a word as unique to an author only to come across it in another contemporary source: moreover, it is still quite common for new, unusual words to have a short, intense vogue and then disappear for good. An apparently invented word may have been picked up from an earlier text, as the eighteenth century plundered Milton and the Romantics Spenser. Coleridge's inventions – sometimes used to add further definition to an existing word ('a temporising, fugacious policy'; 'with as obstinate and unadding a fidelity') – have shown less staying power than Shakespeare's or Milton's.

Favourite words are not always permanent even in the work of a particular author. I cite Bevis Hillier reviewing Roy Strong's *The Spirit of Britain*:

> In reviewing Strong's *Diaries*, I noted his unfortunate addiction to 'luvvie' words: marvellous, wonderful, thrilling, breathtaking, fantastic and horrendous. He has cut back on these – I have found only one 'thrilling' in this book. But his writing still suffers from superlative-fatigue. So much is 'enormous', 'vast' or 'huge'. (In the *Diaries* we even encounter a 'huge miniature'.) And Strong has become besottedly hooked on another word 'efflorescence', which occurs over and over again – it is like being in a Schweppes advertisement. The word does not deserve a total ban; but 'flowering' is simpler and less spluttery.[19]

Clearly Strong listens to Hillier and we can expect no more efflorescence. All writers are pulled up by a reader from time to time for overuse of a particular word and most will respond by retrenching it. Foster points to the way in which certain words enter and depart from Shakespeare's vocabulary, relating this speculatively to his relearning parts in his own plays and those of others.[20]

Alongside the favourite word goes the distinctive use of figures of speech. For Erdman Coleridge is a writer 'who can seldom proceed any distance incognito without being provoked into some ironic comment, some gesticulation of metaphor, or some metaphysical outcry that gives him away'. Particularly characteristic is his inventiveness and precision in using metaphors. Writing of Burke, Coleridge had himself said 'It seems characteristic of true eloquence, to reason *in* metaphors; of declamation, to argue *by* metaphors'.[21] Erdman expands:

> To reason in metaphors is to analyse their implications and employ them purposefully. 'Assumed opinions . . . become real ones; the *suspension* of a tenet is a fainting-fit, that precedes its death.' Efforts at free thought in France may be 'as transient and void of immediate effect, as bubbles. . . . Yet still they prove the existence of a vital principle; they are the bubbles of a fountain, not such as rise seldom and silent on the muddy and stagnant pools of despotism'. In Coleridge's hands the metaphor is a precision instrument. He was acutely sensitive to the difference between good writing, in which 'every phrase, every metaphor, every personification, should have its justifying cause', and writing 'vicious in the figures and contexture of its style'. Alert to structural and postural tensions, he would say of the French Constitution that it exhibits 'a metaphysical posture-master's dexterity in balancing'; of an unimpressive argument: 'How will it fly up, and strike against the beam, when we put in the counter-weights!'; but of the assertion that Jacobinism and Royalism completely counteract each other, that it is 'a childish application of mechanics to the subject, in which even as metaphors, the phrases have scarcely any intelligible sense'.[22]

This combination of boldness, exactness and a self-aware foppishness in Coleridge's use of metaphor is a qualitative, not a quantitative element of style. He was proud of his metaphors: when part of an article he had sent to the *Edinburgh Review* was rewritten by the editor, he spluttered over the 'rancid commonplace metaphors' that had been introduced.[23] This aspect of his mind and writing immediately declares itself to an experienced and responsive reader (or another good writer) but could only be tested for with extreme difficulty using quantitative methods. Shakespeare is another writer who habitually thinks in metaphors and vivid images. One of the problems with 'A funeral elegy' is their uncharacteristic absence.

SYNTAX AND GRAMMAR

Distinctive vocabulary decreases as we move from showy, egotistical authors, such as L'Estrange and Coleridge, to those who pride themselves on the 'correctness' or lack of idiosyncrasy of their writing. Addison would be an example close in time to L'Estrange of a writer who cultivated a 'gentlemanly', urbane style without noticeable idiosyncrasies; or think of Hume trying to purify his prose of Scotticisms. Such writers would be easy enough to separate out from their flamboyant brethren but not from others of their time. To discriminate in such cases, we would need nothing less than descriptive grammars of the practices of the individual authors of sufficient specificity to make anomalies immediately apparent. Such grammars would direct attention to the underlying causes of the quantitative effects registered by statistical studies of word frequencies. A stylistic explanation, where possible, is always to be preferred to a stylometric one, which, however helpful in distinguishing authors, does not show us *how* they write.

Unfortunately such detailed treatments of a single writer are rare for the early modern and modern period. A few do however exist for writers of Old and Middle English and Shakespeare's linguistic practice has been exhaustively described in a number of sources. A. C. Partridge in his study of the shares of Fletcher and Shakespeare in *Henry VIII* and Foster in his account of 'A funeral elegy' both reason effectively about Shakespearean grammatical practice.[24] Partridge is particularly acute in his contrasting of late Shakespearean syntax with the more modern, analytical style of Fletcher, which, moreover, is written to 'given tunes' whereas in Shakespeare, as Ralph Waldo Emerson noted, 'the thought constructs the tune':

> Shakespeare cannot serve as a stylistic model for anyone, because his rhythms are individual and accommodated to the needs of the moment; his ideas outstrip his syntax. On the track of the telling and indelible image, he may leave behind anacoluthons and hanging relative clauses in the most inconsequent fashion; he compresses his meaning and tortures his syntax, so that while the effect of the passage may be poetically grand, the meaning is wrung from it with extreme difficulty.[25]

Fletcher does pretty well the reverse.

In the case of Dr Johnson, whose *œuvre* includes a great deal of unattributed minor literary work and journalism, questions arising from the language of a suspect piece can be referred directly to the grammar contained in his own dictionary. Sherbo brings this into play for its failure to acknowledge the historic present.[26] The weight of the evidence left by Johnson not only of his own language use but in the form of advice to others about how they should use language places him in a handy situation for the verification of dubia. Ben Jonson and Milton have also left us grammars.

The challenge to future scholarship is to establish how comprehensive descriptions of an author's grammatical and especially syntactic practice should be compiled. Here the first step might well be to turn to the models of stylistic analysis given by Gerald R. McMenamin in *Forensic Stylistics*,[27] and his two topic bibliographies 'Descriptive markers of style' (pp. 181–8) and 'Quantitative indicators of style' (pp. 189–207). Literary criticism frequently addresses stylistic questions and, when well performed, does so with a specificity and density of reference that can be of great value to attribution studies. Needless to say, criticism can also be impressionistic and overgeneralised, but that should not lead us to reject it *en bloc*.

PROSODY AND METRE

Traditional stylistics gave considerable attention to prosody and metre. This concern originated with classicists studying Greek and Latin poetry written in quantitative metres, who in turn drew on a heritage of commentary from ancient and mediaeval times contained in grammars and scholia. Establishment of metrical norms for poets such as Horace and Virgil was important for editors, in that a prosodic anomaly was often a sign of textual corruption or interpolation. In 1866 W. M. Drobisch published a comparative study of the use of the Latin hexameter by Virgil and a range of other classical poets. The first four feet of this verse form may be either dactyls (long short short) or spondees (long long) giving twenty-four possible variations. It was easy to demonstrate both period and individual characteristics in preferences for particular patterns.[28] Nineteenth-century students of Old and Middle English devoted considerable effort to the study of the four-beat alliterative line in its evolution from Caedmon to Langland, using their findings to refine datings and from time to time to assist attributions.

Metrical analysis of the English blank-verse line was used by a series of scholars from the early nineteenth century onwards as a means of dating and authenticating the plays of Shakespeare.[29] Their findings recognised a progressive liberation from the rigid Marlovian conception to the far greater variability of the late plays. This could be described by measuring the frequency with which the caesura appeared in certain positions, the percentage of lines ending with unstressed rather than stressed syllables, the ratio of end-stopped to run-on lines, and the ratio of syllables to stresses. The frequency of rhyme proved less useful as being more dependent on genre, though it took some time to recognise this. The purely quantitative approach reached its climax in the work of the Indian mathematician M. R. Yardi who reduced these differences to a formula $u = 0.7204 + 0.07645v$, where u represents a discriminant function derived from the data and v the number of years from the earlier play.[30] By calculating u one can immediately derive a value for v; however, these values are reliant on external evidence for the supposedly imperfect datings that they set out to refine. In the Wells and Taylor Oxford edition, results by Wentersdorf, Fitch and Brainerd are drawn on.[31]

Unfortunately for attributionists English metrical practice is much harder to reduce to rules than that of classical poets. In Latin quantitative verse of the Golden Age and after, a syllable is judged long or short by well-understood rules and there is usually only one way in which a line can be scanned. English metrical verse, as hardly needs saying, is based on accent not length of syllables, and in all but the strictest forms there is likely to be a hierarchy of stress-intensities within the line rather than two distinct levels, meaning that a metrically 'strong' stress at one point may be acoustically weaker than a weak stress at another point, or that the same word may be weak in one position and strong in another. An outcome of this ambiguity is that there will frequently be more than one valid way of scanning any particular line: the actor or reader decides. Shakespeare's later verse is particularly free in this respect, compounding the problem by freely interpolating additional 'weak' syllables between the strong ones.

Attempts have been made in recent years, first by Marina Tarlinskaja and more recently by Peter Groves, to create a formal description of Shakespeare's metrical practice of a kind that might be usable in attribution studies.[32] Tarlinskaja's work was drawn on by Elliott and Valenza for their project to investigate anti-Stratfordian candidates for Shakespearean authorship.[33] The test that has attracted most attention is that for 'leaning microphrases', defined by Tarlinskaja as 'phrases with a "clinging monosyllable", which loses stress by virtue of its metric position'.[34] These may be either proclitic with the destressed monosyllable before the syllable carrying the metrical stress or enclitic with it behind. Her own examples from *Venus and Adonis*, as quoted by Foster, are as follows: of a proclitic

Look how a bird *lies tangled* in a net

and of an enclitic

Now *which way* shall she turn? What shall she say?[35]

Leaning microphrases became one of many bones of contention between Foster and Elliott and Valenza in a heated four-contribution exchange in *Computers and the Humanities* during 1996–8. Elliott and Valenza thought the test was potentially a revealing one but conceded that, despite Tarlinskaja's assistance, it had not been consistently performed. Foster, pouring cold water on both the idea and the performance, thought it 'may be just as well to give the Leaning Microphrase a rest'.[36] My own view is that leaning microphrases are an identifiable component of spoken or subvocally heard verse and a useful contribution to the modelling of the metrical line for analysis, but that there are always likely to be individual differences in realising them. I am also aware that there are individuals with a verbal tin ear (the sonic equivalent of colourblindness) who would never be able to perform such analyses.

Groves addresses this problem by drawing a distinction between the rule-based allocations of syllabic prominence recognised by generative metrics and those instantiated in a reader's performance (performance here including silent subvocalisation).[37] The reader is seen as engaged in an attempt to reconcile the range of possible performances licensed by prosodic form with a variety of abstract metrical patterns or 'templates'. Like the scansions of the generativists, Groves's deal with the underlying prosodic phonology rather than subjective assessments of relative syllabic prominence, registering stress as it is automatically assigned by the syntactic rules that (for example) distinguish phrases (*a blàck bírd*, *the whìte hóuse*, *Chrìstmas púdding*) from words (a *bláckbìrd*, *the Whítehòuse*, *Chrístmas càke*). But the generativists' insistence on the irrelevance of performance means that they cannot distinguish lexical and syntactic stress from pragmatic accent, the kind of performative pitch change by which a speaker makes a syllable or word prominent for contextual, emphatic or contrastive purposes (*It was a BLÀCK bírd, not a WHÌTE óne*). In fact, as Groves demonstrates, these two different kinds of prosodic prominence behave quite differently in respect to the metre.[38]

The chief disqualification of traditional metrics as a serious tool of stylistic analysis is precisely that it cannot distinguish in any principled way between metrical and unmetrical lines. In Groves's system, metricality is determined by the disposition of stress, juncture and accent, which then determines the possible placement of rhythmical beats in the spoken line, thus allowing (or not allowing) the line to conform to one of the available metrical templates that govern the arrangement of beats and offbeats. This is another departure from the generativists, for whom metricality is 'not a positive characteristic of lines but a mere absence of disqualification' (pp. 88–9). The major advantage for attributionists of Groves's system over those of the generativists, of Tarlinskaja, and of Derek Attridge,[39] lies in its greater capacity to perform objective modellings of delicate prosodic effects, and in its ability to identify habitual choices in the mapping of prosodic material onto metrical templates. Groves's analysis reveals, for example, why the model of leaning microphrases, though certainly useful, is limited by its failure to distinguish between metrical destressing, prosodic destressing (embracing syntactic stress-subordination and the kind of destressing that occurs when a stressed syllable neighbours an accented one) and the pragmatic effects of the immediate context. His 'base and template' scansion permits significant generalisations about aspects of metrical style that are either obscured or invisible in less discriminating systems of scansion.

Investigations into rhythm as a characteristic of style should not be confined to verse, as many kinds of prose have quantifiable rhythmical patterns. In Roman and Greek oratory this is often plotted in terms of the rhythms used at the close of a period, the so-called *clausulae*. In English a classic study by George Saintsbury contains many useful suggestions for the analysis of authorial practice.[40] An experienced reader with good aural response can hear the characteristic movement and intonations of a writer's prose as clearly as that of a poet. Martin Battestin writes of Fielding:

> The signal initially was the sense I had as I read the essay for the first time that I was hearing Fielding's voice. The phenomenon is perhaps analogous to the response of a lifetime student of Mozart, say, upon recognizing the familiar cadences of that composer in an unidentified work he had not heard before.[41]

In qualifying himself as competent to make such judgements Battestin cites his experience as an editor:

> . . . in the course of collating numerous editions of Fielding's novels for the Wesleyan edition, and of seeing those works through the press, I have read aloud (or had read to me), pausing at every mark of punctuation, some 13,000 pages of his prose – after which experience even a tone-deaf reader might be expected to develop an ear for Fielding's syntax.[42]

This would be more persuasive if John Robert Moore and his predecessors had not been led by applying the same method into a long series of now rejected Defoe attributions.[43] The challenge is to discover how this absolutely fundamental aspect of style is to be made available for objective rather than subjective measurement. Battestin quotes with approval Schoenbaum's dictum

> The value of intuitions is that they are sometimes right. Their correctness is determined by the evidence. Nothing else counts.[44]

Having made his selection on the basis of intuition Battestin proceeds to buttress it with evidence. Each of his 'new essays' comes with a closely argued introduction and detailed explanatory notes listing parallels with other works by Fielding. There are also stylometric tests which are discussed elsewhere in this book. But the nature of the music remains undefined, so far only accessible to the responsive ear. Occasionally a writer will try to represent intonation patterns in musical notation; but this must always be of a particular verbal realisation.[45]

How might one go about describing Fielding's or any other author's music in a way that makes it directly usable in an argued case for attribution? Eighteenth-century prose of the Latinate kind favoured by Fielding is often strongly periodic in the classical sense of proceeding by a long phase of mounting tension marked by step-like symmetrical phrases to a climax which is followed by a rapid falling away to the initial level. Take the opening sentence of Johnson's *Rasselas*:

> Ye who listed with credulity to the whispers of fancy, and pursue with eagerness the phantoms of hope; who expect that age will perform the promises of youth, and that the deficiencies of the present day will be supplied by the morrow; attend to the history of Rasselas prince of Abissinia.[46]

When a player of a musical instrument is being taught to phrase, a standard question from the teacher is 'Which note are you aiming for?' Having determined that (and the note one is aiming for next, which is usually the real goal) one could begin playing. The principle also works for sentences. In the case of *Rasselas* the long-term goal would be either 'attend' or 'Rasselas' – grammatically the first, as the verb on which everything else hinges, semantically the name of the hero to whom we are being introduced. The earlier major stresses would all occupy places within a hierarchical relationship to the culminating one and to each other. A sentence of this kind possesses a gradient and a sectional structure which make it as apt for formal description as a verse stanza. What is not yet available is a way of modelling this gradient so that it could be used to distinguish between the practice of individual writers.

SPELLING AND CONTRACTIONS

Arguments from spelling have always been risk-prone but have their utility for the period before about 1800 when spelling was still not fully standardised. Indeed, even today many dictionaries will give permissible variant spellings such as artefact/artifact and judgement/judgment, while it is always possible to distinguish writers of British and American English from each other by their spellings. The danger lies in the difficulty of knowing whether a particular spelling (say 'abhominable' for 'abominable', 'scilens' for 'silence' or 'woeman' for 'woman') was genuinely original or one of a number of variants in regular use at a particular time. The *OED* will normally list a range of variant spellings together with dates but makes no pretence of being complete. LION offers a vast body of old-spelling material for searching but is not totally accurate in its reproduction of its sources. It is important to understand the spelling systems current at any given time. That both Rochester and Donne preferred spellings such as 'hee', 'shee', and 'mee' was not an idiosyncrasy but part of a rival system to that eventually adopted by the London printers who gave us our regularised modern spelling. The printers' reason for doing so was the practical one of never having enough 'e's in their cases of handset type, although the 'ee' spellings were truer phonetically (we still use 'see', 'free' etc.).

Today, as hardly needs saying, few speakers of English who are not engaged in writing-related professions have acquired a complete command of its wildly inconsistent orthographical system. The computer spelling-checker has ensured that formal writing is now more likely to be correctly spelled than in the days of the pen or the manual typewriter, but has also been responsible for a further erosion of spelling skills which becomes glaringly evident when students have to produce handwritten examination papers and in such rapidly typed and unchecked documents as emails. Forensic work of the kind described by Gerald McMenamin in *Forensic Stylistics* and anecdotally by Foster in *Author Unknown* is heavily reliant on individual preferences for non-standard spellings. Individual preferences are also likely to be evident in punctuation, hyphenation, spacing and layout – matters carefully illustrated and classified by McMenamin.

A rule that cannot be overstressed is that any listing of an author's characteristic spellings or layout preferences must be assembled from holographs or from printed texts and scribal copies that reveal themselves as faithfully set from holographs. This is particularly important with regard to doublets. Stieg Hargevik instances a text by Defoe whose first edition contained 104 examples of 'farther' and only two of 'further' but which in a nineteenth-century reprint appears with twenty-five 'farther's altered to 'further'.[47] There are cases where the known preferences of an author can be glimpsed through the known preferences of a scribe such as Ralph Crane or a compositor but these are rare and require careful handling. Preferred spellings of certain compositors involved in the setting of important books have been studied to the extent that departures from them can be hypothesised as the result of authorial influences. Some compositors can be shown to have followed copy much more closely than others; but each case of this kind would need to be carefully argued before it could be used as evidence for attribution. One cannot simply assume that a printed edition (which may be further distanced from the original by a scribal transcript) gives us a reliable record of authorial spellings. It goes without saying that trade reprints are of no value for such work.

This has not stopped editors of Renaissance texts making such suppositions, especially as regards contracted forms. Here they may be on stronger ground. Contractions are most common in play dialogue where they often serve to define what is a syllable for metrical purposes: scribes and compositors who were aware of this would have been more prepared to respect them than any run-of-the-mill spellings which came into conflict with their own preferences. The dramatist John Ford had a penchant for the forms 't'ee' for 'to ye' and 'd'ee' for 'do you' which compositors generally preserved. Serious use of contractions as a means of identifying work by Renaissance dramatists began in 1916 with Willard Farnham's 'Colloquial contractions in Beaumont, Fletcher, Massinger and Shakespeare as a test of authorship'.[48] In his detailed study of the role of collaborators in the 'Beaumont and Fletcher' plays, Cyrus Hoy relied heavily on the evidence of contractions. By comparison with Massinger, Fletcher has many more examples of ''em', 'i'th' and 'let's' and is the only one of the pair to use 'o'th', 'a'[=his], ''is'[='he is'], 'h'as', 'in's' and 'on's'. He does not use the abbreviation 't'' for 'to' which is quite common in Massinger.[49] Overall Massinger is much more sparing in his use of contractions than Fletcher. Hoy's figures, drawing on first editions from a variety of printing houses, are impressive evidence of the stability of contractions in transmission. Peter Murray developed Hoy's methods to deal with the disputed authorship of *The Revenger's Tragedy*, having first established that the habits claimed as typical of Middleton and Tourneur stretched across a number of printings and therefore were unlikely to be compositorial.[50] (In Middleton's case manuscripts were also available.)

CONCLUSION

It should be clear that qualitative methods and non-statistical quantitative methods can lead to consensually acceptable answers when carefully and responsibly applied to problems of authorship. These answers are likely to be most persuasive when the problems are of a relatively simple kind such as 'What are the shares of A and B in this joint work', but the discovery of good evidence can offer a purchase on more complex cases, especially in the securing of disproval of a candidacy. But such methods do not give any infallible way of adjudicating between the claims of differing doctors, of whom there have been a great number in the history of attribution studies; so it is best to end with a note of caution. After reviewing the enormous field of scholarship concerned with the attribution of English Renaissance plays and parts of those plays, Schoenbaum was left with an appreciation not of coherent discovery but of disorganised futility:

> For the better part of a century, enthusiasts have devised and applied tests of authorship. They have ransacked scenes for parallel passages. They have pointed to peculiarities of diction and phraseology. They have counted nouns, adjectives, and interjections, rhymes, end-stopped lines, redundant syllables, and double and triple endings. They have strained their ears to catch the elusive notes of the 'indefinite music' permeating the verse. The overall result of so much energetic but uncoordinated effort – some of it brilliant but misguided, some misguided but not brilliant, some lunatic, some (not enough) persuasive – has been predictable chaos.[51]

Elsewhere he speaks of rare triumphs from the application of stylistic evidence being overshadowed 'by the bedlamite antics of the wildmen' (p. 107). His own book brings a good deal of order into that particular chaos but leaves other historical fields of literary investigation as they were. In Chapter eight we will enquire whether new statistical computer-based methods which were only just coming into being at the time he wrote have contributed to any lessening of chaos or simply left confusion worse confounded.

CHAPTER SEVEN

Gender and authorship

Where more exact kinds of identification are impossible, may there be ways by which we can detect the gender of an author? Most readers of fiction will have had the experience of detecting a certain unreality or incompleteness in depictions of characters of their own sex by members of the other. For women this may involve a dissatisfaction with Madame Bovary or Anna Karenina as lacking a true female inwardness, while a male reader of *Wuthering Heights* may recognise shrewd observation of a certain type in Heathcliff but be genuinely puzzled by what makes Edgar Linton tick (or not tick). Readers of either sex would probably assume that if they were given a selection of ten anonymous short stories, half of which were written by women and half by men, they could have a pretty good shot at working out which were which – Red Symons has actually provided such a collection, with the authors listed but not their contributions.[1] Extend the scope to whole novels and we would expect even better results, since we would not only have fuller exposure to tone and style but there would be more chance of encountering the kind of factual detail that immediately betrays. Non-fiction would pose more of a challenge; but even here it is not impossible that we might be able to locate preferred male and female forms of style and exposition. Work by Mary Hiatt and Estelle Irizarry, discussed at the end of the chapter, proceeds on this assumption. Hiatt has no doubt about the existence of a distinct 'feminine style' or genderlect and even offers a theory of how it arose, which is that the male world of action 'emphasizes events and decisions rather than perceptive observations of people'.[2]

We would need, naturally, to acknowledge that there are continuums in writing practices much as there are in other aspects of gendered behaviour. Moreover, even if we were to accept that certain kinds of expression and content were more characteristic of writing by members of one or the other sex, we would still be left with the problem of how effectively these might be imitated by writers who set out to disguise their birth gender. John Clute, for one, rejects the view that

> an artifact of language – in this case the phallocentric *parole* of themes and tropes and rhythms and rituals and syntaxes greased for power which makes up 'masculine discourse' – was in itself inherently sexed, so that only a biological male could utter it. . . . Artifacts – like jungle gyms, like pseudonyms – are in themselves inherently *learnable*. They can be climbed into.[3]

To which one can only reply, learnable enough to deceive the inattentive reader perhaps, but *perfectly* learnable? – learnable enough to defeat every conceivable probe? That surely is an empirical matter to be determined by testing the wits of attributionists or the capacities of neural networks (discussed in Chapter eight) against a range of actual cases. It is not yet possible to declare apodictically that the parsing programme that will unfailingly distinguish bearers of two X chromosomes from those of an X and a Y will never be written.

Clute's comment comes as part of a reproof to Robert D. Silverberg for asserting that the stories of James Tiptree, jr (aka Alice B. Sheldon) could not have been written by a woman because they were 'ineluctably masculine'.[4] In fact Tiptree/Sheldon imitates some aspects of male parole brilliantly. Clute himself confessed to having built a mental image of Tiptree as 'a wiry sharp man whose colour was the colour of marmalade, like a tiger out of Blake': the reality was 'a sixty-year-old woman whose health was precarious' (pp. xi–xii). But her stories would probably have been recognisable as by a woman author had anyone subjected them to the kind of tests Jacqueline Pearson applies in *The Prostituted Muse* to women dramatists of 1642–1737. These were concerned with the relative prominence given to women in plays by men and by other women respectively and the amount of speaking time allowed to them. Some of her findings were as follows:

- Plays by men have an average of nine male characters to four or five female; plays by women have an average of nine male characters to six female.
- Few plays by men have episodes in which only women appear. Such scenes are significantly more frequent in plays by women.
- Female characters are much more likely to open and close plays by women writers.
- Women are more likely to allow female characters the authority to end the play and thus sum up its significance for the audience.
- In plays by women, female characters speak just over one line in three, although in twenty-seven cases they are allowed to speak half the lines

> or more. In plays by men women speak only one line in four and in very few plays [2 out of 100 sampled] are allowed to speak half the lines or more.[5]

The issue here is the prominence given to women and the share of the dialogue assigned to them, which in Tiptree's fiction I would judge to be much more considerable than that of male writers in the same genre.

Tiptree, although she eventually felt obliged to come clean, seems to have enjoyed her mystification. She had been aided in it by possessing anomalous knowledges, acquired during her work as a technical officer for the CIA, and, when she set up her pseudonymous writing identities, she used CIA techniques to prevent discovery. Another woman writer who clearly had a strong identification with her male writing persona was Henry Handel Richardson (aka Florence Ethel Richardson) who in a long correspondence in French with the translator of her first novel *Maurice Guest*, Paul Solanges, refused to concede for a moment that she was a woman. Solanges clearly suspected the truth and would press her gently on the matter from time to time, but always unsuccessfully. When he asked her what she looked like, she referred him to a painting of Goethe as a young man.[6] The nineteenth-century dramatist, Michael Field, was actually an aunt and niece combination, Katherine Bradley and Edith Cooper: their sense of their collaboration is illuminated by correspondence in which they speak of 'Michael' as a third person distinct from either of them. Bradley wrote to Robert Browning:

> Spinoza with his fine grasp of unity says 'If two individuals of exactly the same nature are joined together, they make up a single individual, doubly stronger than each alone,' i.e. Edith and I make a veritable Michael.[7]

In the cases of George Eliot, Richardson and the first appearance of the Brontës as Currer, Ellis and Acton Bell, the pretence was supposedly undertaken in order to get a fair hearing from prejudiced male reviewers; and yet for Richardson, at least, the attractions of the impersonation clearly ran deeper. Among male pretenders we might note William Sharp (1855–1905) who wrote biographies and unsuccessful novels under his own name and highly popular 'Celtic' fiction as 'Fiona Macleod'.[8] Sharp, who was rumoured to have worn women's clothing when he wrote as his alter ego, concealed Fiona's identity until his death through such Tiptreean devices as a bogus *Who's Who* entry.

Sometimes writers record an experience of being possessed and dictated to by a 'character' of the other sex. Consider the following from an interview with Helen Garner:

But I've just finished writing a character, in this new book *Cosmo Cosmolino* – a bloke named Alby. I invented him totally. Well . . . as totally as a character is ever really invented, in fiction. Anyway, he is not based on or inspired by a real person, and I found that writing him was the greatest bliss and joy of anything I've ever done. And then when I created him I had to fight him for control of the book. He almost got the upper hand. I thought: Bugger you – I'm in charge here! He marched into the book and turned everyone around him into wimps. He was like an energy thief. We had a titanic struggle. I *think* I won. Nothing like that has ever happened to me before. I've always felt I was in control of things . . . . I found such ease in him . . . he seemed so intensely familiar to me. It was as if I were he.[9]

The experience described has something in common with that of an actor interiorising a character; but the imagery both here and in similar accounts by other writers is one of an invasion from outside by an alien, already formed personality. In this respect it has something in common with a medium's experience of possession. Garner rationalises in Jungian terms by suggesting that Alby 'was a version of my animus' (p. 68); likewise Aphra Behn located her writing self in 'my Masculine Part the Poet in me'.[10] It has not yet been tested how such powerful forms of identification might modify the primary genderlect. Defoe's prose when he writes as Moll Flanders is not noticeably different from that when he writes as Robinson Crusoe; but then it is agreed that Moll is not an entirely convincing woman. The eighteenth-century epistolary novel would be a good field for further investigation. A methodology is offered by John Burrows's study of differences between the language of Jane Austen's characters in *Computation into Criticism*.[11]

Most of all, it must be remembered that, even when they do not possess any strong subjective identification with the other gender, writers are professional deceivers and will take care to use members of that gender as informants or even as 'half-ghosts'. Samuel Richardson in the eighteenth century and George Meredith and Henry James in the nineteenth were male writers who had a great appeal for women readers of their time, wrote fiction rich in female characters, and drew heavily on their women friends' ideas and advice. Ada Cambridge, who should have known, wrote of Meredith: 'no man in the world ever understood *us* as he does'.[12] Aphra Behn in the seventeenth century was well enough informed about the ways of men to be able, if two recent attributions are correct, to compose the foul-mouthed male political libels known as lampoons.[13]

MEANS OF DETERMINING GENDER

Any attempt to devise an empirical method for identifying the gender of authors would need to consider three main topics. The first would be differences which have been suggested by neurobiologists in the brain structure of males and females and the areas utilised by each for processing language. The second would be evidence from psychology concerning the development of language behaviour in the young. Here there are undoubted differences; but do they leave lifelong, ineradicable traces? The third, and for practical purposes the most manageable, would be evidence from different kinds of socialisation and the characteristic knowledges of men and women in given societies. I will consider each of these briefly.

Genetic differences

It is generally accepted at the present time that slight structural differences do exist between the male and female brain and that centres involved in language activity may well be affected by these. It needs to be said at the start that these differences concern averages, and that there is generally a high degree of overlap between the scores of individuals, as there is in physical height. The most commonly cited finding is that the material connections between the two hemispheres of the brain appear to be richer in women. In the forebrain this affects the corpus callosum and in the rear brain the anterior commissure. Most attention has been given to the corpus callosum which has two parts, the rostrum (Latin for the prow of a ship) to the front and the splenium (Latin for an adhesive plaster) to the rear. The differences are not absolute ones but a question of the organ occupying a larger proportion of the generally smaller female brain as measured by the total number of neurones. (In compensation, women lose brain tissue at a lower rate than males.) It has been speculated that women have a higher capacity for communication between the left hemisphere, which is the primary language centre, and the right hemisphere. According to Rita Carter

> This may explain why women seem to be more aware of their own and others' emotions than men – the emotionally sensitive right hemisphere is able to pass more information to the analytical, linguistically talented left side. It may also allow emotion to be incorporated more easily into speech and thought processes.[14]

It has also been noted that women's capacity for speech is less affected by physical damage to the left hemisphere, suggesting either a greater degree of generalisation of language function over the whole brain or that the right hemisphere shares in this to a greater degree than in males.[15] The male brain, on the other hand, is regarded as relatively more specialised than the female brain: imaging studies show that women are more likely than men to use both hemispheres during the performance of complex tasks, including reading, while autism, a state of excessive specialisation often accompanied by a single exceptionally developed talent, is much more common among males.[16]

While such differences are clearly genetic in origin, they are activated in the foetus and mature body through the release of hormones. (Whether it is significant or not, 'Tiptree' only came into existence after Sheldon had passed menopause.) Ingenious work has been done on the results of breakdowns in the normal functioning of hormonal systems, e.g. in males who produce testosterone but lack the receptors that inform the body of its presence. It has been suggested that a facility in mathematical reasoning is associated with androgen levels in the lower range of males and the higher of females – and that it is not shared by males with very high androgen levels (perhaps an explanation for Einstein's wonderful head of hair).[17] All of this is fascinating but, at this stage of our knowledge, hardly usable for purposes of attribution. One may accept the proposition of there being differences in the way language is processed by the XX and XY brains without having any clear notion of what effect this might have on the language produced. There is also the possibility that language is like a piece of software that can run perfectly satisfactorily on differently configured computers, though one suspects that this kind of claim will become less and less tenable as results accumulate about its neurological activation. Should genetically determined elements in language ever be identified that were so profoundly interiorised as to be ineradicable, they would immediately become imitable, creating opportunities for a new generation of fakers and literary cross-dressers; but this should not affect our analysis of texts written prior to any such discovery.

As with brains, so with bodies: many theorists have proposed physical determinants for characteristic writing styles. Women's writing is frequently characterised as fluent and men's as spasmodic; women's as aesthetic and men's as dynamic; women's as shrill and hysterical while men's, in the amazing words of William H. Gass, exhibits 'an openly lustful, quick, impatient, feral hunger' along with a 'blood congested genital drive'.[18] Mary Hiatt has compiled a bizarre florilegium of such characterisations of which Gass's is the prize specimen.[19] Her text punctures the patriarchal clichés one by one on the basis of actual counts of stylistic features but does not deny that there are significant differences.

Differences in language development

It is undoubtedly the case that males differ from females in the stages and rate at which they acquire language in infancy and childhood. These have been much studied by educational psychologists and can be predicted accurately for a representative child of known age (there will naturally be exceptions and overlaps). At toddler stage females generally talk earlier than males; but males on average are more talkative and assured at the pre-school level.[20] At about the age of five boys tend to turn away from the mother-dominated sphere of infancy towards a new one of masculine identification in the schoolyard and through play, which requires them to master a new genderlect, while girls, by and large, continue fluently in the maternal one. At school, males, while still talkative, are more likely to be bored and disruptive and females to outstrip them in linguistic attainments in the crucial middle years. Two thirds of the 'special needs' children in British primary schools are male and only one third female. Ninety per cent of the prison population is male. Males are generally more successful than females in subjects involving spatialisation but even here are hampered by being, on the whole, less docible. Past generations of pedagogues responded to this difficulty by enforcing male learning with frequent canings but this sanction is no longer tolerated. By young adulthood Anglophone male speech can be statistically identified by its use of interruptions, directives and conjunctions/fillers at the beginning of sentences and female speech by a preponderance of questions, justifiers, intensive adverbs and personal pronouns and by the use of adverbials at the beginning of sentences.[21]

It is also accepted that males and females tend to construct narratives in different ways. These preferences have been studied in children aged from two to eight by Brian Sutton-Smith[22] who uses a folklorist's model based on the ways in which a story deals with a perception of danger (p. 20). He found no gender-related difference in the length of stories or in the rate of progression to employment of the higher levels of the model, but did so in the 'style of solution' in that 'boys more often reach level iii or iv by having their hero overcome the villain; the girls more often reach that level through an alliance' (p. 24). Similar differences have also been recorded for dreams and games, with the boys' displaying more complex kinds of organisation. Interestingly, 'Both sexes told more imaginative stories to male storytakers and more realistic tales to female storytakers' (p. 36). As would be expected, the stories told by girls and boys also differed in content:

> the boys told significantly more tales of villainy, and the girls more of deprivation; the boys told more of contest, and the girls more about domestic animals. (p. 27)

J. A. Appleyard cites a number of additional studies which agree that boys are more interested in conflict, violence and the search for autonomy and girls in stories that emphasise security and the need to sustain relationships.[23] That this distinction also governs adult reading tastes would be accepted by anyone working in the book or video trade; that it arises very early in childhood would suggest that it is part of our evolutionary heritage; but that it is a reliable marker of gender in authorship can be no more than a probability in any given case, especially when pretence is involved.

Effects of socialisation

Genetic differences and differences in language development interact with those of social conditioning to an extent that makes it impossible, in many instances, to tell whether nature or nurture holds the greater responsibility for their production. What is clear is that an immense amount of social effort is expended on confirming 'biological' gender roles, not least by small children themselves. The liberalisation which has taken place over the last century is only relative.

It hardly needs to be said that, until relatively recent times in the West, most middle-class women were brought up to lead more dependent, restricted lives than men and were denied comparable formal education, or sometimes any education at all. By the same social conventions men were barred from many of the most absorbing and character-building of human activities, particularly those concerned with the nurture of very young children. Prior to the introduction of compulsory schooling, literacy levels among females were generally much lower than among males, and even among those women who were functionally literate only a few, and those chiefly from privileged backgrounds, would have possessed the higher level of literacy needed to become authors. In English-speaking countries until the mid-nineteenth century most male writers of literature had received a classical education which left indelible marks on their written style. Very few women, on the other hand, were allowed to learn classical languages, though they were often fluent in French and Italian. John Burrows has demonstrated that this is reflected in patterns in the use of common function words.[24] Though the difference is also encountered in some uneducated male writers (others could mimic the classical style without a knowledge of classical languages), it serves as a useful gender marker in combination with other evidence.

Yet, for most attribution enquiries the nurture/nature difference is not a significant one, since our concern is simply with what might mark the work of a woman within a particular historical society. Here various common-sense discriminators come into play, of which the most important is expertise in matters regarded by the society concerned as the province of one or the other gender. Even today a female is much more likely on the whole to write convincingly about the experience of buying baby clothes and a male writer about what it is like to be a professional furniture removalist. (It is no less important that on the whole they would be more inclined to write about such things in the first place.)

Samuel Butler's *The Authoress of the Odyssey* (1892) has had no detectable effect on Homeric scholarship, and is usually regarded as a literary joke undertaken to shock the erudite; but the tests it proposes for assigning the poem to a woman poet are often quite good ones.[25] Butler sets out from Richard Bentley's claim that the *Odyssey* was written for women and the *Iliad* for men, which he takes a step further by asserting that 'The history of literature furnishes us with no case in which a man has written a great masterpiece for women rather than men.'[26] His first and most persuasive class of criteria is similar to that established by Pearson in her analyses of plays written by women, being drawn from their prominence in the narrative, the priority in encounters given to them over men, as in the underworld of Book xi (pp. 105–24), and the power they are repeatedly given of directing the actions of men. ('Never mind my father', instructs Nausicaa at v. 310, 'but go up to my mother'.) The argument from socialisation enters with examples of the author's familiarity with female knowledge and with mistakes of a kind that would not have been made by a male, e.g. that the rudder of a ship was at the bow, that a hawk can tear its prey while still flying, or that well-seasoned timber can be cut from a growing tree (p. 9). Finally, and more controversially, he introduces a series of observations based on the assumption that women's behaviour and attitudes in archaic Greece would have had much in common with those of his own late-Victorian day. Only a female poet, he argues, would have had Odysseus supervise the washing of the seats and tables immediately after killing the suitors (p. 118) or Helen give Telemachus a wedding-dress for a present (p. 150). He assumes without considering the matter further that a male poet would not have included the episode of the murder of the twelve errant serving women as we have it:

> Fierce as the writer is against the suitors, she is far more so against the women. When the suitors are all killed, Euryclea begins to raise a cry of triumph over them, but Ulysses checks her. 'Hold your tongue, woman,' he says, 'it is ill bragging over the bodies of dead men' (xxii. 411). So also it is ill getting the most hideous service out of women up to the very moment when they are to be executed; but the writer seems to have no sense of this; where female honour has been violated by those of woman's own sex, no punishment is too bad for them. (p. 119)

Here Butler lapses into special pleading. The continuing value of his book lies in its challenge to present-day classicists to find a way of proving that its revolutionary attempt to insert female authorship into the founding moment of Western culture is a failure. Until that is done its argument must continue to hover like an unpropitiated Elpenor in the realms of the dead.

CROSS-GENDER COLLABORATION

It is very likely that much male writing contains unacknowledged contributions from women. A case of this which seems fairly well documented is the composition of Brecht's *Dreigroschenoper*, as recorded in John Fuegi's controversial *The Life and Lies of Bertolt Brecht*.[27] It was also often the case in the past that women's writings were heavily edited by men before publication. Germaine Greer has documented male interference in the published writings of the Restoration poet Katherine Philips (Orinda), and regards it as likely that this kind of supervision applied to much women's writing of that period.[28] Philips's letters, now available in the comprehensive Stump Cross edition, reveal an insecurity over matters of grammar and idiom that is unexpected in so gifted a writer, but becomes explicable once it is realised that these matters were in many cases undetermined at the time: there was no seventeenth-century Fowler's for her to consult! Hester Piozzi writing in the late eighteenth century was caught both ways: when she wrote 'correctly' she was accused of doing it with the help of Samuel Johnson and when she wrote in her lively, more conversational style, modelled on the conversation of her bluestocking friends, the charge changed to one of illiteracy (see p. 106 above). Today when the majority of skilled publisher's editors are female the boot is on the other foot. John Burrows and Anthony Hassall have used statistical methods (among others) to distinguish the contributions of Henry Fielding to his sister Sara's novel, *David Simple*, and Sara's to Fielding's *A Journey From This World To The Next.*[29] Many more cases of this kind await investigation.

QUANTITATIVE ANALYSIS OF GENDERLECTS

Considering the interest that attaches to the intrinsic differences between female and male writing, it is surprising that, since the publication of Hiatt's *The Way Women Write*, so little stylometric work has been done on the subject.[30] Hiatt used an archive of four 500-word samples from each of fifty books by men and fifty by women, equally divided between fiction and non-fiction, and all except one first published in the late 1960s and early 1970s. She returns a series of results indicating differential tendencies in men's and women's writing but always with a considerable overlap of populations.[31] Unfortunately these results are presented within an interpretative framework which restricts their usefulness to attribution studies. Her aim was to rebut unfair accusations made by men about woman writers and her choice of aspects for testing is made on this basis and such attendant assumptions as that exclamation marks are an index of excitability and parentheses and dashes of self-abegnation. The most one could hope for is that agreement across all of the tested preferences would create a probability (it could be no more) of male or female authorship; but it is also likely that there are other preferences that might be indicative but were not sought for by Hiatt because they had never been a topos of male put-downs.

The problematic nature of Hiatt's findings was revealed by Estelle Irizarry in a computer-assisted investigation of gender-based differences in the Spanish writings of two leading Mexican authors, Octavio Paz and Rosario Castellanos.[32] The idea of basing such a study on a single example of each sex might seem to have derailed it from the start, as also might the fact that the only data examined was a single 10,000 word article by each. One would certainly have to be very careful in generalising from her results. But her study does provide a handy summary of the suggestions made by Hiatt, Burrows and other earlier writers for distinguishing genderlects. Irizarry's conclusions are as follows:

- Hiatt found that women's sentences were generally shorter than men's. In this case Paz's sentences were shorter than those of Castellanos.
- Hiatt, in showing that women used more sentences under six words, suggested that women's writing is more fragmented and segmented than men's. Again this does not apply to Castellanos.
- A number of writers have proposed that conjoined constructions leading to a 'cumulative' style are more common among women, while men's writing favours a 'complex, subordinating style' (p. 108). Again this does not apply to Castellanos with regard to Paz.
- Hiatt found that men used exclamations more than women. Not so Paz. However, Castellanos asks many more questions than Paz (another suggested characteristic of women's discourse). Paz's questions come at the beginning of his essay whereas Castellanos's are spaced more regularly throughout.
- Hiatt's findings on the use of logical sequence indicators are borne out by Paz and Castellanos. Paz makes three times as much use of case-building additives ('words expressing "also", "in addition" and "at the same time" ') (p. 108). Castellanos uses 'causatives corresponding to "since" and "because" more than three times as often as Paz' (p. 108). Hiatt (p. 57) suggests that this is because women 'offer more reasons and justifications'. Adversatives ('words that change the direction of argument' (p. 109)) were twice as common in Paz, although Hiatt had found no obvious gender preference. Walter J. Ong regards 'adversativeness' as a feature of male speech.[33]
- Castellanos uses more comparisons than Paz and intensifies them by using '*mucho*', which Paz never does.
- Hiatt found that women used similes half as much again as men. Castellanos uses them nearly four times as often as Paz. The content of the similes is also indicative of gender in both cases.
- Castellanos's vocabulary is more varied than that of Paz. She also uses more diminutives, euphemisms and words expressive of tenderness and fewer 'strong words' such as *mierda* and *puta*. Her spatial references tend to be to interiors. There are few geographical references by comparison with Paz (who, however, was a professional diplomat). She is more given to understatement: words corresponding to 'always' and 'never' are more frequent in Paz.
- Paz is 'decidedly more aggressive and emphatic in his use of forms in the first-person plural' (p. 110), seen by Irizarry as the pronoun most expressive of power.

- Both use about the same number of negative words but Paz is more likely to put them at the beginning of a sentence. Paz has a higher frequency of the strong affirmative '*sí*' than Castellanos. Paz makes greater use of the assertive form of the verb 'to be' and is much more likely to place it at the beginning of a sentence. Castellanos prefers less assertive impersonal constructions.
- Castellanos makes much more use of verbs of obligation. She prefers 'a softened, indirect (female) way of commanding' (p. 113).
- Castellanos refers to 37 females and 25 males. Paz refers to 15 females and 35 males.

Irizarry's paper is of greater interest for the range of topics it addresses than for its particular findings. A new quantitative study built on larger English-language samples would clearly be of great value. It hardly needs saying that the issues raised regarding gender also apply *mutatis mutandis* to other ways of dividing people off into genetically defined categories: particularly race. (Several examples of gender impersonation have also been transracial.) The answer to the question asked in the opening sentence of this chapter would seem to be 'potentially, but not yet'.

CHAPTER EIGHT

Craft and science

We saw in Chapter six that stylistics, variously understood, has been one of the most important tools of attribution studies but that in the past its effectiveness rested on the erudition and intuitive flair of the investigator. When Aulus Gellius called some lines from *Boeotia* 'Plautinissimi', he was working from an intuitive holistic response to the text intensified by a local activation of the pleasure principle. There is nothing wrong with intuition: we use it successfully every time we manage to cross a busy highway in one piece; but its results are not always shareable. We might not have such success in guiding a blindfolded experimental subject across the same road by mobile phone. Erasmus in rejecting the Jerome-spuria was forced to look more closely at aspects of language and style, but still relied strongly on his intuitive sense of authentic Jerome as a unique integration of style, matter and ethos. By the time of Richard Bentley, arguments over authenticity had acquired a strong philological emphasis, informed by a newly acquired understanding of the historical development of languages. Cases began to be argued in a more forensic way from systematically marshalled evidence. It was also understood by this time that a negative case was easier to make than a positive one in that a single anachronism or historically impossible form might overturn an otherwise persuasive attribution.

At a certain stage stylistics so practised passes into stylometry, considered as the exact quantitative measurement, tabulation and interpretation of designated aspects of verbal performance. The recording of such data has quite a long history. Jewish Bible scribes in the Masoretic tradition used to keep counts of the numbers of verses, words and even letters in a book to ensure accuracy in transcription. Both Jewish and Christian cabalists looked for occult meanings in letter patterns and the numbers that could be derived from them. Quantitative approaches to metrical practice have already been described. By the beginning of the twentieth century, in English studies, there was a general acceptance of the usefulness of rudimentary stylometric methods, encouraged by their compatibility with those of philologists in dating and localising Old and Middle English writings. Results were expressed in direct numerical terms or as simple ratios that posed no difficulties for unmathematical humanists.

As early as 1851 the mathematician Augustus De Morgan had proposed that the old problem of the authorship of the Epistle to the Hebrews could be solved by comparing the average number of letters per word in the Greek text with that of the other Pauline epistles; however, he did not actually carry out the calculations proposed. Such straightforward methods can still yield acceptable answers to undemanding problems. The 1880s saw attempts at tabular and graphical representation of features of style by a number of scholars, of whom the most persistent was Thomas Mendenhall. Mendenhall's paper 'The characteristic curves of composition' (1887) contended that authorial characteristics could be detected in the distribution of the frequencies of words of given lengths.[1] In a later publication Mendenhall used his method to address whether Bacon might be the author of the plays attributed to Shakespeare. He found that the graph of Bacon's preferences peaked, typically of writers in English, at the three-letter word but that of Shakespeare at the four-letter word; however, the graph of Christopher Marlowe's preferences proved to be very similar to Shakespeare's, meaning that the test that could distinguish between Shakespeare and Bacon (or possibly just between dramatic blank verse and ratiocinative prose) could not distinguish between the two playwrights.[2] This result continues to be quoted by those who believe that Marlowe was the true author of the plays attributed to Will the player (as he will be christened in Chapter eleven). John Michell claims contentiously that 'It was as rare a coincidence as finding two people with identical fingerprints.'[3] In fact, Thomas Merriam has demonstrated that Shakespeare and Marlowe can be separated by as simple a test as the frequency in their work of the letters 'a' and 'o' (see p. 159).[4] Nonetheless, Mendenhall's work must be regarded as ancestral to the modern numerical investigation of attribution.

With the growth to maturity of statistics as a branch of applied mathematics, new possibilities presented themselves for the analysis of stylistic data. An important advance was made in 1944 when G. Udny Yule, the author of a standard textbook on statistics, published *The Statistical Study of Literary Vocabulary*.[5] In this work Yule used the relative numbers of nouns occurring once, twice and so on as an indicator of authorship. This method was used to test whether a famous mediaeval devotional text, the *De imitatione Christi*, was by Thomas à Kempis, as normally accepted, or by Jean Gerson. Yule found in favour of à Kempis. In 1970 C. B. Williams, a biologist with a long-standing interest in stylistic problems published his *Style and Vocabulary: Numerical Studies*, a still valuable summing-up of work from the first (pre-computer) phase of statistical stylometrics.

THE STATISTICAL INVESTIGATION OF AUTHORSHIP

While the mathematical study of probabilities goes back to the Renaissance (having been of pressing interest to gamblers), statistics as a discipline remained identified for a long time with the collection and analysis of demographic and economic data. The 1922 edition of *Chambers's Encyclopaedia* defined it as 'a branch of political science', with the account of the relevant mathematics relegated to the article 'probability', and even this chiefly concerned with the actuarial calculations used in the life-insurance industry. It was only several decades into the twentieth century that developments in physics and biology and the growth to maturity of sociology and psychology as experimental disciplines elevated statistics into a major instrument for the mathematical investigation of reality. The middle decades of the century saw much refinement of its methods.

The arrival of the computer and the availability of a growing body of texts in machine-readable form gave further impetus to the investigation of the statistics of style. In the pre-computer phase the accumulation and processing of data were unbelievably time-consuming and its accuracy difficult for other researchers to verify. The earliest days of computer applications were still labour intensive. Texts had to be key-punched onto cards or paper-tape and software had to be written 'cave-man' style, command by command, in languages which were not designed for verbal manipulation. The memories even of physically imposing mainframes were tiny by present-day standards. These limitations led to a need to squeeze the maximum amount of information from very small samples, which lingered in the work of researchers such as Andrew Morton long after it was strictly necessary. It also took some time to discover which kinds of data and which methods of analysing that data were likely to be productive. Investigation proceeded by trial and error guided by precedents from other disciplines.

Erdmann and Fogel's *Evidence for Authorship*, published in 1966, stands close to the borderline between manual and computational methods, between stylistic and stylometric approaches, and, in the case of the latter, between statistical and non-statistical forms of analysis. Stands close to but does not cross: its index has no entry for computer! Yet, inspired by the work of Mosteller and Wallace on the *Federalist* papers, the second half of the 1960s was a period of great creativity in attributional stylistics.[6] This celebrated study addressed itself to the authorship of twelve uncertainly attributed periodical essays from a series of seventy-seven written in 1787–8 to encourage the ratifying of the American constitution. The rest of the series was securely attributed to one or the other of Alexander Hamilton, James Madison and John Jay, with three papers known to have been written collaboratively by Hamilton and Madison. After several false starts the problem was approached from the viewpoint of individual preferences in the use of function words. By obtaining an overall value from these preferences the investigators were able to assign the dubious papers unambiguously to Madison. The *Federalist* problem has since become a testing ground for the trialling of new statistical approaches. Another long-standing journalistic mystery, the authorship of the late eighteenth-century letters published in the *Public Advertiser* under the signature 'Junius', was successfully resolved in 1962 by Alvar Ellegård, using a similar approach.[7]

In briefly surveying developments since the 1970s I will look, side by side, at the statistical study of individual language behaviour and the use of computers to extract information from databases. My discussion assumes a basic understanding of statistical concepts and reasoning such as is possessed by those who have studied the subject at an introductory level in social science courses. Those without prior experience should begin with one of several available books which set out to explain the founding concepts of statistics in an approachable way without getting too involved in details of practice. Among these, John L. Phillips, jr, *How To Think About Statistics*, is useful for the clarity of its expositions and for being explicitly directed to the 'mathphobic' while Anthony Kenny's *Computation of Style: An Introduction to Statistics for Students of Literature and Humanities* concentrates on the issues of greater relevance to aspiring attributionists.[8] Having mastered the basics, the beginner should be able to follow a fair deal of the argumentation of papers in the field. Those with a background in statistics but none in the technical side of attributional stylometry should proceed straight to David Holmes's 1994 article 'Authorship attribution', a masterly short review of work up to that time.[9] More recent developments can be followed by turning to the last few years of the two major journals in the field, *Computers and the*

Humanities (*CHum*) and *Literary and Linguistic Computing* (*LLC*). The present author writes as no more than an involved spectator of the field and has no pretensions to teach statistics to statisticians.

STATISTICAL STUDIES OF *THE REVENGER'S TRAGEDY*

A sense of developments in stylometry and computational stylistics over recent decades can be gained from the debate over the authorship of *The Revenger's Tragedy*. This brilliantly macabre drama had been published without an author's name in 1607. Long admired by scholars and critics, it re-entered the classical acting repertoire in 1969 with a stunning production by the Royal Shakespeare Company.[10] The fact that it was listed in the Stationers' Register under the date 7 October 1607 together with a second play known to be by Middleton suggested that he may have been its author. A lost play, *The Vyper and her Broode*, mentioned by Middleton in a court case as having been completed by 6 May 1606, sounds from its title as if it could have been identical with *The Revenger's Tragedy*, though Schoenbaum in 1966 was sceptical.[11] However, a playlist of 1656 attributed *The Revenger's Tragedy*, without giving evidence, to Cyril Tourneur, author of the similarly titled *The Atheist's Tragedy*. The difference in style and quality between the two works was noted by a number of scholars from the 1890s onward and in 1926 E. H. C. Oliphant formally proposed Middleton as the author of *The Revenger's Tragedy*.[12] This identification was widely though not, for a time, unanimously accepted. (Schoenbaum after initially supporting Middleton became a fence-sitter.) Careful comparisons of the frequencies of usage of Middleton's favoured spellings and contractions, made in 1964 by Peter Murray, were overwhelmingly in favour of Middleton against Tourneur.[13] Murray was also able to demonstrate by elaborate cross-checking that the compositors in the two printing houses concerned were reproducing authorial forms with reasonable fidelity – a vital point for all such demonstrations (pp. 161–5).

In 1975 David Lake published a major attributional study of the Middleton canon, which included an examination of the evidence for Middleton's and for Tourneur's authorship of *The Revenger's Tragedy*.[14] Not possessing machine-readable texts of the plays he assembled all his evidence by hand from the original printings, meaning that the word lengths of plays had to be estimated rather than exactly measured. Lake followed the method of Cyrus Hoy's work on the Fletcher canon by concentrating principally on the use of contractions, supplemented by exclamations, oaths, 'connectives' (among/amongst etc.) and characteristic spellings. These are presented in tables which in many cases establish his argument without further processing; however, where Hoy and Murray had been content to sum their results, Lake conducted statistical comparisons of the frequencies of these features with those of twenty-three plays of similar date and related genre to *The Revenger's Tragedy* and *The Atheist's Tragedy*. Among his conclusions, based on two methods of testing, was an estimate 'for the fraction of the population of Jacobean dramatists who write as much like *The Revenger's Tragedy* as Middleton does' of one-hundred millionth or one fifteen-thousand-millionth (p. 156).

These cosmic probabilities were challenged in a subsequent paper by Wilfrid Smith, an insistent voice for reasonableness and good practice during the founding decades of attributional stylometry.[15] While accepting Lake's broad contention that Middleton was the most probable among the authors tested, and Tourneur among the less likely, he found that, in applying the non-parametric chi-squared test to pairs of plays, 'one or more plays by other dramatists always appeared indistinguishable from a Middleton comedy' (p. 32). Concerned that the features used to determine Middleton's authorship could have resulted from his acting as a scribe or play doctor, Smith later returned to the question using principal component analysis (described below).[16] This was a narrower investigation based on complete machine-readable texts of four other plays by Middleton, together with *The Atheist's Tragedy* and two plays by John Marston, as another suspect requiring investigation. The effect of this test was to confirm Middleton as the most likely of the three to be the author of *The Revenger's Tragedy*, though in one plot 'one Middletonian act is seen to fall within the territory encompassed by Tourneur and *The Revenger's Tragedy* could be partly by either playwright, or indeed, by neither' (p. 510). Lake's careful findings as qualified by Smith require us to question Morton's later dismissal of Middleton's participation on the strength of an analysis of only twenty-five sentences (see p. 140).

The relationship of *The Atheist's Tragedy* and *The Revenger's Tragedy* was treated incidentally in a study by Thomas Merriam contesting Smith's criticism of one of his own earlier studies of the Shakespeare dubia. Two scatter plots (PC1 vs PC2 and PC1 vs PC3) show the pair always close together and at some distance from the other two Middleton plays in the test, *Women Beware Women* and *A Mad World My Masters*.[17] However, these tests, based on Andrew Morton's method of proportional pairs and collocations, are disqualified from authority with regard to the Middleton/Tourneur question by their original orientation of distinguishing between Shakespeare and non-Shakespeare and the fact that only eight wholly non-Shakespearean plays were tested. In the most thorough study to date, Hugh Craig in 1999 applied discriminant analysis to 110 Middleton 2,000-word segments (drawn from the twelve plays for which Middleton's authorship is uncontested) and 775 non-Middleton ones drawn from 97 plays.[18] The data used were counts of 155 high-frequency words, generally the most common but with a few specific content-determined words omitted. In the first, verificatory, stage of the test all but one of the Middleton segments were classified correctly as by him and all but eight of the non-Middleton segments classified as not by him, giving a success rate of ninety-nine per cent. The application of the same function to a reserve set confirmed the validity of this result. When the function was applied to *The Revenger's Tragedy*, eight of its ten segments fell into the Middleton group and two outside it. On this basis Craig judged that 'Middleton would seem to have had a large but not exclusive part' in the play (p. 109). For *The Changeling*, an acknowledged collaboration between Middleton and William Rowley, eight of the nine segments fell into the Middleton area and one outside it. Another dubium, *The Second Maiden's Tragedy*, came out as wholly by Middleton. *The Atheist's Tragedy* fell into the non-Middleton section. The only new result likely to disturb the acceptance of Middleton's authorship would be one that still allowed him a major role as, say, the reviser of a rudimentary script by a tyro dramatist such as Richard Braithwaite. Braithwaite is suggested as he was a brilliant verse satirist in both English and Latin, and claimed to have written a number of plays successfully performed on the London stage; however, *The Revenger's Tragedy* would seem to be a year or two early for his arrival in London.[19]

THE DEBATE OVER MORTON'S METHODS

The year 1978 brought the publication of one of the most influential texts in stylometry in Andrew Morton's *Literary Detection: How to prove authorship and fraud in literature and documents*.[20] Morton had originally been drawn to the field through an interest in the authenticity of the Pauline epistles. The two pressing questions confronting him were which features of style were to be measured and which statistical procedures were most appropriate for their analysis: there would be no point in choosing a feature whose frequency did not conform to one of the standard distributions recognised by statisticians.[21] Morton came to the conclusion that 'by far the most effective discriminator between one writer and another is the placing of words' (p. 107). Working with Greek texts, Morton rejected Yule's proposal of studying the frequencies of words of given lengths in favour of comparing variation in sentence length and in the position of certain key words within the sentence. In the case of sentence length he was able to demonstrate that by adjusting the Pauline data it could be fitted to a log normal distribution. The result confirmed the 'German' position that 1 and 2 Romans, Corinthians and Galatians formed an inner core, with the remaining epistles being by other hands. Tests of positional distributions within the sentence relied on the fact that, being an inflected language, New Testament Greek is not tied to a rigid order of the parts of a sentence but can vary the sequence of elements in order to suit the expressive need of the moment or the taste of the author: so 'και' (and) might appear as the first word, the second, the third and so on. Here Morton's results not only supported those obtained with sentence lengths but suggested that Romans contained an interpolation by another hand and that 2 Corinthians was a composite of two Pauline letters (pp. 182–3).

English with its rigid, analytical syntax does not offer this liberty of order. Here Morton preferred the immediate context of a given word irrespective of its placing in the sentence. This gave rise to the measuring of collocations, defined as 'the placing of two or more words in immediate succession' (p. 130). These are notated in the form '*and* FB *the*', '*and* FB *a*', '*and* FB *adj.*', '*as* FB *the*' and so on. Proportional pairs of words (e.g. on/upon) were also tested and the various totals processed statistically through the use of Cusum charts, a graphical technique that allows rapid identification of changes in the mean for a series of observations.

Morton's early results were well received and encouraged a widespread acceptance of collocations and proportional pairs as the most suitable data for the investigation of authorship. This was challenged by Smith in several papers which were critical both of the method and of Morton's application of it; however, Smith also noted that when he applied the method to 'two cases for which the evidence of authorship derived through traditional literary approaches was already strong, almost all groups of tests confirmed the scholarly position'.[22] Burrows identified one weakness of Morton's approach in its assumption of the independence of its separate tests, whereas linguistic analysis showed that many of them were mutually dependent. Morton's astronomical probabilities were reached by multiplying the results for separate tests when they should only have been summed.[23]

In Morton's later research he attempted to work with more sophisticated statistical tools on very small samples in cases where larger ones were freely available (a kind of rapture of the deep which few stylometrists are able to resist). A popular presentation of his method in an article in the *TLS* raised eyebrows with its abrupt dismissal of Middleton's authorship of *The Revenger's Tragedy* on the basis of tests on twenty-five successive sentences taken from that work, from *The Atheist's Tragedy* and from *The Changeling* (which was a collaborative work to start with).[24] Morton also became controversially involved in forensic work, particularly the analysis of police 'verbals' – statements supposedly made by prisoners in their own words but sometimes suspected of being fabricated. His account of his experiences with criminals, police and lawyers, as given in *Literary Detection*, pp. 195–207, makes clear that such work presents enormous difficulties to the researcher. It was possible for Morton, in a number of highly publicised cases, to overturn written confessions by engendering astronomical probabilities that certain features of these were not characteristic of other writings by the accused.

In June 1993 Morton was challenged to test his methods publicly on a British television programme. When they failed this particular trial, stylometry itself was felt by many to have failed. The Cusum test was already distrusted by other workers on the grounds specified by Holmes as 'the subjectivity of the interpretation of the charts themselves and that the underlying assumption regarding the consistency of habits within the utterances of one person is false'.[25] This last remark if taken literally would derail the whole project of attributional stylistics: what is meant is that frequencies for capriciously chosen features cannot be relied upon to conform to any of the standard distributions. Morton and Michaelson had made this assumption about the frequency in Jane Austen's sentences of words beginning with vowels, demonstrating that this worked for a short segment. A graph for the entire text of *Mansfield Park* prepared by Hilton and Holmes showed that this was not the case.[26]

Morton's work rested on the twin assumptions of the uniformity of individual habit and that a certain measure of statistical difference (significance at five per cent or less probability of occurring by chance) indicated a difference in authorship. In the early stages of the stylometric enterprise these assumptions had to be taken on faith. Morton added to this a third assumption, which was that this uniformity was most likely to be found in wholly unconscious habits. He went to extraordinary lengths to find aspects of style of which the author could never have been conscious. Holmes argues that some unconscious habits may well conform to a recognised statistical distribution but that others do not. Nancy Laan points out that for a habit to be unconscious is no guarantee of its remaining stable across an entire career:

> Attribution studies claim that the unconscious aspect of an author's style stays the same throughout his or her life: an author unwittingly leaves his or her stylistic fingerprints on each and every one of his or her works . . . Chronological studies, however, claim that the unconscious stylistic features change in the course of an author's life and that they develop rectilinearly. That is, the decrease or increase in these features is gradual and thus provides a criterion for dating an author's works, at least relatively.[27]

Laan's solution is to turn to conscious aspects such as metre. Another classicist, Gerard Ledger, questions the second assumption of the Morton method when he says 'We are not at liberty to deduce that difference of population equals difference of authorship, because there are many instances where this is not so, and the probability levels indicating a separation between two populations, even though they are from the works of one author, can be extremely high'.[28] It is also now generally accepted that stylometric methods alone cannot tell us conclusively whether a group of anonymous works in an otherwise unrepresented style are by the same or different authors.[29]

Morton's choice of method rests on a particular view of the linguistic unconscious which is now being questioned. A possible defence of his preference for measuring hidden, apparently arbitrary features of style is that they arise from the interactions of simpler, concealed structures. A version of this position is put by Ledger. Having chosen to represent the text of the New Testament by nineteen ALETS (the percentage of words containing a specified letter of the alphabet), nine BLETS (the percentage of words containing a specified ultimate letter) and the type/token ratio as a standard measure of vocabulary richness, he justifies the choice thus:

> This gives a total of twenty-nine variables, measurements which are taken on each of the 126 samples of the NT divided into 1000 word sections. . . . Since each of these orthographic variables probably records variation caused by a number of diverse factors, many of them expressive of an author's style, they give immediate access to a cumulative result derived from these underlying stylistic features.[30]

This kind of reasoning is almost second nature to statisticians; yet to apply it to verbal texts requires a leap of faith when the basis both of the assumed regularities and the governing concept 'style' remains totally unexamined. Smith in 1985 questioned the assumption that 'every author exhibits his own multinomial distribution of the features compared and that the figures compiled for each test are random samples from such distributions'.[31] This topic will be revisited in Chapter twelve.

Morton's adoption of the Cusum test was simply one of a number of experiments of the time conducted on what was virtually a trial-and-error basis aimed at determining which statistical technique and which kind of data were most productive for attributional stylistics. His methods and the Cusum still have their defenders[32] but recent work has largely passed them by. This is not because they did not have utility but because they rested on assumptions about representativeness and individuality which were never properly examined. Morton himself concedes that 'the subject under investigation is the storage mechanism of the human brain' but presents no theorised view of the nature and functions of that enigmatic entity.[33] The huge advances made in recent years in the neurological, psychological, philosophical and linguistic fields of cognitive studies have made this omission more serious than probably appeared at the time.

GRAPHICAL AND 'BLACK BOX' METHODS

The late 1980s and 1990s were a period of intense experiment with new techniques and different classes of data, the general tendency being to replace detailed statistical analysis of the frequencies of particular features with graphical representations derived from a richer sampling of textual evidence. Not all of this has proved to be of permanent value but there have been some remarkable successes. One very influential method, pioneered by John Burrows, has been built on the application of principal component analysis, a form of multivariate analysis, to frequency lists of function words. PCA is a technique which, in Holmes's words, 'aims to transform the observed variables to a new set of variables which are uncorrelated and arranged in decreasing order of importance'[34] – in other words, those elements are isolated which are most productive of variation. 'By arraying the words,' Burrows explains, 'relative to each other, in a sequence (or "vector") of comparative resemblance, the process of eigen analysis enables the words to be entered in the graph as neighbours or non-neighbours.'[35] The first vector is the eigenvector corresponding to the largest eigenvalue. How many vectors are treated will depend on their relative strength. Sometimes this declines abruptly, but in other cases the third vector may be only marginally weaker than the second and may offer a more indicative outcome. Since the early vectors will not account for all the information in the data some sacrifice of information is inevitable. Results are most commonly presented as scatter plots of Vector A (PC1) against Vector B (PC2). In the following case the plot represents a test run on a group of late seventeenth-century poets, including the Earl of Rochester, and two Rochester dubia (Figure 1). This is then converted into a scatter plot of authors (Figure 2), in which each author, apart from Rochester (HHL-E and HHL-O), is represented by a single point. In less populous tests it is usual to represent each text or author by a number of samples of a given length which show as separate points on the plot. Material of like origin should cluster together allowing a judgement to be made of the affiliations of further points representing samples from the unattributed text.

PCA is now regarded as more reliable for work of this kind than Morton's tests and other methods based on cumulating the scores from individual variables. A particular advantage of Burrows's method is the greater fullness with which it represents textual data. Where earlier statistical analyses had attempted to locate specific stylistic markers which would act like fingerprints, Burrows builds on a list of the fifty or more highest frequency word types, which usually account for half or more of the total number of tokens in the sample. In subsequent processing these may be refined down to those which show most power to create the desired discriminations. With a body of writers such as those tested in the two plots given, the technique is to establish a second smaller list for each author consisting of those words for which they exhibit unusually high or unusually low frequencies. Burrows does not exclude content words or words that have a necessary connection with each other (e.g. 'neither' and 'nor'), accepting that anomalies in the plots may need stylistic moderation. Characteristically his demonstrations move between the scatter plots for the individual words tested and those for the authorial segments, with each being used to make sense of the other and, where justified, to interpret its meaning. A good demonstration of the method at work is given in his 1992 article 'Not unless you ask nicely: the interpretative nexus between analysis and information', in which he demonstrates the effects of a number of versions of his techniques applied to samples from novels by Henry James and Jane Austen.[36]

More recently stylometrists have explored the possibilities of neural networking, an artificial intelligence technique which teaches a system to discriminate between pairs of writers before letting it loose on dubious works.[37] In the most elementary form of network, a number of input units in the form of quantitative measurements of features of style are linked to two output units which assign the text to one or the other author.

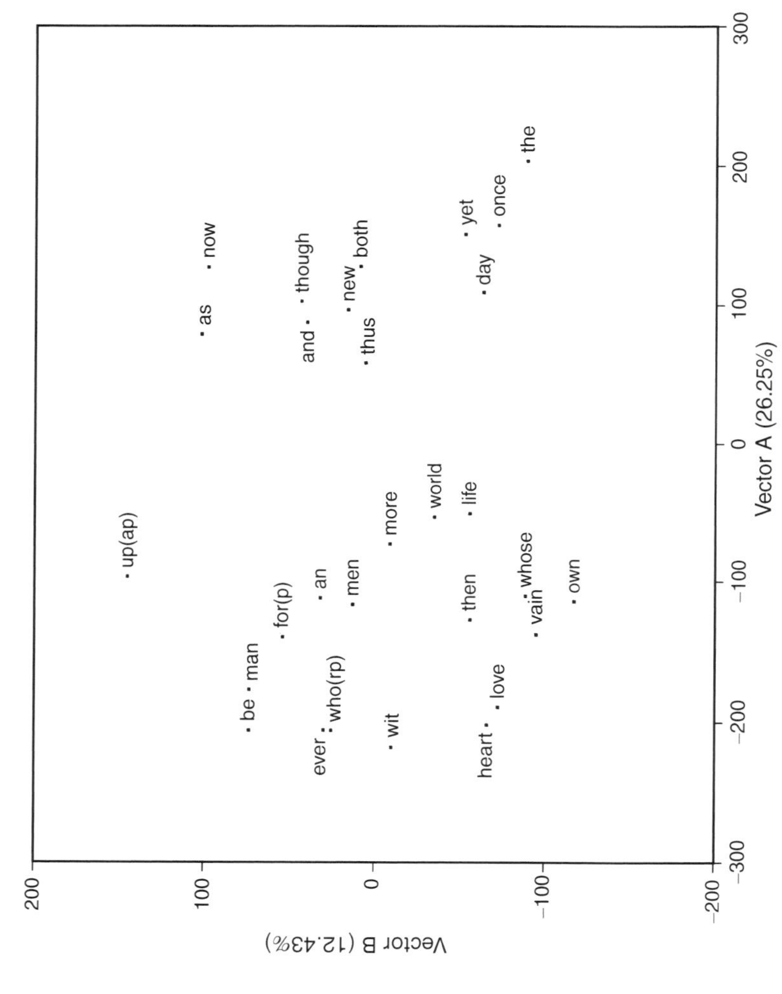

Figure 1 Twenty poets and two test cases (word plot for the 29 most common uninflected 'Rochester markers')

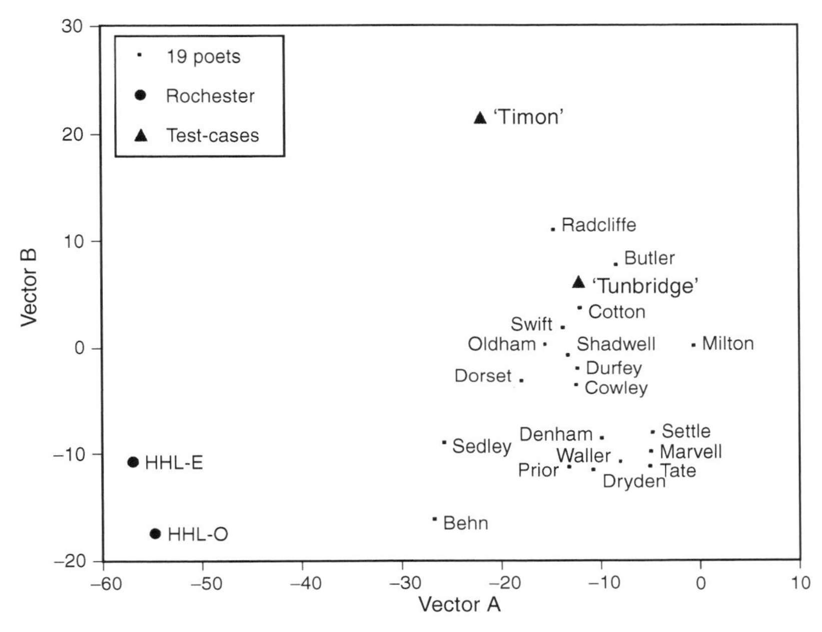

Figure 2 Twenty poets and two test cases (text plot based on the 29 most common uninflected 'Rochester markers')

In between lie one or more 'hidden' layers consisting of a number of nodes, each of which is independently connected to each node in the layer immediately preceding and succeeding it, whether that is the input layer, the output layer, or another hidden layer. At the commencement of training a provisional 'weight' is assigned to each of these connections. The network is then put to work on data from works of known authorship, and by a process of trial and error (technically back-propagation)[38] learns to modify the values of the weights until they are able to produce the correct identifications. More than one complex of internal settings will often be capable of achieving the desired result. Having been trained on samples of known authorship, the network is then applied to a testing set, also of known authorship. If the results are still satisfactory, the network can then be applied to texts which might be by one or the other author.

Results obtained from using networks have varied in their persuasiveness. Bradley Kjell, after a not entirely happy experience with the *Federalist* papers, suggested that their chief use might be for rough screening of large bodies of data; however, Holmes considers that Kjell's network was inadequate for the high number of input variables it was asked to handle, citing his own and Tweedie's results on the same data from a more parsimonious and differently configured network.[39] Merriam and Matthews reporting on their use of a neural network to distinguish between Shakespeare and Marlowe warn that a network may become so expert at producing the desired result for the training set that it is incapable of generalising to the testing set. For this reason they accepted an error rate at the training stage of ten per cent. At the testing stage the network distinguished credibly between the two dramatists, with the striking exception of Marlowe's *The Jew of Malta* which produced the highest of all readings on the Shakespeare scale and the lowest on the Marlowe scale. Seeing that the network was trained to distinguish between these two dramatists only, this does not count as an attribution to Shakespeare but simply as an indication that, according to the tests selected and the decisions of that particular network, the play is strongly uncharacteristic of Marlowe. (In Merriam's simpler letter-frequency test the play sits securely in the Marlowe group.[40]) Tests by Hoorn with networks trained to distinguish between the works of three Dutch poets presented as overlapping three-letter 'trigrams' scored better results than were obtained from the same material by Naive Bayesian classification (as used by Mosteller and Wallace) and Nearest Neighbour classification but still only achieved eighty to ninety per cent correctness in distinguishing between two poets and seventy per cent with three.[41] It would be a pretty inept reader of English poetry who could not achieve a one hundred per cent score in assigning unseen passages from, say, Browning, Tennyson and Swinburne to their correct authors.

Neural networking, and its more recent derivatives, appeal to Ledger's ideal of obtaining 'a cumulative result derived from . . . underlying stylistic features'[42] but do so by intensive processing of a small number of characteristic frequencies. Kjell's error, so interpreted, arose from his desire to represent the work too richly to his network. Yet, in reducing the number of input variables, one runs the risk of inadequately representing the work. The testing phase is all important. Merriam and Matthews in their Marlowe-Shakespeare study short-circuit the testing phase when they allow the failure of their network to deliver the expected result for *The Jew of Malta* to count as an argument against its Marlovian authorship instead of evidence of imperfect training. It should also be noted that neural networking offers none of the ways of assessing reliability offered by statistical methods: when it works it is simply because it works; nor are more than a few problems in attribution capable of being reduced to a straight competition between two unambiguous contenders. In skilled hands working with adequate data, and with support from other tests, neural networking offers discriminations of a kind which we could hope to obtain from no other source. In unskilled hands it is more like taking the suspect down to the basement of the police station and beating him until he incriminates both himself and everyone else on his interrogators' wish-list. We should also note that its apparent freedom from philosophical allegiances is illusory, and that, if it was genuine, this would be a weakness rather than a strength.

A full survey of the range of new statistical and AI techniques experimented with over the last decade lies beyond this study but may be followed instructively in the pages of the two principal journals and their associated websites.

THE CASE OF 'A FUNERAL ELEGY'

Computer-enhanced stylistics returned to the public arena in 1996 with Donald W. Foster's conclusive identification of Joe Klein as the author of *Primary Colors*, a novel satirising the Clinton administration.[43] Prior to this, in 1989, Foster had set off one of the most hotly contested debates in the field with his claim that a 578-line poem called 'A funeral elegy in memory of the late virtuous William Peter', published in 1612 as the work of 'W. S.', was by Shakespeare. As published in book form as *Elegy by W. S.: A Study in Attribution* (1989), Foster's arguments rested on an exemplary consideration of evidence *pro* and *con* and claimed no more than a likelihood, with at least one other candidate still in consideration; however, late in 1995, with the encouragement of Richard Abrams, Foster advanced the case for Shakespeare with much greater confidence, leading to a period of intense debate in *Shakespeare Studies*, the *TLS* and the SHAKSPER online discussion group. This soon assumed a transatlantic character, with British critics almost unanimously rejecting Shakespeare's authorship and American ones predominantly supporting it. Foster's scholarly discoveries projected him, like Morton, into a forensic career, of which he gives a lively personal account in *Author Unknown*.

Eschewing stylometrics, Foster's work relies on versatility in deploying external, internal and stylistic methods. His most characteristic technique is a trawling of the vast electronic databases now available in search of phrasal parallels and rare vocabulary. In the case of *Primary*

Colors this led him to the correct author with relatively little fuss; but considered as a method for establishing attributions for older texts it runs all the dangers that Greg and Schoenbaum identified with the 'parallelographic school' of the early twentieth century. Chief among these is knowing when a similarity in expression actually constitutes a parallel close enough to be enrolled as evidence for derivation or common authorship. The cumulative totals extracted from Foster's rare-word testing of the 'Funeral elegy' are certainly impressive but arguments based on them have an inescapable circularity. By the laws of chance alone there should also be a list of rare words which are exclusive or near-exclusive to the published works of, say, Abraham Lincoln and Queen Victoria, but no one would argue for a moment that this proved that one was ghosting for the other. It has been the author's personal experience that LION searches for characteristic words and phrases from anonymous satires from the 1660s and early 1670s almost inevitably generate numerous concordances with the works of Ned Ward (1667–1731), presumably because, like Shakespeare, he wrote a good deal and had an exceptionally rich vocabulary. (Ward's first published works did not appear until the 1690s.) Whether Foster's examples are found persuasive or otherwise is dependent on what is ultimately an intuitive assessment by the reader. Foster also regularly breaks Schoenbaum's addition to Byrne's rules forbidding the use of attributions as evidence for other attributions.[44]

That the 'Funeral elegy' is now generally included as a dubium in complete editions of Shakespeare is largely a consequence of the unwillingness of Foster's critics to put the same kind of effort into their demonstrations that he put into his and the absence of a convincing alternative author, though there has been no shortage of suggestions.[45] Whatever one's own view of his case (and I personally am unconvinced) there is no doubt that Foster still dominates the ring like a TV tag-team wrestler calling on all comers to step up for a serious slog over the matter. Until now his critics have been content merely to heckle from the bleachers, and the few who have accepted his invitation to combat have retreated rather the worse for wear. The main stumbling block to acceptance is the crude quality of the actual writing: the poet of the elegy seems often to have only the cloudiest idea of what he wants to say and several times lapses into turgid near-nonsense. Even Foster and Abrams are disinclined to make much claim for the poem as a work of art. There is general agreement that even if it is Shakespeare it is pretty poor Shakespeare. That American critics tend to a higher opinion of its merits may be owing to their having a different way of hearing its music: much Elizabethan poetry sounds better with an American accent simply because it is closer to that of Elizabethan times than modern RSC English. Most importantly, to date there has been no rigorous statistical testing of the language of the poem by one of the acknowledged leaders in the field.

Foster's work can be seen as a new phase in the evolution of attributional stylometry whose theorist, as far as it has one, is Ian Lancashire. Both from their different perspectives attempt to anchor individual authorship in Morton's 'storage mechanism of the human brain', or rather the words that are stored by that mechanism. Instead of using the mathematics of probability to compare frequencies of stylistic usage, the new attributionists look on the widest of available scales for characteristic words and word clusters, which are assumed either to be conscious recollections of earlier texts (including those of the same author) or subconscious examples of authorial idiolect. Foster generally works on the first assumption, and has made fascinating suggestions about the way in which texts memorised by Shakespeare the actor may have influenced his current working vocabulary as a dramatist.[46] Lancashire is more concerned with the underlying idiolect, as something independent of previously memorised texts, while conceding that its study is still 'a science in waiting'.[47] His ideal would be to identify 'clusters of traits that cannot be imitated by any other writer' (p. 173). Lancashire distinguishes this method from that of Mosteller and Wallace on the ground that the problem of the *Federalist* papers, with only two possible candidates, 'does not rely on a firm theory of authorship fingerprinting' (p. 173); however, he would also have to reject the assumption made by Foster and Abrams that the parallels to, say, *Richard II* in 'A funeral elegy' arise from conscious recollection, because it would be irrelevant to the search for any such 'fingerprint'.

Lancashire's approach has its starting point in the commonsense position that 'a person's speaking or writing is routinely exercised semiblindly' (p. 177), i.e. that it is only through the process of writing that we become aware of the meanings that we wish to encode. Writing so performed does not draw on recollections of earlier texts but is a fresh activation of conceptual pathways established by association.

> Most researchers regard our long-term memory store as an associative network. It constrains us to remember, not by direct look-up (e.g., 'go to the concept starting with the letters *ex*') or according to any logical or scientific schema ('go to *Richard II*, 3.1.10'), but by casting out a line for any things directly or indirectly

associated with the object of our search. The organization of memories thus reflects the person's own past experience and thought rather than a shared resource of cultural knowledge. While people may remember the same things, they seldom store them in similar associational matrices. The associational matrix seems to me to require that a person's speech or writing will exhibit a unique idiolect. (p. 178)

As a general principle, this was already familiar in the eighteenth century to the author of *Tristram Shandy* who got it from Locke. Edward Armstrong assumed it in advancing the notion of 'image clusters' as a possible determinant of Shakespearean authorship. Likewise, R. W. Chambers used it in drawing a connection between an associatively linked sequence of images in *Sir Thomas More* and similar sequences in other Shakespearean plays.[48] But to apply it to Shakespeare in the way suggested by Lancashire requires us to assume that he was a highly spontaneous writer, like Jack Kerouac in writing *On the Road*, who never revised and did his best to block out memories of other texts.

Both assumptions are dubious. To start with, an early modern writer would be quite likely to draft material in what was called a table-book, composed of erasable wax tablets. Hamlet uses one, so why not Shakespeare? Beyond that, the early modern memory was, unlike ours, a trained one, and that of a professional actor would need to be exceptionally so. There are well documented stories of Mozart, Dr Johnson, Keats and others which reveal a capacity for the mental composition of lengthy texts prior to their inscription, which therefore was not a process of discovering meanings but a fair copy of words already composed and memorised. Flora Annie Steel, we are informed by a late-Victorian contemporary, 'spends a great deal of time in thinking out a new subject, and does not write until it is as clear before her mental vision as the printed page; then it is transferred to paper with scarcely an erasure'.[49] We cannot assume to suit a particular theory that Shakespeare did not possess the same capacity. Such a trained memory would also be well stocked with texts and topoi: it was the central aim of Renaissance humanist education to supply these. The process of conceptual association described by Lancashire would still operate in any act of composition but alongside and indistinguishable from the consultation of memorised texts and processes of revision and reworking conducted prior to inscription. In this respect Foster probably has a better grip of the functioning of the mechanism.

Foster and Lancashire could no doubt discover common ground on this issue. What is more of a challenge is how the interrogation of what Foster would call the working vocabulary and Lancashire the associational matrix might generate a reliable means for determining attributions. Findings with a firm basis in the mathematics of probability can at least offer that part of their reasoning for examination: if it is formally correct, objections have to be mounted on the basis of the choice of data or distribution or the assumptions made about the relationship of differences in recorded frequencies to differences in authorship. Artificial intelligence methods surrender this form of verifiability but can point to the performance of trained circuits on samples of known authorship to validate their findings. These circuits, in turn, are specifically trained for that particular textual task: it is not the same as to say that because Foster was right about *Primary Colors* he is always going to be right. What I will call as a convenient shorthand the 'memory mechanism' approach, with all its promise, offers no *formal* method of verification, but relies on the inherent plausibility or implausibility of the patterns presented. And yet a search for close, exclusive parallels with the word-rich Shakespearean corpus would yield positive results with any writer of the time whose work was preserved in reasonable quantity. Apart from the obvious regional and educational influences, these parallels might either be derived from a common source (which need not survive or even be a written one), be the outcome of common experience (sitting by the fire on long winter evenings), or be purely fortuitous (two different minds independently finding the same words for the same idea). What is singularly lacking to date is any way of calculating the level of significance that applies to such findings. This problem will have to be solved before lasting and fruitful alliances can be forged between stylometry and the scientific study of memory.

HAVE THE NEW STUDIES REACHED MATURITY?

Today attributional stylometry is an exciting, statistics- and AI-based discipline on the fringe of applied linguistics, which is delivering important results to literary scholars and historians. After four decades of energetic experimentation one would expect it to enjoy general acceptance. This has not quite happened. Despite expectations to the contrary, the field is as littered with affirmations and rebuttals as the work of scholars using older methods: many responsible practitioners are themselves agreed on this point. The state of affairs at the end of the twentieth century was summed up in the 1998 articles by David Holmes and Joseph Rudman already mentioned and in a more recent article by Rudman.[50] While Holmes's chief concern was with statistical techniques, Rudman set out in his first article to review every aspect of 'non-traditional' attribution studies; and while Holmes was generally optimistic about the soundness of at least some methods currently available, Rudman took a far more sceptical view:

> Non-traditional authorship attribution studies – those employing the computer, statistics, and stylistics – have had enough time to pass through any 'shake-down' phase and enter one marked by solid, scientific, and steadily progressing studies. But, after over 30 years and 300 publications, they have not. . . . There is more wrong with authorship attribution studies than there is right. (p. 351)

In his second article he presents the issue even more forcefully:

> Do the more than 700 published non-traditional studies constitute a Rosetta Stone allowing us to name virtually every anonymous author, as Andrew Morton and many others would have us believe? Or, are these studies an ignis fatuus with just enough legitimate, successful techniques and results to lure unsuspecting practitioners into a quagmire full of half truths and flawed techniques? Do these studies show non-traditional authorship attribution to be simply 'aspiration' and not a science, as Furbank and Owens claim? (p. 163)

This is followed by a list of weaknesses he finds in some (thankfully not all!) of the accumulated work. It is a daunting list including 'No agreement on experimental setup and techniques', 'No agreement on style-markers', 'Studies governed by expediency', 'A lack of competent and complete research' (found in 'the majority of published non-traditional attribution studies'), 'Poor statistical techniques' (there have been over a hundred different statistical tests used), 'Sloppy primary data' and 'Lack of expertise in allied fields'.[51] His broader charge is the failure of the field to have shape *as a field*. Rudman would not deny that much excellent work is being done, and concludes his article on an optimistic note by foreshadowing a coming phase of enhanced co-operation, self-regulation and a vast expansion of data. But it can hardly be denied that many of his anxieties are shared. At the risk of sounding like a Luddite (which I hope I am not) I would like to examine them more closely before offering a qualified endorsement of his optimism for the future.

There are several reasons for the problems Rudman identifies. One is that they are not unique to 'non-traditional' attribution studies but might be directed at the field as a whole. Writing in 1966, before the large-scale advent of stylometric methods, Schoenbaum found the history of attribution study in the Elizabethan field 'on the whole unexhilarating', adding that 'Triumphs have been few and scattered, failures numerous and sometimes of appalling magnitude; one can take small comfort from the interludes of unpremeditated comic relief.'[52]

A second reason is that stylometry does not want to stand still in the way Rudman recommends – at least not yet. There is a perpetual search for more refined methods capable of extracting fuller results from small samples or asking more searching questions of larger samples. The request for a stable body of method denies the fact that the parent disciplines, AI and statistics, remain highly innovative. Statisticians are always pushing against the limits of their techniques, and as new ones become available stylometrists are keen to experiment with them. Stylometrists are also fond of testing the limits of their own established routines, often in adventurous ways. There can be no holding back this process. A third reason is that the problems to which the techniques are directed are often of a particularly challenging and intractable kind. Attributional stylometrists in this respect are a little like Napoleon's generals marching without orders towards the sound of the cannons. Easy solutions to easy problems hold little interest. A fourth reason is that work on attribution, whatever the technique employed, often attracts a particular kind of larger-than-life personality, typified by Richard Bentley in the eighteenth century. (His present-day successors will remain nameless.) Attribution studies often employs metaphors of detective work, treasure hunting or oil drilling – the treasure being not only the new work by a great author but the possibility of attention through the media. There can be a brash dogmatism in the proclaiming of results which seems meant to invite disagreement and more than once has given rise to gladiatorial combats in the pages of *Computers and the Humanities* and elsewhere. (For a recent example see Foster versus Elliott and Valenza over the Claremont Shakespeare project;[53] for an older one F. G. Fleay's aggressive use of the terms 'certain', 'conclusive', 'infallible', 'absolutely', and 'unquestionably' as noted by Schoenbaum.[54] The appearance of any of these words today should ring warning bells.) Finally, communication between exponents of traditional and non-traditional scholarship working on the same project may be less than perfect, especially when, as Rudman notes, many scholars come to attribution studies in order to solve a particular problem and leave it once that is done without ever having reflected on broader principles.[55]

SOME HUMANISTS' MISGIVINGS

Rudman's papers represent a frank acknowledgement of the problems by a scholar who is firmly committed to the project and has a profound understanding of it. As such they can only do good, and it will be helpful, in the same spirit, to review and extend them. Granted that some interjections from humanists have been monumentally silly, others acknowledge perfectly genuine difficulties. One concerns methodology. Good research requires that the data subjected to analysis should have been assembled with the highest scholarly care. Conscientious humanists approve when Farringdon removes all quotations from other authors from the samples used for his Fielding tests; but they note that some other stylometrists regularly cut corners by using suspect texts and failing to conduct essential documentary research of the kind discussed in Chapter nine. Scientists dabbling in stylometry have been known to take short cuts and make approximations which if applied in laboratory disciplines would invalidate their results. There is an air of taking a holiday from real work about some of these interventions. In other cases one is led to wonder how well the 'real' work itself is done: are stylometric results being delivered by admirers of the Cyril Burt school of twin research? Humanists appreciate that statistical methods are specifically designed to deal with sampling errors and skew but they wonder also about the wisdom of assuming in advance that this will solve the problem of poor-quality data in those cases when better could be provided with a little labour. They also note that, at the end of the day, significant discriminations may rest on a handful of instances. Even the innumerate have heard of the 'butterfly effect', by which a tiny alteration in the initial conditions from which a system is generated leads to enormous differences in the outcome, and are entitled to wonder how or whether this applies to the results of stylometry. Observing in the weaker examples what, from their perspective, is spectacular carelessness they are led to speculate about the validity of other parts of the investigation which they are not capable of cross-checking. That results from such studies should (as sometimes happens) be offered with a dogmatic assumption of correctness is almost to guarantee suspicion. The other extreme of presenting results in a spirit of 'We just want to throw our stuff out there, and let other people see if our tests are any good' is no more reassuring.[56]

These objections do not apply to those many investigations which even humanists can see are well designed and conscientiously conducted; but even here a broader distrust may apply that concerns the value of statistical methods in themselves. In considering statistics as a method of interrogating day-to-day reality we are regularly faced with its failure. The stock exchange does not behave as predicted. A hedge fund headed by Nobel Prize winners for economic modelling goes spectacularly broke.

Election results defy the professionalism of highly paid pollsters. In 2000 it was discovered that, owing to poor statistical method, all estimates of age at death made by archaeologists from the study of skeletons were invalid. Using this method it had been calculated that a Mayan prince had died at forty. When the inscription on his tomb was finally deciphered, it transpired that he had lived to be eighty.[57] There is another problem: do the impressive tables of numbers actually describe anything significant to start with? Stylometrists themselves sometimes assure us otherwise. Consider Morton:

> It may seem difficult to create a set of figures which contain no information but it is much easier to do so than most people suspect. There are papers full of figures which describe nothing more substantial than the legendary and invisible snark. Like the assets of bogus companies, figures are used to conceal a vacuum; they literally describe nothing at all.[58]

Rudman presumably has such papers in mind. Michael Farringdon puts the matter more subtly, but the objection is the same:

> If the data collected by computer can be relied upon as accurate, and the statistics are precise, the question then to be asked is whether the data thus cited constitute evidence of any kind. If the answer is affirmative, such evidence does not, of course, become conclusive and exhaustive; other related questions will remain, since admissible evidence does not necessarily resolve a problem for all time and for all people.[59]

Humanists have also observed that stylometrists frequently contradict each other, even when using the same, or related, methods on the same data. Eric Sams equates stylometry with phrenology, adding 'nobody has ever proved that minds can be measured by bumps, or style by numbers'.[60] He makes effective play with stylometrists' own disagreements (including Smith's with himself):

> The Morton-Merriam method identified *Edmund Ironside* as the work of Robert Greene, not Shakespeare, at odds announced as 890 million million milllion to 1. This calculation much impressed many readers, including at least one stylometrist [D. Foster]. But even Dr Smith has denounced such investigators as 'mesmerised by their arithmetic at the expense of their critical faculties'. . . . Not only do Morton and Smith contradict each other; they are both contradicted by other stylometrists such as Brainerd and Slater, each of whom inferred from his own separate statistical system that *Ironside* was in fact Shakespeare-compatible. (pp. 471–2)

Furbank and Owens describe the periodical literature on the subject as 'a scene of carnage'.[61] They also point to the obverse of the problem of rival methodologies, which is that they offer means for validating virtually any preconception:

say that you were to apply yourself to finding a feature of *David Copperfield* and of *Oliver Twist* which would suggest, to someone ignorant of literary history, that these novels were by two different authors, would you not fairly soon find one? (p. 243)

Responsible stylometrists and computational stylisticians, who would never base an argument of this kind on a single feature, can be excused a degree of exasperation at the tone of such criticisms but are not absolved from the need to reply to them. Moreover, such objections are not always raised in an anti-scientistic spirit, or without an understanding of the aims and methods of stylometry, but may simply reflect an expectation that the relentless sceptical questioning of results characteristic of good research in the humanities should be shared by stylometrists and disappointment when this does not happen. Humanists must also be allowed their commitment to the longer view, since they will have to live and work with the results handed across the fence. These results will become foundational – perhaps at several removes – for other theories and conclusions. They need to be careful they are not taking a papier-mâché rock for their foundation stone.

The challenge for stylometrists is not to reject disagreements that are in some cases misguided and in others perfectly understandable but rather to consider under what conditions Sams's objections might be overcome. One way of satisfying humanists would be for stylometrists to show more of Burrows's concern with the linguistic causes of quantitative distinctions. But this, as we will shortly see, is exactly what is not being done in most published research. Another would be to look more closely at the disciplinary relationship of stylometry to the humanities, to the social sciences, and to science, a matter that has not received much attention.

IS STYLOMETRY A SCIENCE?

'Stylometry', writes Morton, 'is a science and a powerful one.'[62] McMenamin defines it as 'the scientific comparison of written or spoken utterance habits in questioned and authentic samples'.[63] Since the work of many of the scholars mentioned was influenced by this aspiration, we need to consider its validity. For a start, it is not correct to say that prior to the developments of the 1960s stylistics had been an 'art' or a mode of 'subjective impressionism', since even as practised by a Bentley it drew on huge erudition and was required to argue its positions with diligence and rigour (and would be criticised when it failed to do this, as was sometimes Bentley's case). We might describe it as a department of reasoned evidential scholarship. The difference, which will be further discussed in Chapter twelve, is essentially one between rhetorical methods and mathematical methods of arriving at a proof, each of these having its own validity under appropriate circumstances.

Uncertainty about whether stylometry is a science or not is further compounded by differences over what constitutes a science. It is necessary to ask just how this change in status might be recognised if it ever took place. One view is that stylistics becomes scientific when it argues by means of numbers; but this is to take a very restricted view of science which leaves out experimental method, means of confirming hypotheses, repeatability of results, the capacity to induce universal laws from particular data and, most importantly, the power to generate explanations.

This aspiration to scientific status on the part of practitioners of attributional stylometry has not found universal acceptance. Eric Sams cites the view of 'a very distinguished mathematician [J. Littlewood, writing in 1953] that probability inferences about any field of human endeavour are bound to be flawed and misleading'.[64] Furbank and Owens argue that 'While . . . there is so little basic agreement about methods and aims, let alone the underlying rationale of the whole business, stylometry cannot be classed as a "science".'[65] Laan has already been cited in a similar demurral.

There are other reasons why we should not regard stylometry as a science or even as a science in embryo as chemistry was in the seventeenth century. The first is that it has no general body of theory to which its results can be referred. If this existed it would presumably be in the discipline of linguistics; but linguistic theory is spectacularly absent from reports of results in attributional stylometry. In science particular results gain their meaning by being placed in relation to general hypotheses which they either confirm or contradict, in the latter case leading to modification or replacement. Characteristically these hypotheses are arranged in a hierarchy of increasing generality. Nothing of this kind takes place in attributional stylometry. It is not even clear what form such a theoretical superstrate might take: perhaps a kind of universal grammar. It is possible to imagine other forms of stylometry that were sub-disciplines of experimental psychology or neurobiology and drew their explanatory paradigms from those disciplines, but only Lancashire among present-day attributionists seems to be building bridges in this direction. Morton concedes, in words already cited, that 'the subject under investigation is the storage mechanism of the human brain' but makes no use of the technical literature on that subject.[66] Lancashire is more specific:

> Word, phrase, and collocation frequencies . . . can be signatures of authorship because of the way the writer's brain stores and creates speech. Even the author cannot imitate these features, simply because they are normally beyond recognition, unless the author has the same tools and expertise as stylometrists undertaking attribution research. Reliable markers arise from the unique, hidden clusters within the author's long-term associative memory. Frequency-based attribution methodology recognizes these and depends on a biological, not a conceptual, paradigm of authorship.[67]

To Lancashire's credit he has proposals about how the work of cognitive linguists could help refine the goals of attributional studies; but what he is claiming as the founding assumption of stylometry is not elsewhere an *examined* assumption but something that stylometrists (rather hopefully) take as an article of faith, and in which on occasions they are clearly deceived. The majority of stylometrists are oil drillers not geologists: most of the time they behave like oil drillers who have no interest in geology. This is particularly so when they make use of 'black box' techniques, such as neural networking, which are justified solely by their ability to provide results. A fairer analogy might be with the medical discipline of epidemiology, in which statistical relationships are sought between the incidence of disease and geographical, environmental and economic factors. The controversy over the status of epidemiological arguments, such as their linking smoking and lung cancer, has a structural similarity to those over statistical arguments for authorship. The difference is that a relationship proposed by an epidemiologist can be tested across a range of scientific disciplines concerned with the human body, which remains the primary object of medical study. Stylometry in its present form has no such higher-level discipline to appeal to.

This brings us to the second and more serious reason for not considering stylometry as a science, which is that, while often highly persuasive in its primary task of identifying authors, it possesses little explanatory power. What it presents are the effects of the workings of language; what is needed is an understanding of those workings. One criticism that might well be made is that, in its groping for modes of testing and categories of data which will provide a *passe-partout* to the identification of individual language behaviour, attributional stylometry has a lot more in common with magic than with science. The shaman or witch tries this ritual and that one until he/she is successful in bringing rain or restoring health, and then sticks with it, but could never explain to you why the successful ritual is more pleasing to the gods than the others are. The magic of stylometrists has the advantage that when properly done it has a much higher likelihood of working than the magic of the shaman, but many of its practitioners often seem no better informed than the magicians why this should be so.

An example! 'The result', Thomas Merriam reports, 'of counting the letters in the 43 plays was the implausible discovery that the letter "o" differentiates Marlowe and Shakespeare plays to an extent well in excess of chance. If the cut-off ratio of 0.078 is adopted, then six of the Marlowe plays are grouped together at less than 0.078, 36 of the Shakespeare plays are classified correctly at greater than 0.078, and one Marlowe play, *Edward II*, is very marginally out of place by reason of its being greater than 0.078. The likelihood of 42 out of 43 correct chance classifications is infinitesimal.'[68] Further discriminations of the same kind were made with 'a', 'n', 'r' and 'y'. A graph with frequencies per play for 'a' as the vertical axis and those for 'o' as the horizontal one shows the Marlowe block to the left and the Shakespeare results to the right, creating an image rather like a duck with Marlowe the head and neck and Shakespeare the body. The meeting point of the two (the collar bone?) is at *Edward II* and the *Henry VI* trilogy; however, the presence of the mature plays *The Tempest*, *Macbeth* and *Antony and Cleopatra* towards the left of the Shakespeare group indicates that the effect is not simply one of chronology. This is by any standards a dazzling result achieved with the simplest of means; but it explains nothing and is itself unexplained. Merriam has no interest in the particular reasons why the relative frequencies of the letters 'o' and 'a' should be able to distinguish between Shakespeare and Marlowe or what an investigation of this might contribute to the discipline of linguistics:

> Differences in letter frequencies in modern spelling either reflect personal differences in the use of common words such as 'no' and 'not', or reveal deeper registers of phonetic expression. These could be rather more regional than personal, as, say, between Kent and Warwickshire, than between Marlowe and Shakespeare as individuals.[69]

Possibly so, but also possibly not so: the matter cannot be finalised until we know why as well as what. Moreover, if we did know why, it might be possible to home in on the real basis of discrimination rather than counting letters of the alphabet. This, I take it, is precisely what a scientist would want to do. Merriam's lack of curiosity suggests that his real interest is in finding better kinds of magic.

For that very reason some workers in the field, including Burrows, make a distinction between stylometry and computational stylistics. The computational stylist will be much more concerned to discover the structures responsible for the numerical pattern and as a result is better placed to assess the significance of those patterns and to correct in cases where they have been skewed by the influence of a particular rhetorical context. Craig's 1999 paper, already cited, with the provocative title 'Authorial attribution and computational stylistics: if you can tell authors apart, have you learned anything about them?' asks the question 'How much confidence can one have in an ascription, if the linguistic mechanism behind the results remains a mystery?'[70] In an endeavour to answer it, he uses frequencies established in a stylometric study of three Middleton dubia to ask what makes Middleton distinctive as a stylist.

> A substantial passage of Middleton, so the present argument goes, will accumulate meanings of a stylistic kind in the notable abundances and scarcities summarized in the table. The reader or hearer will become aware of an open, casual, commodified reference; a dialogue of emphatic cross-reference and insistent deixis; and a thinning out of expected conjunctions, suggesting improvisation and fragmentation. (p. 111)

Middleton's characters live in the present using 'now' a lot; they 'point instead of tell', something evident in the high frequency of 'there'; they have close, in-your-face relationships; they avoid, to quote the dramatist himself, using 'mighty words to lean purposes'. Middleton's exceptionally high frequency for the indefinite article 'a/an' betrays 'a disposition on the part of his characters to make reference general rather than particular' (p. 110). This is illustrated by an example from *A Chaste Maid in Cheapside*: 'The idiosyncratic locution "this will make a poore S[i]r Walter" (v.iii) shows how even a proper name and a human individual can be transformed by the article into a class' (p. 111). Such explorations are to be strongly commended as a form of bridge-building between stylometry and linguistics; but they do not as yet frame and test general hypotheses about the nature of language, or human perception and cognition, or brain function.

What stylometry offers, then, is not a science but a mathematisation of stylistics – a new way of discriminating between forms of language behaviour that is of great potential value but not as yet a way of accounting for them. While it is possible to foresee that results being obtained may become of interest to scientists in several fields, at present they are being produced almost solely for the use of humanists, whose main interests are likely to be interpretive rather than descriptive. But even here, it is only in rare cases such as Craig's article just cited and Burrows's *Computation into Criticism* that this challenge is being met. The real problem with attributional stylometry is not the organisational one highlighted by Rudman but a profound unwillingness on the part of its practitioners to pursue the wider theoretical questions that its results are constantly posing. While it is important to know who wrote what, or what bits of what, it is more important to ask what such determinations and the means by which they are obtained have to tell us about why they were successful in the first place. Strong questions have to be asked about habit, about individuality, about the brain's storage and retrieval mechanisms, about writing and about language. But most of all stylometry needs to question the widespread assumption that it is a science in its own right, or at least an aspirant towards scientific status, and accept the more challenging possibility that it is an academic cyborg, only half of which is computational and the other part interpretive, and that its full potential will only be reached when, like Robocop in the movie, it comes to an understanding of its double nature.

For all these reasons I would argue that attributional stylometry, as it now exists, is not a science in the sense claimed for it by a large party of its practitioners. That does not stop me from being greatly excited by its advances as a body of quantitative techniques for determining authorship and by the results it is beginning to offer. There can be no doubt that it is by far the best game in town at the present moment. Rudman was right to draw attention to the difficulties and inconsistencies in its practice, since they exist, and are not by any means all the product of prejudice and ignorance among its consumers. Rudman goes on in his article to describe a search for a degree of methodological stability and mutual communication among the community of scholars with a permanent interest in the field. Two professional bodies, the Association for Computers and the Humanities (ACH) and the Association for Literary and Linguistic Computing (ALLC), are involved in this process and a programme of meetings has been established.[71] All this is to be welcomed. At the very least it shows an increased sense of responsibility on the part of attributional stylometrists towards their consumers, who, as mentioned, are mostly literary scholars, historians and, with some reservations, the judiciary.

Certainly, what has been collectively achieved so far is impressive. Anyone wishing to conduct serious research in attribution studies cannot do so today without a good general understanding of the nature and basic techniques of statistical reasoning. This includes literary scholars working with a professional statistician, who, while they may not be able themselves to inaugurate methods or perform calculations at an advanced level, must understand what is being claimed in their joint names, and why. The results being offered by stylometry and computational stylistics are much too important to be neglected. In a great many cases they will be by far the best evidence we have in cases of disputed authorship. Humanists should not turn back from the ascent of the peak in Darien because the road is a rocky one and our guides keep arguing with each other about the best path and may not be quite sure what the trip is for in the first place.

CHAPTER NINE

Bibliographical evidence

No one would wish to venture very far into attribution studies without an acquaintance with the specialist disciplines loosely linked under the rubric 'textual criticism and bibliography'. Codicologists, palaeographers and descriptive bibliographers study aspects of the material records used to transmit texts and the ever-changing forms of the signs inscribed on them but without concerning themselves more than necessary with the meaning of those signs. Textual bibliographers study the relationship between physical manufacture and semantic change. Stemmatologists analyse verbal variants between sources in order to determine the direction of transmission. Historians of the book contextualise the work within contemporaneous cultures of authorship, book-manufacture, distribution and reception. Scholarly editors have to be able to do all of these things.

Each of these specialisms has vital information to offer attributionists. Each also has a large professional literature to which entry may be obtained through introductory texts such as Philip Gaskell's *A New Introduction to Bibliography* (1972), David Greetham's *Textual Scholarship: An Introduction* (1992), Peter Davison's collection *The Book Encompassed: Studies in Twentieth-century Bibliography* (1992) and Geoffrey Glaister's *Encyclopedia of the Book*, 2nd edn (1996). For handwriting one might begin with Anthony G. Petti's *English Literary Hands from Chaucer to Dryden*[1] before proceeding to more specialised studies such as Michael Finlay's *Western Writing Implements in the Age of the Quill Pen*[2] and Tom Davis's 'The analysis of handwriting: an introductory survey' which summarises contemporary forensic methods.[3] P. J. Croft's *Autograph Poetry in the English Language*[4] reproduces examples from William Herbert (died *c.*1333) to Dylan Thomas.

A drawback of existing published studies is that their advice peters out as they approach the present day. Ancient papyri, mediaeval codices, incunabula, Elizabethan play printings and Victorian three-deckers have been investigated in enormous detail from a bibliographical perspective; category fiction of the 1980s relatively little. To date there is no comprehensive reference work for manual typewriter imprints nor an electronic archive from which one might extract dated examples of word-processor fonts, though organisations such as the FBI are known to possess data banks of such materials. The physical study and description of cinema, TV and audio records is still in its infancy, while that of e-texts is hampered by the frightening rapidity with which they disappear from their web sites and archives or simply mutate into other forms. Yet variation between the material texts of a popular film (alternative cuts, other-language sound tracks, TV, airline and rental versions) is as marked as any transmissional changes found in written texts. Here attributionists will often need to create their own methods of analysis and description on the model of those developed for manuscripts and printed books.

In this chapter, we will look initially at the value of the 'bibliographical' disciplines for the selection of versions to be used for stylometric or other kinds of testing, then consider ways in which they assist in their own right in establishing attributions.

EVALUATING THE TEXT

One goal for stylometric study, projected by Forsyth and Holmes, is to create 'methods of textual feature finding that do not need background knowledge external to the text being analysed'.[5] Well and good if this can be done, but any such procedure will stand or fall by the quality of the versions which are its raw materials. There would be no point in using a neural network to assess a mediaeval text that had been heavily reconstituted in scribal transmission or a novel which included innumerable verbal changes made at the insistence of an interventionist editor. Nor does it make sense in searching for authorial markers to treat a text which originated as an oral performance on the same footing as one that has passed through the numerous, professionally supervised stages which characterise modern print publication. A printed version of an oral event is always at least two removes from the original and to that extent can never be treated as a transparent witness to authorial style or to content. From the Elizabethan and Caroline periods we have parliamentary speeches circulated in manuscript either from notes taken during delivery or from the recollections of other members after the event.[6] Sometimes there are two or more different versions, each recording what seemed important to the particular hearer. The member who delivered the speech might also put out a version, which would naturally be fuller and more polished but which need not be as reliable a record of what was said in the House. Most of the time we have a single version, compiled from notes or from the memory of someone present, surviving in a number of contemporary manuscript copies circulated for gain or as an extension of the political process. Challenged in 1671 over how much was his own in a speech so transmitted, Lord Lucas stated that 'Part was, and Part was not' – a nice problem for attributionists.[7] What is more to the point is that few of the large retrospective printed anthologies of such materials, including those intended for modern students, indicate that there is any textual problem at all. Leah Marcus describes a similar pattern in the process by which the 'more vivid, vehement, direct and verbally eloquent' wording of the impromptu speeches of Elizabeth I was transformed in subsequent 'official' versions into 'more measured, abstract, often (to us) windy and convoluted, but more formal and politically neutral wording and syntax'. The translator of these texts into 'Tudor bureaucratese' was as likely to be Burghley or some other assistant as the queen herself.[8] Attributionists should not be misled into looking for authorial fingerprints in texts that rest on a reporter's transcript or have been recomposed by a reviser. Where formal and informal versions survive of the same oral performance, the second are likely to be more characteristic of the speaker, but will also be dependent on the accuracy of the reporter. The formal versions, even when revised by the speaker, will have been adjusted to the reigning norms of written discourse.

Similar caution needs to be exercised with texts which, while not oral, have come to us through scribal transmission. In the cases of such provident writers as the fifteenth-century poet Thomas Hoccleve, the seventeenth-century scribal-publishing poet, Thomas Traherne, or, in the nineteenth century, Emily Dickinson, we are fortunate to possess virtually entire *œuvres* in their own manuscript fair copies; but prior to the nineteenth century this is most unusual. The more common situation is that represented by Chaucer and Langland in the fourteenth century and Rochester in the seventeenth of a profusion of scribal copies derived by a multiplicity of routes from lost originals which themselves may have existed in several variant forms.[9] Even the most relied on of these manuscripts, such as Hengwrt for the *Canterbury Tales* and 'Hartwell' for Rochester, come to us through the medium of scribes who made their own changes and adjustments. Hartwell has carefully purged the corpus of indecencies, and in Chaucer's case we have a poem of reproof to his unreliable scribe Adam. We also know that the problem of creating an order for the elements of the *Canterbury Tales* was one that Chaucer himself had not solved at his death and that this gave rise to several experimental orders. In the case of Langland, three quite different versions of *Piers Plowman* (the A, B and C texts) exist in a multitude of sources collectively containing thousands of variant readings. The stupendous modern editions of the three versions, by Donaldson, Kane and Russell, are confessedly dependent on the ceaseless exercise of editorial judgement.[10] It is difficult to see how editions of this kind could be used for attributional research. If they were, it must be with a full acknowledgement of their intensely constructed nature.

There were of course scribes, probably the majority, who mechanically copied out what they saw before them, or thought they saw. These are the kind of whom modern-day editors approve, since all they will have contributed to texts is their honest mistakes. But for much of the history of scribal circulation, the task of the copyist was held to include a textual repair function together with an obligation to adjust the text to the form of the language then current – making them in effect modernising editors of the work rather than just transcribers.[11] The repairs would be performed either by consulting other copies, thus promoting what stemmatologists call conflation, or speculatively, in which case they would often advance variation rather than reducing it. It is also the case that certain transcribers regarded themselves as authorised to revise the work to their own liking, or to prune it of expressions which they regarded as heretical or indecent, or to augment it.

Insight into the problems posed to attributionists by manuscript transmission is given by the case of the *Scriptores Historiae Augustae*, a late-classical collection of biographies of Roman emperors, which is represented in the manuscripts as the work of six different authors responsible for between one and nine lives each. In three papers published between 1889 and 1918 Hermann Dessau argued firstly that the work was a century later than its professed date and secondly that all the biographies had been produced by a single author, a position now generally accepted by historians of the period. In recent years the postulate of common authorship has been subjected to stylometric tests with inconclusive results.[12] The kinds of textual changes likely to affect a work of this kind are shown by a manuscript of the *Historia* written in the ninth century and now in the Vatican library. 'Over a period of some six centuries', P. K. Marshall records, 'this book was worked on by a succession of scholars, making it a splendid example of cumulative editorial acumen.'[13] The markings comprise the corrections of the original scribes, improvements made in a hand from the tenth or eleventh century, and corrections and annotations by five different Italian humanist scholars, including Petrarch and Poggio. The difficulty does not lie in these visible corrections but in the suggestion they leave of a history of similar, perhaps more radical, interventions in the five centuries of manuscript transmission from which we have no surviving witnesses. (Apart from everything else the work is assumed to be extensively interpolated.) Rudman does not exaggerate when he describes the *Historia* as 'a morass' (p. 153).

Like the *Historia*, the majority of our texts of ancient works descend from single copies written centuries after the death of their authors. That these, rather than other copies circulating in early times, survived was usually a matter of chance. *Beowulf*, which we possess in a single, decaying tenth-century manuscript, and for some of whose details we are now reliant on eighteenth-century copies of that manuscript, illustrates this perfectly. To judge from the evidence of place-names, the poem, or at least the legend behind it, must have been very well known. Fossilised linguistic forms show that the version we have, which is in West Saxon dialect, was derived from an Anglian original, perhaps of the eighth century. One of the two scribes of the MS carefully replaced Anglian forms with West Saxon ones; the second was more respectful of the exemplar. We are still a good way from the earliest written version, and even further from the origins, whatever they were, of its oral forerunners. If history had saved us one of the Anglian versions rather than a West Saxon one, we might well have had a significantly different poem. Scholars do their best to peer backwards from the existing text towards its forerunners, but in doing so are inevitably speculating. Questions of authorship in such a situation have to give place to more manageable questions concerning the cultural genetics and historical and inscriptional context of the version.

The transition to print replaced the radiating copies of manuscript culture with a preference for linear descent in which one edition takes over the readings of its predecessor. Where there is no evidence of later intervention by the author, such a chain should always be represented by its first member, as later editions will inevitably introduce non-authorial readings. Yet, since nearly all printed texts from the last millennium are descended from a manuscript or typescript of some kind, and sometimes from a whole series of them, the problems of the handwritten text are not evaded, just less immediately visible. Editors of English Renaissance drama have devoted considerable ingenuity to inferring the nature of lost manuscript copy from the resultant print. Fredson Bowers, in a well-known passage, identifies thirteen different possible categories of

Elizabethan printer's copy which may have been used for the setting of play quartos.[14] Such reasoning is often crucial to the determination of authorship. *The Excellent Comedy, called The Old Law: or A new way to please you* (dealing with the compulsory euthanasia of the elderly, complete with the cooking of birth data to speed up the process) comes down to us from an edition of 1656 whose title-page attributes it to 'Phil. Massinger. Tho. Middleton. William Rowley'. George Price's analysis of the respective shares of the three authors concludes that the play began as a collaborative work between Middleton and Rowley written around 1614–15.[15] Sorting out their respective shares was not an impossible matter, as not only did each leave a body of uncollaborative work, but they also collaborated on four other plays. Middleton was by far the more accomplished dramatist of the two and normally handled the serious parts of their plays, with Rowley, an actor specialising in comic roles, providing the farcical scenes. Middleton's share is identified by the appearance of 'characteristic diction'. Massinger appears to have revised the play for a revival some time between 1625 and 1636 (this part of the argument involves a consideration of how the script may have passed from company to company). Price next considers what the errors and anomalies in the printed text tell us about the now lost manuscript. He concludes from spelling, punctuational and stylistic evidence that it was partly in Massinger's hand and had been marked up as a promptbook, but that it also contained what were either original pages by Middleton and Rowley or a scribal transcript that preserved some of their idiosyncracies. Price's allocations (published in 1953) are due for reconsideration through more exact, up-to-date methods – Massinger's responsibility for one speech is argued impressionistically from his 'rhetorical, solemn manner, as well as his freer rhythm and his inadequate punctuation' (p. 127) – but at least there is a clearly articulated model to treat as a starting point.

Cyrus Hoy in his survey, already referred to, of shared authorship in the Beaumont and Fletcher canon[16] also had to grapple with the problem of known or suspected revision undertaken for revivals, while the Shakespeare corpus contains a number of cases in which plays exist in both an original and revised form. *Timon of Athens* is currently seen by many scholars as a revision by Middleton of a work left incomplete by Shakespeare; the Oxford editors of both dramatists accept the surviving text of *Measure for Measure* as another Middletonian revision. When the revised and the unrevised form both survive, as in the cases of *Q2* and *F1 Hamlet* and *Q1* and *F1 King Lear*, the problem is to determine whether or not the primary author was responsible for the revisions. Demonstrations of this kind nearly always depend heavily on assumptions made about the nature and affiliations of the lost manuscript sources. The editors of the Oxford Shakespeare relied in preparing their text of *Hamlet* on the premise that *Q2* was descended directly from the dramatist's 'foul papers', but with a second, revised authorial copy intervening between the foul papers and the promptbook. The promptbook was in turn the ancestor of both the folio text and, through memorial reconstruction, of *Q1*. They further hypothesised that *Q1* was consulted during the printing of *Q2*, and that *Q3* (descended from *Q2*) may have been consulted during the printing of the folio.[17] This position involves accepting as authentically Shakespearean a large number of folio readings that were rejected by some earlier editors. As with the Langland example considered earlier, attributionists need to be aware of the many kinds of argued constructedness embodied in such editions. Researchers coming to attribution studies from a science or maths background naturally expect literary editors to have done that part of the work for them; but what many editions – including some of the greatest – present is not a solution but a case that has to be assessed like any other case. With *Hamlet* a decision would have to be made whether to load both the second quarto and the folio variants into the database, the issue being that to omit genuine readings might be just as damaging as to include non-authorial ones.

Difficulties arising from transmission are compounded by those arising from the covertly collaborative nature of much literary writing. While this issue has already been raised in Chapter three, it will be useful to reinforce what was said there with a couple of examples from printed texts which on first encounter would appear to be reliable repositories of authorial readings. Consider the pre-printing history of Keats's 'Isabella' (1820) as recorded by Jack Stillinger:

> Keats wrote two manuscripts, a draft and a fair copy, and then his friend Richard Woodhouse made a shorthand transcript from the fair copy, a longhand transcript from the shorthand, and then a second longhand transcript from the first longhand version. The last of these successive transcripts was the setting copy used by the printer of Keats's book. Woodhouse began attempting to revise Keats's lines even in the holograph fair copy itself while he was making his shorthand transcript; he further changed Keats's text substantively in all three of his transcripts; Keats himself made additional revisions in the transcript used by the printer; and the publisher of the volume, John Taylor, also made changes. The upshot is that Keats wrote most of the poem as we have it in the standard

text, but Woodhouse and Taylor between them were responsible for the title of the poem, for most of the punctuation and other accidentals throughout, and for some of the wording of about sixty of the 504 lines – roughly one line out of every nine in the poem.[18]

While this information is advanced by Stillinger in the course of an argument about collaborative authorship, its point for the present section is its unveiling of the intricate manuscript history that may lie behind a straightforward printed edition of the nineteenth or twentieth century.[19] To this example, let me add Tony Parsons's account of the writing of his highly successful 1999 novel *Man and Boy*:

> Throughout the writing and editing process I had guidance from Nick Sayers at HarperCollins and Caradoc King at my agents, A. P. Watt. There were countless discussions about every theme, every chapter, every line. We made sure that every scene in the book was played in exactly the right key.[20]

Despite the amount of well-intentioned alteration recorded by Stillinger, Keats's printed text was probably closer to his original draft than that of an average present-day first novel which has passed through the hands of an interventionist publisher's editor. This has implications for all investigations of attribution which depend on the exact measuring of style.

In the course of the eighteenth century, changes in cultural attitudes towards writers made it much more likely that their manuscripts would be preserved after their death. In our own century research libraries are so keen to possess literary manuscripts that they will pay for them to be sent in regular batches while the writer is still alive, with the result that, in a complete reversal of the Elizabethan predicament, we often possess complete records of the textual history of individual works, including drafts, fair copies, corrected proofs and relevant correspondence. Knowledge of this history is essential to the planning of tests involving stylistic measurement; but it also reminds us that important evidence for attribution studies may lie concealed in those parts of the heritage that did not survive the drafting stage – the rare word, the consciously suppressed stylistic reflex or the abandoned allusion. A writer's drafts and revisions will often reveal innate individual habits more clearly than the completed work. Manuscripts are also likely to offer visual clues concerning the contributions of the various specialists or co-authors who may have collaborated on a work.

THE MATERIAL RECORD

Many scholarly arguments stand or fall by the accurate dating and location of records. We all know that the attribution of easel paintings is crucially reliant on an understanding of the historical evolution of paints, canvases and artists' tools, as well as particular schools' and artists' ways of using them. The work must also be examined for repairs and overpainting: if possible X-ray or beta-radiograph images should be taken to reveal what lies underneath the opaque surface. How the canvas was primed and stretched and colours prepared must be determined. The work of generations of repairers may need to be distinguished from that of the original creator or creators. To this must be added an understanding of the ways in which manufacture was organised (often in the case of easel paintings on a kind of co-operative system with assistance from apprentices), commissioning practices, and the relationship of the artist to dealers and patrons, all of which may have influenced choices of medium or technique.

For literary scholars the object of investigation is the manuscript, typescript, printed book, tape, computer file, video or film. A manuscript on papyrus or vellum is written on a processed form of an organic substance which can be subjected to various forms of scientific testing. Manuscripts or printed books composed of paper (still organic but more radically processed) can be dated according to the visible evidence of their mode of manufacture. Until the early nineteenth century, paper was hand made in moulds from a solution of fibre in water, the fibre being obtained by breaking down linen rags. By looking through the sheet to a light source, the markings of the mould will be clearly visible, as may a watermark and possibly a countermark, both created by images in wire attached to the top of the mould. (In the smaller formats fragments of the watermark will be distributed over several leaves, obscured in gutters or partly lost through trimming.) Machine-made papers may also be watermarked, but in this case the mark is applied by a roller to the top of the sheet rather than being an element of the base on which it rests in manufacture, meaning that the sheet has indentations on both sides. John Bidwell's 'The study of paper as evidence, artefact, and commodity' offers guidance to the published scholarship on this early period.[21] Papers can also be tested for their constituents and additives: the forger of Romantic 'pre-first' editions, T. J. Wise, was exposed through his use of a paper containing esparto grass which was not available at the time of the supposed production.[22] The failure to conduct such tests was one reason for the initial acceptance of the faked Hitler diaries. An experienced documentary scholar will always want to look through paper as well as at it – sometimes to the discomfiture of librarians who, however, will often be able to supply a flat light surface for this purpose. Lord Keeper North presided over a trial in which an account was read as covering purchases from a cook up to 1677. The cook replied 'quick and loud' that it was only to 1676. The judge 'turning towards the light looked thro the paper, and saw plainely, . . . 6 in rasure and in ink . . . 7', then handed it to the jury to confirm the matter for themselves.[23] H. Robbins Landon's suspicion that the Haydn Op. 3 quartets, including the famous 'Serenade', might be a fraudulent attribution was verified when, looking through the title-page in the same way, he realised that Haydn's name had only been engraved on the plate after that of Romanus Hoffstetter had been scraped out. The works are now generally accepted as by Hoffstetter.[24]

The scholarly study of handwriting has determined many disputed attributions. While broad tendencies in styles of writing may easily be traced, there will always be a multitude of individual sub-styles within those broader movements, associated with particular localities, writing schools and copy-books. That a hand learned in youth may vary over decades is something most of us will have experienced in our own lives. We will also be aware of variations in the same hand between hurried and careful writing and between writing performed with different implements. In a further complication, writers of the early modern period would frequently have mastered several different hands – say, a secretary, an italic and possibly one or more specialised legal hands. The secretary tended to be more expressive of individuality than the relatively invariant italic. Mary Ann O'Donnell's claim for the presence of Aphra Behn's hand in a Bodleian manuscript anthology was argued from a relatively small body of holographs widely separated in time.[25] In such cases it is essential that samples be reproduced for the judgement of the reader. Shakespeare's authenticated handwriting is represented by the words 'by me' and signatures, not all of which are certainly authentic. The claim that he was the writer of the 'hand D' passages in the manuscript of *Sir Thomas More* could not be sustained on this basis alone and has been most persuasively argued from the evidence of parallels in thought and expression.

Forged documents are a special problem which will be considered in Chapter ten. Hardly less challenging are fraudulent imprints on printed books. A case from England is the 'Antwerp' editions of Rochester's *Poems on Several Occasions* (1680), which in fact ranged over more than a decade and were all surreptitiously printed in London. The bibliographical relationships of these editions were first unriddled by James Thorpe; their contents – only partly by Rochester – were the subject of David M. Vieth's classic attributional study.[26]

How is one to determine the date, place, printer and publisher of an anonymous, pseudonymous or disputably ascribed work in cases where this problem cannot be resolved from legal records? Watermarks may help with the date and compositorial practice may yield clues to location.[27] In early printing there is often a link between specific authors and specific publishing booksellers and between the booksellers and particular printers, who may be identifiable from characteristic woodcut ornaments or combinations of typefaces. A single face may also permit identifications if it contains damaged sorts which can be shown to have come from the same cases that were used for a piece of signed work. Hand-set type got considerably knocked around during its lifetime and, since a single sort might well be used several times in printing a book, such identifications are perfectly practicable. Charlton Hinman's *The Printing and Proof-reading of the First Folio of Shakespeare*[28] demonstrates the technique. Damage to a long-used woodcut may also assist in dating.

MODES OF PRODUCTION

A further kind of scholarly study of meaning-bearing records is concerned with the processes of their manufacture and the professional skills employed in these processes. For an introduction to the specialist literature the reader is referred to the studies listed earlier in this chapter; but it will be helpful to examine a case when such evidence has been of importance for attribution.

In 1950 Donald F. Bond analysed the 555 numbers of Addison's and Steele's famous periodical the *Spectator*, which appeared six days a week between 1 March 1711 and 6 December 1712, and later had enormous circulation in multi-volume book form.[29] Like its heavily studied United States successor, the *Federalist*, the *Spectator* was the work of two primary authors with occasional assistants. While a number of booksellers had a hand in the publication, the principal ones were Samuel Buckley and Jacob Tonson II. Bond's key realisation was that in order to reach the reputed circulation of over 3,000 copies a day (and probably much higher) from a single setting of type, two not one day's work was needed on a common press of the time. Examination of reused standing type, broken rules, the width of the type line, and the type size and fount confirmed that this was indeed the practice in the early numbers, Printer A being responsible for the odd-numbered papers and Printer B for the even-numbered ones. Variations from this pattern later in the run did not mean a departure from the basic principle of distributing the load. Additional evidence was given by advertisements, some of which only appeared in copies from one or the other printer. Among these were advertisements for books published for Buckley and Tonson respectively. Buckley's advertisements appeared mostly in copies printed by Printer B and Tonson's in books printed by Printer A. The connection between Printer B and Buckley is confirmed by the fact that this printer was also responsible for Buckley's other paper, the *Daily Courant*. Similar evidence links Printer A with Tonson: he was actually Tonson's partner, John Watts.

The next stage in the argument was to examine the printing of the large number of papers whose authorship was already known through their being signed with single letters (R and T for Steele, C, L, I and O for Addison – the name of his Muse – and Q, T, X and Z for other contributors). This showed a clear, though not exclusive, link between Steele and Printer B and Addison and Printer A. Working from this, Bond was able to make persuasive allocations of the unsigned papers and to question assignments of certain papers to the minor contributors.

In neither this nor any other field is it valid to project the relatively disciplined procedures which attend the progression of a modern work into print back into the past; but neither should we suppose that the situation in the past was one of 'anything goes': different stages of the history of publishing and journalism have had their own accepted trade practices. It is certainly important to distinguish texts which come to us via authorised publication from those that, prior to the acceptance of authorial copyright, were put into print from casually circulating manuscripts. A passage from George Wither sums up the situation as it prevailed in the early seventeenth century when many works were intended for manuscript rather than print publication but might still in the course of their copying and recirculation come into the hands of bookseller-publishers:

> If a seller of Bookes . . . gett any written Coppy into his powre, likely to be vendible; whether the Author be willing or no, he will publish it; And it shallbe contrived and named alsoe, according to his owne pleasure: which is the reason, so many good Bookes come forth imperfect, and with foolish titles.[30]

A publication of this kind, often in mutilated form, would sometimes bring a counter-publication from the aggrieved author designed to supply an accurate text. (Sir Thomas Browne's *Religio medici* is a famous example; *Q2 Hamlet* might well be another.) This solves the problem of attribution but may leave a new problem of whether passages and readings in the unauthorised printing which do not reappear in the authorised one were interpolated by other hands or simply omitted in the author's revisions.

A key realisation is that any printed book always *looks* more reliable than it is. The symmetrical, evenly marshalled lines of the type-page, the invariance of letter forms, and the overall sense of a mechanised impersonality stripped of human presence all enact an authority which is not, as Walter J. Ong has reminded us, possessed by the same text inscribed in manuscript.[31] Where these attributes of typographical dignity are lacking they can be supplied. Looking at a handsomely bound Shakespeare quarto under glass in a library we may be misled into thinking it is an expert piece of bookmaking, but nothing could be further from the truth. Like most single-play publications of the period (and indeed for much later), it began its existence as a disposable piece of cheap print. Its binding is invariably modern: if it was bound up in its own time it would usually have been as part of a collection of similar works rather than singly. A modern binder working on such a rare survivor might well resize the paper, calendar it between hot plates to make it smooth and glossy, and gild the edges. All this leads to the endowing of a humble original with a factitious timelessness. By contrast, faced with a shelf of paperbacks in a modern bookshop we make accurate judgements about their intended market and likely readership on the basis of the most cursory of glances. Experienced readers can walk into a house for the first time and sum up the personalities of its occupants from a quick inspection of their bookshelves. The trained eye does the same for the material books of the past, viewing them always as time-bound products not as timeless icons. Such expertise is greatly enhanced by an understanding of the way a book is constructed out of folded sheets of paper and the technologies that have covered the surfaces of those sheets with markings.

TEXTUAL ANALYSIS

Textual bibliography has the same perspective on the verbal text, seeing it always as time-bound and subject to the prevailing contingencies of manufacture, transmission and commerce. When a work survives in a variety of copies from a relatively young manuscript tradition, not fatally affected by conflation, it is sometimes possible to recover lost original readings by a combination of directional judgements and topological study of agreements in variation. However, there are many traps in this process, one of which is the difficulty of determining whether any particular dividing of the tradition took place through a single multi-branch junction or a series of binary ones, and a second being a need to distinguish genetically significant groupings from the many that arise fortuitously or through conflation. When it works, the process can deliver valuable evidence. Rochester's *To all Gentlemen, Ladies and others* is a bogus medical brochure produced during a practical joke in which he posed as a quack named 'Alexander Bendo'. In a reprint by Edmund Curll, published in 1709, an additional paragraph appears which looks suspiciously like an interpolation:

> *I have likewise got the Knowledge of a great Secret, to cure Barrenness . . . which I have made use of for many Years with great Success, especially this last Year, wherein I have cured one Woman that had been married Twenty Years, and another that had been married One and twenty Years, and two Women that had been Three times married; as I can make appear by the Testimony of several Persons in* London, Westminster, *and other Places thereabouts. The Medicines I use, cleanse and strengthen the Womb, and are all to be taken in the Space of seven Days. And because I do not intend to deceive any Person, upon Discourse with them, I will tell them whether I am like to do them any Good. My usual Contract is, to receive one Half of what is agreed upon when the Party shall be Quick with child, the other Half when she is brought to Bed.*[32]

The false note here is the unaristocratic inclusion of monetary terms, whereas the rest of the brochure presents Dr Bendo as a high-minded public benefactor. It also appears to be playing by implication with Rochester's reputation as a rake. A note at the beginning of Curll's volume claims: '*Since the finishing of this Work, there has been transmitted to us a perfect Copy of my Lord* Rochester*'s Mountebank Bill, under the Feigned Name of* Alexander Bendo. *Tho' this Piece has been printed, yet 'tis so imperfect that besides several words which alter the Sense, there is one large entire Paragraph omitted.*'[33] However, stemmatological analysis shows clearly that, apart from its addition, Curll's text is descended from Rochester's own 1676 printing via the Tonson 1691 collected edition: the passage is unlikely, therefore, to be authentic.[34]

Where stemmatological analysis fails, the textual bibliographer reverts to what is called *divinatio*, using philological knowledge and an understanding of the errors habitually made by scribes to choose between alternatives offered by the tradition. Once again, the edited texts which result from such a process will be constructed ones, and must always be acknowledged as such. A third possibility is to choose the most satisfactory of the surviving sources and to reproduce it with minimal alteration. Divinatory and 'best manuscript' editing will produce different styles of text which need to be understood for what they are. One is likely to contain a large number of readings which have been settled by editorial judgement and the other to have a substantial residue of scribal alterations. The choice of versions for authorship tests has to be made in the light of this knowledge.

Textual bibliography will also be called on to assess the circumstances of origin of individual documents. One famous case of a deceptive manuscript is that already discussed in Chapter five – Diderot's *Paradoxe sur le comédien* in the hand of Jacques-André Naigeon. This work, dealing among other things with the acting of David Garrick, was published nearly fifty years after Diderot's death from an autograph manuscript acquired by Catherine the Great of Russia. Then in 1902 a second manuscript was discovered in the hand of Naigeon, a close associate of Diderot, which had been heavily revised in a way that suggested that Naigeon was its author: in particular numerous words and passages had been struck through and alternatives written interlinearly and in the margins. It was recognised that much of the work was adapted from earlier writings by Diderot; more was traced to other sources of the time, some of which were thought to date from after Diderot's death, though it was conceded he might have seen them in manuscript. The matter was not resolved until the great textual critic Joseph Bédier made an inspection of the second manuscript. He perceived that Naigeon, while making numerous corrections to the originally inscribed text, had made no corrections at all to his corrections – a most unusual thing for an author revising a draft. Bédier's interpretation was that Naigeon, having transcribed a manuscript by Diderot, had then altered its readings to incorporate those of a lost manuscript containing a version of the work further revised by Diderot. Thus, instead of the authorial manuscript of a text by Naigeon, the source comprised a scribal record of two versions of an original work by Diderot.[35]

CONCLUSION

In this necessarily skimpy review of the disciplines of the book much that would be of pressing interest to editors has been omitted because it is not of direct interest to attributionists. It should be stressed after so much textual scepticism that many editions of works *do* exist that offer an accurate record of the text in the form in which its author or authors sent it to the scribe or the press. All this chapter has attempted is to point out that this state of affairs is not universal and that the credentials of a source should always be examined before scholarly use is made of it. Naturally, a version does not have to be wholly authentic in order to yield ample evidence for authorship; but when the whole text is to be drawn upon to generate word frequencies or a record of stylistic practices, or when a large weight of argument hangs on a single reference or allusion, it is important that the version be the best available. If the text chosen for attributional study is that of a scholarly edition, the researcher must understand the assumptions that lie behind the choices made by the editor between alternative sources and alternative readings – something which should be clearly explained in the textual introduction. If the version is drawn from a manuscript or printing of the author's own time, it is only fair to the readers to whom the results of analysis will be presented that a careful investigation is made of the path by which its text has travelled from the author's desk to the hands of its original readers. It should also be explained why that record, rather than any others that may be available, has been chosen to represent the work for the purposes of the study. This explanation should come early in the article concerned so that the reader can be saved the labour of reading any further, should the attributionist's house prove to have been constructed on sand.

The texts of both original and scholarly editions exist in history as intersections of contingencies. To treat them as if they belonged to some ideal order of authorial textuality is to miss the point both practically and philosophically. Most to be suspected are those records which proclaim themselves as containing an authorially sanctified text. The title-page of the first folio of Shakespeare assures us that its contents were 'Published according to the true original copies'. This was a fib.

CHAPTER TEN

Forgery and attribution

John of Salisbury's *Polycraticus* is one of the major works of twelfth-century literature. Belonging to the traditional genre of the 'advice to princes', it draws on a remarkable range of classical and patristic learning. Among the works paraphrased, but in this case not directly quoted, is the *Institutio Traiani* supposedly written by Plutarch to the emperor Trajan. These excerpts are the only evidence for the existence of such a work and have been much discussed. While Plutarch and Trajan were certainly contemporaries, there is no other reference to any connection between them; moreover, if such a work did exist it must originally have been written in Greek and later circulated in a Latin translation. It has been suggested that it was a late-classical fake: another theory would spread its composition over several centuries. Janet Martin has argued that there never was such a work and that John invented it in order to give authority to a number of his own morally improving stories. The evidence for this lies in John's treatment of his other classical sources, particularly in one case when we know the very manuscript on which he drew and where we see him interpolating material of his own which is then sourced to the classical author.[1]

Welcome to the busy arena of literary forgery! John may have assumed that the cognoscenti among his audience would have picked up the fraud and been amused by it – or by their own superior acumen in spotting it. His readers would in any case have been aware that in the world around them much more self-interested acts of forgery were a common occurrence, particularly those of faked deeds, faked charters and faked wills: Anthony Grafton has speculated that 'perhaps two-thirds of all documents issued to ecclesiastics before A.D. 1100 are fakes'.[2] A famous example was the Donation of Constantine, one of an early mediaeval collection of bogus decretals which were used to support the claims of the Papacy to secular power. This attribution was first overturned on church-historical grounds by Nicholas of Cusa in his *De concordiantia catholica* presented to the Council of Basle in 1433–4. A more celebrated demolition was performed in 1440 in the humanist Lorenzo Valla's *Declamatio de falsa et ementita donatione Constantini*.[3] Other Renaissance scholars exposed allegedly first-hand accounts of the Trojan War by Dares Phrygius and Dictys Cretensis as late-classical forgeries, along with the *Sybilline Oracles* and the Hermetic corpus. Dionysius the Areopagite was demoted from the authorship of the neo-Platonic writings that passed under his name. The letters of Heloise and Abelard were also questioned but present-day scholars mostly regard them as genuine.[4] Richard Bentley's later demonstrations that Aesop's *Fables* and the *Epistles of Phalaris* could not have been written by their putative authors had both been anticipated in the sixteenth century.[5] Martin Luther, who had great respect for Aesop, surmised (no doubt correctly) that the fables were the product of many hands over a long period of time rather than works of a single author.[6] Erasmus was aware of the late-classical date of the pseudo-Phalaris but could never have demonstrated the matter with Bentley's depth of erudition. A skilful fake of the Renaissance itself was the fraudulent Chaldean chronicle *Berosi antiquitatum libri quinque*, one of a number of forgeries published together by Giovanni Nanni (Annius of Viterbo) in 1492. It took several generations for scholarly understanding of the ancient world to recover from this particular deception. Grafton regards Nanni as an archetypal figure of the ideologically motivated faker: his skills might have made him a great attributionist.[7] In 1693 a French literary postfabricator, François Nodot, published a version of that defective masterpiece, the *Satyricon* of Petronius, supplemented by extensive new passages supposedly found in a manuscript from Belgrade.[8] While in this case the deception was quickly revealed, the colourful new passages were often retained in later French and English translations.

Eighteenth-century Britain was another great age of literary forgery. Macpherson's fabrication of the poems of Ossian, Chatterton's 'Rowley' poems and Ireland's pseudo-Shakespearean *Vortigern* were only the best known of a whole series of literary fakes put forward with different levels of competence and seriousness.[9] George Psalmanazar's *Description of Formosa* (1704) belongs to a different category, as there was no doubt that he had written the work, only about his claim to be a Formosan. Sticking to Latin, Charles Bertram (1723–65) fabricated a mediaeval account of Roman Britain and a late-classical Itinerary, which were good enough to fool Gibbon. It was not until 1886 that he was finally exposed.[10] In the highly deceptive world of early eighteenth-century political journalism and pamphleteering, Swift and Defoe were far from exceptional in their fondness for borrowed and invented identities. The artistic point of such works as Defoe's *The Shortest Way with Dissenters* and Swift's *A Modest Proposal* is that perceptive readers would recognise irony where the imperceptive assumed sincerity. Defoe's fate in being put in the pillory for writing the *Shortest Way* shows the practical dangers of such a practice. *Robinson Crusoe*, *Moll Flanders* and the rest were soon recognised as works of fiction, but a glance at the original title-pages will show that they were intended as fakes.[11] There is not the slightest hint given that Robinson and Moll were not real people writing real memoirs, nor of Defoe having any involvement in their production. The invention of an intervening editor for *Moll Flanders* is designed to heighten, not to disperse, the air of verisimilitude.

Richard Savage's *An Author To Be Let* (1729) is a satire on the use of false attributions by booksellers of the time but probably not far from the truth:

> At my first setting out I was hired by a reverend Prebend to libel Dean *Swift* for Infidelity. Soon after I was employed by *Curll* to write a merry Tale, the Wit of which was its Obscenity. This we agreed to palm upon the World for a posthumous Piece of Mr. *Prior*. . . . 'Twas in his Service that I wrote Obscenity and Profaneness, under the Names of *Pope* and *Swift*. Sometimes I was Mr. *Joseph* [i.e. John] *Gay*, and at others Theory *Burnet*, or *Addison*. I abridg'd Histories and Travels, translated from the *French*, what they never wrote, and was expert at finding out new Titles for old Books. When a notorious Thief was hanged, I was the *Plutarch* to preserve his Memory; and when a great Man died, mine were his Remains, and mine the Account of his last Will and Testament.[12]

Edmund Curll has remained notorious for such deceptions; but they were the general stock-in-trade of professional pamphleteering. Bentley's lament that 'to forge and counterfeit books, and father them upon great names, has been a practice almost as old as letters' applied just as pressingly to his own time as it did to the classical past.[13]

In the nineteenth century, with the advent of Romanticism, there were a number of imitators of Macpherson's and Chatterton's faking of mediaeval ballads and sagas. Sir Walter Scott would write stanzas to place as epigraphs to the chapters of his novels which he would credit to 'Anon.' or 'Old song'. The shortage of information about the life of Shakespeare was attended to by a number of fakers of whom the best known was John Payne Collier, who specialised in the modification of genuine documents. Inevitably, there were numerous deceptive attributions to such scandalous writers as Byron and, later, Wilde. Anonymous journalism was massively conducive to authorial role-playing. Consider the following from George Gissing's *New Grub Street* (1891):

> On an evening of early summer, six months after the death of Edwin Reardon, Jasper of the facile pen was bending over his desk, writing rapidly by the warm western light which told that sunset was near. Not far from him sat his younger sister; she was reading, and the book in her hand bore the title, 'Mr Bailey, Grocer.'
>
> 'How will this do?' Jasper exclaimed, suddenly throwing down his pen.
>
> And he read aloud a critical notice of the book with which Dora was occupied; a notice of the frankly eulogistic species, beginning with: 'It is seldom nowadays that the luckless reviewer of novels can draw the attention of the public to a new work which is at once powerful and original;' and ending: 'The word is a bold one, but we do not hesitate to pronounce this book a masterpiece.'
>
> 'Is that for *The Current*?' asked Dora, when he had finished.
>
> 'No, for *The West End*. Fadge won't allow any one but himself to be lauded in that style. I may as well do the notice for *The Current* now, as I've got my hand in.'
>
> He turned to his desk again, and before daylight failed him had produced a piece of more cautious writing, very favourable on the whole, but with reserves and slight censures. This also he read to Dora.
>
> 'You wouldn't suspect they were written by the same man, eh?'
>
> 'No. You have changed the style very skilfully.'[14]

Like the Savage example, this is from a work of fiction but one directly and knowledgeably concerned with the conditions of professional writing at the time.

In the modern world the faking of visual art works, especially easel paintings, and antiquities, is a major international industry. The faking of musical works is rarer, though Fritz Kreisler's repertoire of recital pieces was largely composed of his own works retailed under various historical names. Art forgery brings in money; music forgery is usually playful or malicious; literary forgery may be pursued for either of these reasons. The fabrication of longer texts for commercial publication is a risky business, and in two well-known cases, the Howard Hughes biography by Clifford Irving and Richard Suskind and the Hitler diaries, fabricated by Konrad Kujau, came spectacularly unstuck. The literary forger is most commonly active with smaller textual elements such as letters, inscriptions in albums and marginalia in books. The aim of these is nearly always commercial: basically any kind of document sought by collectors can expect to attract fakes. In one famous example, Mark Hofman invented documents that cast an unfavourable light on the early Mormons in order to sell them to the church itself. In danger of exposure, he committed two murders in order to buy time before injuring himself with a home-made bomb in the course of attempting a third.[15] T. J. Wise's famous forgeries of nineteenth-century 'pre-first' editions belong to another category, as it was the printings not the texts which were fraudulent.

There are also informational fakes such as bogus business documents and professional qualifications, plagiarised student essays and theses, police 'verbals' of the kind investigated by Andrew Morton, forged wills, and documents and photographs invented to cause political embarrassment.[16] Clinching evidence in such cases is more likely to be of a physical than a textual kind – handwriting, layout, paper types, the chemical composition of inks and colouring matter – but there are cases where stylistic evidence will be of importance.[17] McMenamin, whose main concern is with present-day forensic practice, cites a case of 1728 which was determined by stylistic comparison. William Hales had been charged with the capital offence of forging a promissory note for £6,400, using the wording

> I promise to pay to George Watson, esq. or bearer, the sum of six thousand four hundred pounds, at demand, the like value received. For my self and partners.
> Tho. Gibson

Gibson's clerk testified that his employer 'generally begins with I promise to pay, and concludes his notes For Self and Co. but never mentions value received'. Hales was convicted.[18] The covert faking of verbal texts is actively pursued by the world's intelligence organisations, sometimes for private and sometimes for public consumption.[19] Two notorious examples from the past are the anti-Semitic forgery *Protocols of the Elders of Zion*, a widely circulated fake of the 1890s, and the Zinoviev letter of 1924, though some historians regard the latter as genuine. One must be careful not to use one fake as evidence for another, as when the handwriting of the Hitler diaries was 'verified' against that of a supposedly genuine letter which was an earlier Kujau fake.

We have not yet defined a fake: for attributional purposes it is a work composed with the intention to deceive and then promulgated under the name of another. The problems of detecting fakes are thus similar to those of detecting incorrect attributions which have arisen by other means. The employment of ghostwriters is not regarded as a species of faking because the role of declarative author is assumed by mutual agreement and in return for payment. Fakes are secretive: the real authors go to great pains to conceal their presence. Plagiarism, while no less reprehensible than faking, is distinct from it, though some fakes contain plagiarised elements: the true fake is a creative achievement. Texts emerging posthumously from a writer's *Nachlass* have always been regarded with a degree of suspicion. Even when not in any sense fakes they are often heavily reconstructed from imperfect materials and may, as in the well-known cases of Nietzsche and Jung, have been subjected to ideological censorship.[20] When a totally invented work makes its appearance under the name of a major writer it is most commonly, as Savage indicates, after the writer's death, when there is less chance of its being challenged.

SPOTTING THE FAKE

The first aid to spotting a fake is that it is usually a little too good to be true. What is provided has to be something so desirable to the victim, or the public, that normal scepticism is suspended: something either long desired or that provides support for a passionately held theory. *Qui vult decepi decipiatur*. It is for this reason that many shamelessly inept fakes have had long and successful lives. If the fake touches on some matter of deep and desperate importance to its readers, this may restrain those who can see through it from expressing their disbelief. When the ideological moment that brought forth the fake has passed it should be easier to see it as the product of contrivance.

The second clue is that the faker can rarely resist justifying the fake with an elaborate narrative or provenance. The introduction to Nodot's fraudulent edition of Petronius tells a typically circumstantial story.[21] The supposedly complete manuscript had been acquired at Belgrade by a French nobleman named du Pin, serving in the imperial army, from a Greek convert to Islam who had inherited it from his father, a man of great erudition. Du Pin, being unable to read the book's difficult hand, hired an amanuensis to write it out in '*notis italicis*' from which he discovered that it was the *Satyricon*. Du Pin was unable to show Nodot the manuscript in Paris as he had left it at Frankfurt, where he passed the winter between campaigns. Nodot in turn was unable to travel to Frankfurt but managed to persuade a merchant of that city to act as an intermediary in bringing a transcript to Paris. The process described was a leisurely one, attended with difficulties. Fakers all appreciate the value of a good story but their stories tend to have a betraying sameness. No faker ever makes a discovery by simply looking in the catalogue of a library, which is how most real discoveries are made.

The third way in which fakes betray themselves is that even the most skilful of fakers will invariably make slips. These may be in expression, no matter how hard the original has been studied, or in details relating to the life or manners of the time, which should be detectable by those with specialised knowledge. Stylometric testing by John Burrows of novels written in an assumed period style has shown that it is virtually impossible to erase the subconscious speech habits of the modern author.[22] Lastly, one should note that fakers can rarely resist a concealed joke or two, just to rub home how supremely clever they are. Nodot's decision to locate the discovery of his bogus document in Alba Graeca (Belgrade) may have been because with a change of gender it becomes *album graecum*, a chemical manufactured from dog's excrement. Fortunately for scholarship, fakers who pursue their art purely in order to lead others to admire their cleverness will often feel obliged after a time to reveal the fact, as happened with Nodot. But the truly malevolent fakers have no such aspiration. Their pleasure lies in watching the world embroiled in a deception from which only they are free and they die happy in the belief that this will continue to be the case. And no doubt in some cases they are right.

This section has not attempted to deal with the detection of fraudulent transcripts and printings of texts which are not themselves forgeries. For this the reader is referred to the large specialised literature which has been assembled by museums, libraries and the rare-book trade. A good beginning can be made with Kenneth W. Rendell's *Forging History: The Detection of Fake Letters and Documents*, which includes accounts of the author's role in the Kujau and Hofmann investigations.[23]

FAKING AND DEATTRIBUTION

The exposure of fakes is a crucial and very necessary part of deattribution, a practice which is something more than a mirror image of attribution. This book has given its main attention to the process of seeking authors for texts; but the most valuable scholarly results are often those in which a received attribution is shown to be valueless and the scholarship based on it called into question. The influential work of David M. Vieth on Rochester and Furbank and Owens on Defoe was deattributional in this sense. In each case there was a huge body of writing which had been attributed to one or the other author by annotators of manuscripts, shady publishers in search of a sale, booksellers anxious to enhance the price of a catalogue item, imaginative librarians, overconfident attributionists of an earlier generation and well-intentioned readers. These ascriptions, often made on the slightest of grounds or no grounds at all, hardened with amazing rapidity into received wisdom, to be repeated unquestioningly by other librarians, booksellers, bibliographers and scholars. The deattributional investigations proceeded by searching out the source for each attribution and making an assessment of the authority with which it was bestowed. Both canons emerged from scrutiny very much reduced.

It goes without saying that, while such sifting is essential, it will occasionally – perhaps often – reject a perfectly genuine work which just happens to come to us with a late or dubious ascription. But it is not the job of deattributionists to conduct the more detailed assessments that might establish this; their task is to act as gatekeepers and verifiers. They are entitled to use subjective impressions to counter attributions that themselves rest on subjective impressions, though not, of course, to reject evidence of a more substantial kind.[24] The subject matter of deattribution is attribution itself as a system for attaching names to works and parts of works.

However, the urge to deattribute can easily get out of hand. The outstanding example of this was the Jesuit Jean Hardouin (1646–1729) who in a series of studies culminating in his *Ad censuram scriptorum veterum prolegomena* (London, 1766) developed the thesis that the greater part of classical Greek and Roman literature, along with most Christian patristic literature, had been composed by forgers working in the late thirteenth and fourteenth centuries. Latin works had been written by those who claimed to have discovered them at this time in monastic libraries or who had engineered that discovery, the Greek works by refugees from Constantinople. The only genuinely ancient works, among pagan writings, were those of Homer, Herodotus, Pliny the elder, Virgil's *Georgics* (but not the *Eclogues* and *Aeneid*), Horace's *Satires* and *Epistles*, and, in one enunciation of the theory, Cicero and in another Plautus. Hardouin also held that the Latin vulgate was the original version of the New Testament and that the Greek texts were inaccurate translations from it. In an article published in 1727 he argued with great ingenuity that the *Divine Comedy* was not the work of Dante but composed by a disciple of the English reformer John Wyclif.[25]

Hardouin's *Prolegomena*, like Valla's denunciation of the forgers of the Donation of Constantine, is a set piece of forensic invective. The forgers (stigmatised as a quasi-masonic, atheistical body operating across the centuries) are denigrated as the *scelestus grex*, the *impia caterva*, the *improbus grex*, the *inimica Catholicae veritati cohors*, the *cohors impia*, the *impia factio*, the *factio improba*, the *impius cœtus*, the *impii libertini*, the *agmen impium*, the *agmen pestiferum*, the *nefaria coitio* and the *coitio pestifera*.[26] Hardouin's notion of their historical identity wavered: at one period he located them among the Benedictines, at another he classed them as disciples of Severus Archontius, by whom he seems to have meant the Emperor Frederick II.[27] But their aim was always the single one of replacing Christianity with the worship of nature. In inventing works attributed to Church fathers, especially Augustine, they deliberately set out to put heresies into circulation which would corrupt the faith of sincere Catholics. In fabricating historical works they pretended to disagree with each other so as to mask the conspiracy while sowing further seeds of contention. They wrote out their forgeries by preference on parchment and, having given them an appearance of great age, left them in libraries where they would be discovered. They wrote commentaries on works they themselves had forged, so as further to darken counsel. When they got their hands on real patristic works they altered and interpolated them. Only the Vulgate defeated them because that was already in the hands of the people; but by manufacturing spurious Greek versions they were able to diminish its authority. (The Greeks, Hardouin was convinced, had themselves used the Latin Bible and service prior to the fourteenth century.)

Before we dismiss these views as more than a trifle deranged, it should be acknowledged that there was always a sharp mind at work behind them. Hardouin was genuinely erudite: he produced learned editions of a number of classical and patristic texts, wrote on theological questions, edited a twelve-volume collection of the Councils of the Church, and published several works on ancient coins (most of which he regarded as bogus). He was also a skilled debater in the seventeenth-century paradoxical tradition that resurfaces in Archbishop Whately's nineteenth-century *Historic Doubts Relative to Napoleon Bonaparte*.[28] One can even enlist him as an extreme adherent of seventeenth-century Pyrrhonism, the form of classical scepticism that taught distrust of all appearances. In support of his theory he could instance a large number of acknowledged fakes from late antiquity and the Middle Ages, some of which have already been mentioned in this chapter.[29] Was it not likely that there were many others undiscovered? He even demonstrated how easy it would be for him to do some faking himself. If he were to write to Oxford, where a new edition of the Greek New Testament was in preparation, enclosing a list of invented variants from some codex he had forged, would not these be listed with pride in the apparatus as an important new advance in scholarship (p. 70)?

Hardouin's doubts about the date of classical texts had begun when he edited Pliny the elder's *Natural History* and was so impressed by its style that everything else in the Latin language seemed inferior and derivative.

Once the first suspicion had been aroused and his contention defended with regard to the pagan writers, the enormous significance for religion of his discovery began to dawn on him. Protestantism with its reliance on patristic Greek writings and the Greek texts of the New Testament would become an absurdity; the fierce debates within the Gallican church between the Jansenist followers of Augustine and the orthodox would be snuffed out in a flash; secular philosophers and modern atheists would be shown up as credulous fools. And such a purging was not hard to conduct, for the moment that the composition of a work attributed to Ovid or Augustine was relocated in the fourteenth century all supposedly early works that quoted or commented on that work must also have been products of the same infernal factory of fraud. A quotation from the *Aeneid* or Justin Martyr was by definition a mark of imposture or interpolation. Forgeries not detectable in this way revealed themselves by their departures from the doctrine of the Catholic church as secured by tradition and papal infallibility. Whereas Père Simon had been prepared to sacrifice much of the Old Testament in order to destabilise the Protestants, Hardouin was willing to ditch the Fathers and most of the pagans in the same cause.

Hardouin's radical reduction of the corpora of both received learning and controversy was a characteristic response to the information overload which Hobart and Schiffman identify as a defining characteristic of early modern print culture:

> People had available a much wider range of material than ever before. In sheer scope this material would have resisted assimilation, even if much of it had not been so diverse and contradictory. The common response to overload (now as well as then) is to shut down, to ignore information (about strange peoples, for example) that cannot easily be assimilated, and to disregard information (about religious and scientific matters) that contradicts accepted beliefs. But humanistic education had unwittingly opened a few minds to the effects of relativism. And information overload filled these minds, which had been fashioned according to the traditional system of places, with so much diverse and contradictory information that the places burst from within, necessitating that order be improvised.[30]

The press as a multiplier of knowledge and argument was seen by Hardouin as a menace to faith. For three hundred years it had vexed and wounded the church by its publication of the 'armamentaria atheïsmi et hæresium' planted by the forgers in the monastic libraries (p. 199). As a media theorist foreshadowing the work of a greater Jesuit scholar in Walter J. Ong, Hardouin regarded the period when religious knowledge had been transmitted largely through the oral medium as in every way preferable to the age of print, and would have liked to see it return. Documentary succession could and often was broken and once broken could be manipulated and corrupted; but truth passed on from generation to generation, pope to pope and year to year moved in an unbroken and unbreakable continuum. It followed that, for the first thirteen centuries of the Christian era, faith was stabilised through a living imitation of Christ transmitted from individual believer to individual believer (p. 109), it being only in the fourteenth that the atheists and their written fakes appeared to confound this process. Writing, because it encouraged differences in opinion, was inherently duplicitous. In this preference and his consequent rejection of the larger part of the written corpus, Hardouin's project can be seen as a response to the same cultural pressures experienced by Descartes, whose solution had been to turn from the complexities of written discourse to the radical simplicities of mathematics (one of Hobart and Schiffman's most telling arguments). However, Hardouin would have had no answer to Leibnitz or Newton had they pointed out to him that reducing cultural transmission to a series of infinitesimals did not abolish the reality of change: his scheme is ultimately no more than a weak adaptation of the paradox of Zeno. Locke, who might have set him right on these matters, was unfortunately a Protestant.

Hardouin's case shows how the rhetoric of suspicion has its particular seductiveness, and that it can take over a mind to the extent of making it incapable of accepting any proposition unsupported by an impossible degree of verification. It also shows that submission to this seductiveness is often an attempt to evade cultural anxieties. It will be helpful here to turn to a superficially more commonsensical plea for deattribution directed at a single text.

In 1925 C. L. Stainer published his *Jonson and Drummond their Conversations: A few Remarks on an 18th Century Forgery*. The famous 'Conversations', supposedly recorded by Drummond when he was visited by Jonson in Scotland, contain many of Ben's best known remarks: that his wife was 'a shrew yet honest', that Donne 'for not keeping of accent deserved hanging' and that Shakespeare 'wanted Arte'.[31] Apart from the police verbal of Thomas Kyd's interrogation under torture, they are our most substantial record of unprofessional spoken words from an English Renaissance dramatist.

Stainer became convinced that the text had been fabricated by Bishop Sage and Thomas Ruddiman, the editors of the edition of Drummond's works published in Edinburgh in 1711, and that the antiquarian

Sir Robert Sibbald had also been part of the plot. The edition's version, and a second which survives in Sibbald's hand, are quite different from each other. There is no autograph, only a piece of paper in the hand of a Drummond descendant that might or might not once have been attached to one. It is known that Jonson was in Scotland in September 1618. Stainer uses a reference to Drummond's being '*Eight Years abroad*' following the death of his wife in 1615 (p. 11) to propose that he was not even in Scotland either for Jonson's visit or during one by John Taylor at around the same time, nor when James I visited Scotland in 1617 (though this last supposition depends on a tendentious interpretation of the titles of celebratory poems). If this were true, there would be no need to pursue the matter further. Stainer also has to deny the authenticity of letters to and from Drummond included in the 1711 edition. One of these from Jonson to Drummond, dated 10 May 1619, announces that he had been received 'with a most Catholick Welcome, and my Reports not unacceptable to His Majesty: He professed (I thank God) some Joy to see me, and is pleased to hear of the Purpose of my Book' (p. 13). But from March to 1 June, Stainer tells us, the king had not been present in London but seriously ill in the country. Did or did not Jonson visit him there? Stainer finds a number of other discrepancies with known or semi-known facts, including the death dates of Jonson's wife and eldest son. Certainly, some things in the 'Conversations' were strange blunders if they were actually said by Jonson; yet they could equally result from Drummond's inadequacies as a notetaker. Having convinced himself that the work was a forgery, Stainer proceeded to demonstrate how the information might have been assembled from Jonson's published works and other available sources.

These arguments have never been taken seriously by Jonson scholars and must be assumed to rest on a misapprehension. Once one accepts that Stainer got it wrong, a number of features of his pamphlet immediately arouse suspicion from their resemblance to the style of the wilder anti-Stratfordian arguments against Shakespeare. For a start there is a cavalier assertion of amateur status. On page 1 Stainer announces: 'These few notes are not the work of an expert . . . rather, the stray thoughts of one who constantly reads Ben Jonson, and who experiences mild surprise and amusement when he holds the *Conversations* in his hand.' After advancing the vital suggestion that Drummond may have been overseas when Jonson was in Scotland he continues: 'Let me say at once that, as far as I am concerned, the question as to whether Drummond was in Scotland really is not very important. It requires too much research'

(p. 12) – which again turns the burden of proof back to the amateur's private intuition. As with Hardouin there is much tendentious terminology: no sooner has the suspicion of forgery been raised than Sibbald and the two editors become 'the forgers' and 'the conspirators'. Points are established not by demonstration but by rhetorical questions, e.g.:

> Who, for instance, could possibly accept the letters of Michael Drayton, either in style or subject matter? And by what rare fortune did *Drummond's letters to Drayton* find their way back to Scotland to take their place in the folio of 1711! (p. 12)

The second question would have no force at all if Drummond, like many correspondents of his time, had kept a letter-book with a copy of letters sent. A point is made of the Scottish editors having normalised Jonson's name to Johnson, as if this was evidence of inauthenticity, whereas it was the universal spelling of their time. The publication, while Stainer's book was still in the press, of the relevant volume of the great Herford and Simpson edition of Jonson removed one piece of evidence and immediately provoked a defence. Stainer had cast doubt on whether Drummond and Jonson even knew each other: the Oxford edition mentioned a copy of Buchanan's *Rerum Scoticarum historia* given by Drummond to Jonson and containing the signatures of both. Having reiterated that 'the Conversations could be forged even though we proved Drummond to have been in Scotland and to have been a close friend of Jonson' (pp. 79–80), Stainer nevertheless implies that these inscriptions may have been another forgery by Sibbald. But his conceding of points so central to his argument demolishes it.

What dissuades one most from taking Stainer's case seriously is not its content (which is capable of being checked) but its impatient, exasperated tone – the tone of one to whom some unorthodox view is so blindingly obvious that the processes of proof are superfluous and only undertaken as a preliminary to using the great secret to interpret the text from which it was derived. If Stainer had really made an important deattribution, he had chosen the worst possible way to persuade others of it. As with Hardouin we are led in the end to look for the underlying anxiety – the overload – which this performance is meant to address. Clearly in this case it is the anxiety of the amateur scholar reacting to the growing professionalisation of English studies. Until the 1920s most of the foundational research on Elizabethan and Jacobean drama had been done by scholars who were technically amateurs – clergymen, gentlepersons with private incomes, civil servants, librarians, or dons in disciplines other than English. The arrival of the new bibliography with the generation of Pollard, McKerrow and Greg had led to a remarkable rise in scholarly standards, but even these three never held a university post in the discipline most directly concerned with the texts. By the 1920s all this was changing: publication in the field was beginning to be dominated by academic teachers of English studies who subscribed, for better or worse, to the scientistic ideals of the academy. Stainer's appeal against all this nonsense to the commonsense and good taste of the educated lay reader is the response of a dying generation to new forces it could no longer control and new kinds of power over the interpretation of literary texts which it could no longer resist. Characteristically, and no doubt correctly, the new experts did not even regard him as worthy of powder and shot.

Anxieties still bring on the desire to escape from the intractable contingencies of real history. The kind of stylometry whose ideal is the neural network which can operate independently of any consideration of either content or context is simply a modern reprise of the Cartesian retreat from the engulfing corpus of real-world particulars to the comfortable simplicities of number. Literary theory in our time has in much the same way retreated from the problematics of individual language to the production of endless permutations of a few no less comfortable epistemological paradoxes. To balance the ledger we should note that humanist rejections of stylometry are also the product of cultural anxiety – in this case that power over the authorship of texts and the authority to determine their cultural meaning is passing out of their control into that of neural networks. Hardouin in his mania to erase all questioning of a naive fideism and Stainer in his refusal to accept the disciplines of historical argument assist the experienced reader in identifying earlier and present-day crises of the same kind.

CONCLUSION

Fakes are, as said, an incessant and serious challenge to attribution studies. No one should get involved in the field who does not have inbuilt antennae for spotting them. We are all likely to be fooled from time to time, but we should never accept it with a good grace. What for the faker is a joke is a despoiling of serious efforts to understand the present and the past. Faking is the cancer of scholarship. The appropriate punishment for fakers should be public execution, with a last-minute interruption when a reprieve is brought to the gallows, only to be disregarded when it is discovered to be a fake.[32] Likewise there is nothing amusing in the fact that a fellow scholar may have been misled by a fake: it is a sign of incompetence and dereliction in the individual concerned. If one finds oneself in that situation one's response should not be one of wry amusement expressed in an ironic chuckle but profound self-disgust at failing in one's fundamental duty as an attributionist. Finding evidence of inauthenticity in work which is actually genuine is regrettable but an error in the right direction.

CHAPTER ELEVEN

Shakespeare and Co.

A book on attribution can hardly avoid discussing the authorship of what are conventionally known as 'Shakespeare's works'. These comprise a body of plays and poems from the late sixteenth and early seventeenth centuries which are widely, but not universally, accepted as composed by Warwickshire-born William Shakespeare (1564–1616). For this chapter this individual will be referred to as Will the player, but with the warning that a small splinter-group of dissidents maintain that Warwickshire Will was not the same person as the actor of the same name.[1] The plays are distinguished as a corpus by having been published in 1623 in the folio format also used for Jonson's works (1616), the authorship of which has never been doubted, and Beaumont and Fletcher's works (1647), which are believed to incorporate contributions by several other dramatists, including Will the player. The poems comprise two mythological narratives, a collection of 154 sonnets, 'The Lover's complaint', published with the sonnets, and a few shorter pieces.

External attributions are strongest for the two mythological poems, *The Rape of Lucrece* (1593) and *Venus and Adonis* (1594), both of which were published under Will the player's name during his lifetime in editions dedicated to his patron, the Earl of Southampton. The first edition of the *Sonnets* (1609) may not have been authorised (though Katharine Duncan-Jones has argued persuasively to the contrary[2]) and comes attended by mysteries which have aroused much speculation. Its title, *Shake-speares Sonnets. Never before Imprinted*, indicates that the name of the playwright was regarded as likely to attract readers. The publication of the plays was desultory at the start. Only eighteen out of the traditional canon of thirty-six were published during the lifetime of Will the player. Not all these lifetime editions bore his name, and none includes a formal dedication. This lack of authorially sanctioned editions, which so confuses editors, is what we would expect from a major company's 'ordinary poet' (i.e. house dramatist): Fletcher, Massinger and Shirley, who succeeded

Will the player in that office for the King's Men, also abstained from publishing contracted plays during their tenure.[3] In the contract signed by Richard Brome with the Salisbury Court company in 1635 – the only one from which we have actual wording – there was a clause specifically prohibiting publication without the permission of the company.[4] The 1623 folio, published by two of Will's fellow actors in the King's Men, bore the title *Mr William Shakespeare's Comedies, Histories, and Tragedies. Published according to the True Original Copies*, confirming that the name of Shakespeare possessed considerable drawing power. The work was a success, having three seventeenth-century reprints as against two for the collected Jonson and one for Beaumont and Fletcher. It was published with a dedication, a short preface, and four commendatory poems, three more being added in the second folio of 1632. Taken at face value this is very strong evidence indeed for Will the player's authorship of the plays comprising the first-folio canon. Had he been any other writer, it would never have come into question.

Objections and qualifications to the 'Stratfordian' thesis come in four forms. The first kind concerns the content of the corpus: some would add and others subtract. In the third and fourth folios it was extended by additional plays of which only *Pericles* is now accepted as containing work by Will the player. Recently there have been a number of suggested additions both of plays and poems (discussed below). A second qualification concerns the integrity of particular plays, with some generally recognised as collaborations, some suspected to contain revisions by other hands, and others believed to incorporate material taken over from earlier source-dramas. The extent of this indebtedness has been the subject of much discussion. A third and more radical questioning would accept the integrity of the corpus but would assign it to another author, the most favoured candidates being Christopher Marlowe, Francis Bacon, and the Earls of Derby, Oxford and Rutland. Finally there is a 'groupist' argument that would see Will the player as an unscrupulous plagiarist putting together contributions from a whole stable of (mostly) titled authors. This last position is that of John Michell's *Who Wrote Shakespeare?* (1996) which may be consulted as a handy source of information on the history of the debate. I will deal with these objections in order. It should also be noted that other works ranging from sections of the Authorised Version of the Bible to Masonic rituals have been attributed to Will the player. This I will not pursue.

At the very beginning of his career it is likely that Will the player wrote much as other professional dramatists did at that period, which is to say opportunistically and collaboratively. His role within the Lord Chamberlain's–King's Men from 1594 must have involved him in serving as a play-doctor for work by others and as a reviser of older scripts when they were brought back into the company's repertoire.[5] The hand-D section of the surviving manuscript of *Sir Thomas More* is believed to show him at work in the first of these roles, while the 1610 additions to *Mucedorus* may show him in the second. That the same treatment was given even during his lifetime to his own plays is shown by the surviving variant texts of *King Lear* and *Hamlet*, though most scholars would accept that he was himself the reviser in the first case and in one of the two revisions (*Q2* to *F1*) of the second. The search for Will the player's polishing or revising hand in the work of other dramatists is a valid project though one for which it is difficult to propose a methodology. Spellings and punctuation are only of circumscribed use at a time when such details were primarily determined by the compositor, who need not in any case have been working from an authorial manuscript. Parallels and echoes can work both ways: Will the player's well-stocked actor's memory may as well be recalling dramatist X as X imitating Will.[6] There may also be as yet unsuspected cases where Will the player worked as a collaborator (see below) rather than as a reviser. Two plays from outside the canon which have been claimed as wholly or substantially his are *Edmund Ironside* and *Edward III*.[7] There are also a number of flagrant Shakespearean fakes, the most notorious being W. H. Ireland's *Vortigern* (1796).

The corpus of the poems also comes under question. The collection called *The Passionate Pilgrim* (1599), published as by Will the player but presumably without his authority, contains several poems which are known to be by other hands as well as dubia. Two recent attempts to enlarge the corpus are the lyric 'If I die' advanced by Gary Taylor and the funeral elegy on William Peter claimed by Donald W. Foster.[8] Common sense would suggest that the huge body of anonymous lute-song and madrigal verse of the time contains unrecognised examples of his workmanship. Special significance naturally attaches to works published as by 'W. S.'; however, it is important to remember that this was an extremely common pair of initials.

Assent to the integrity, give or take a work or two, of the accepted Shakespeare corpus does not imply an acceptance of Will the player being the sole author of each and every play. We have already considered the likelihood that he was a reviser of the plays of others. Three late plays, *Henry VIII*, *The Two Noble Kinsmen* and *Cardenio* (the last of which survives only in an eighteenth-century *rifacimento*), are known to be collaborations with John Fletcher. *Timon of Athens*, *Measure for Measure* and the folio *Macbeth* probably contain contributions by Thomas Middleton and are to be included in the new Oxford University Press edition of Middleton's *Works*. In the first case it seems most likely that Middleton was working on a script which Shakespeare had abandoned; in the second and third Middleton appears to have revised the play for a revival. With *Pericles* it is widely held that Will the player's hand is most evident (or his words best preserved) in the last three acts, with the first two being the work of George Wilkins. Several plays, among them *Hamlet*, are believed to be based on earlier dramas by other hands and may take over lines from them. Few readers of the closing scenes of *Richard II* can fail to feel that a passage such as

> Kind vncle Yorck, the latest newes we heare
> Is, that the rebels have consumd with fire
> Our town of Ciceter in Gloucestershire
> But whether they be tane or slaine we heare not . . .
> (ll. 2648–51)

represents a considerable falling off from

> Not all the water in the rough rude sea
> Can wash the balme from an annointed king,
> The breath of worldly men cannot depose,
> The deputy elected by the Lord . . .
> (ll. 1353–6)

All of this offers work for attributionists, the task, as always, being one of turning suspicion into reasoned probability. Some plays from the folio corpus incorporate extensive material from non-dramatic sources. The 'history' and 'Roman' plays often show a verbal dependence on Raphael Holinshed's *Chronicles* and Thomas North's translation of Plutarch's *Lives of the Noble Grecians and Romans* that is sufficiently close to justify enroling the writers of these works as 'precursory authors' in the sense established earlier. The changes made to these passages are of great interest for what they reveal of the skills and intentions of the reviser.

One message for attributionists is that any attempt to establish a database of assured 'Shakespearean' usage and parallels has to involve careful assessment of the originality of the passages tested. Alternatively, one may accept the canon as a whole, hoping that its content of work by other authors is small enough not to affect broad results.

ALTERNATIVE AUTHORS

That Will the player was not the author of the plays assembled in the Shakespeare corpus has been asserted since the early nineteenth century by supporters of a number of claimants, beginning with Francis Bacon. The Baconian claim was one of a cluster of 'modern' attitudes that took shape in the 1840s. In the case of William Thomson (1819–83), who published seven works in support of Baconian authorship, anti-Stratfordian conclusions went hand in hand with economic views of an anti-free-trade persuasion, political reformism, evangelical Darwinism, and polemics in favour of the contagionists in the great medical debate against the miasmatists over the mode of transmission of infectious diseases. He also advocated improved methods for disposing of nightsoil.[9] The Baconian cause, with its reliance on ciphers and elaborate mathematical arguments, represented an attempt to appropriate Shakespeare for the emerging, number-based culture of scientists, engineers, evolutionary biologists and political arithmeticians. Subsequent attempts to claim authorship for such colourful characters as Marlowe and the literary aristocrats of the Elizabethan court represent an anti-scientistic move to reappropriate the plays for the older literary culture.

The arguments used to support the anti-Stratfordian case can be sampled in Michell's study. The problem that confronts all such attempts is that they have to dispose of the many testimonies from Will the player's own time that he was regarded as the author of the plays and the absence of clear contravening public claims of the same nature for any of the other favoured candidates. In order to do this, those who believe that other authors were responsible for the canon as a whole (rather than individual plays or parts of plays) have been forced to invoke elaborate conspiracy theories. So, to take one example, the fact that very few documentary records of Shakespeare's life and business dealings survive becomes evidence for a deliberate suppression. Consider Michell:

> A significant feature of Shakspere's life-history, which has often been commented on, is that virtually all the records that would have referred to him have mysteriously vanished. . . . The suspicion is that someone or some agency, backed by the resources of government, has at some early period 'weeded' the archives and suppressed documents with any bearing on William Shakspere and his part in the Authorship mystery.[10]

The simpler explanation would be that there was never any authorship mystery and that the imagined records 'that would have referred to him' never existed or have suffered from the normal accidents of time. As almost a routine move, the character of Will the player has systematically to be blackened: he must be branded as deceptive, unscrupulous, a plagiarist, violent, mercenary and ignorant. Two rhetorical strategies are customarily deployed. By the first, any piece of existing evidence has to be given the most unfavourable spin possible. So, when in 1596 Will the player was enjoined to keep the peace in a petition by a shady character named William Wayte, this becomes part of a battle for 'control of the local vice trade and organized crime'. By the second, the absence of evidence, e.g. the fact that we possess only one apparent literary manuscript, has to be interpreted in a pejorative rather than a neutral or positive sense (Will the player was illiterate).[11] This process of character assassination must then be extended to those among Shakespeare's contemporaries who attest to his authorship. Ben Jonson has to be made a liar in his expressed admiration for Shakespeare. Hemming and Condell must have regarded 'the office of their care, and pain' in the compilation of the First Folio as a vast practical joke. A substantial part of the aristocracy also has to be allowed a giggle. And so on!

The weakness of arguments based on conspiracy theories is that they are by definition unfalsifiable. On the one hand, any evidence in favour of the position attacked simply becomes part of the conspiracy; on the other, because the 'real' author's identity is, by definition, something concealed by the conspirators, and only to be revealed in oblique and allusive ways, fortuitous verbal formulations can be presented as loaded with covert meaning. Anything that sounds a bit odd to modern ears becomes an excuse to plumb for hidden messages. A further weakness of the anti-Attributionist case is that appeals are constantly made to probabilities without any attempt being made to assess the statistical weight of those probabilities, which when they exist as elements of a sorites rapidly multiply into impossibility.[12] Finally there is an insistent tendency in such writings to present 'orthodox' scholars as conservative and unquestioning simply because they are not prepared to discard clear documentary testimony.

Such methods cannot fail to impart a paranoid tone to the arguments of the anti-Stratfordians, which is accentuated when, as often happens, extensive reliance is placed on coded messages of various kinds extracted from the Shakespearean text. The Baconian cause has been a magnet for cryptographers, whole books of messages having been extracted by such means. Supporters of the Earl of Oxford, whose family name was De Vere, also appeal to alleged coded versions of his name; however, seeing that this is likely to happen whenever the common words 'ever' and 'never' occur in the proximity of a 'd', few are even remotely persuasive. Usually anti-Stratfordian arguments rest on the prior assumption of what is to be found. (Bacon is the real author: therefore any reference to hogs or pigs must be part of a coded message.) Michell gives the game away when he quotes a predecessor recommending exactly this procedure:

> If one follows Looney's advice, becomes familiar with Oxford's biography and then reads *Hamlet* and the other plays with him in mind, numerous references to him and his associates can be identified. (p. 171)

Vladimir Nabokov's *Pale Fire*, in which a demented editor misreads a text as referring to himself when nothing of the kind was intended, is the clinching refutation of this mode of reasoning. It has more than once been claimed that the combination of 'biographical-fit' and cryptographical arguments could be used to establish a case for almost any individual of Shakespeare's (or our own) time selected at random.[13] The very fact that their application has produced so many rival claimants demonstrates their unreliability.

Shakespeare claimants tend to have their half-century of fame and pass on. Bacon has few if any remaining supporters, with the smart money now directed at Marlowe or the Earl of Oxford. The case for Marlowe rests on the assertion that he was not really killed at Deptford in 1593 but was spirited away to write plays under the name of Shakespeare. I find it hard to accept current theories that the death of Marlowe was a political assassination. To do so we would also have to believe that if British intelligence had wanted to murder a modern Christopher Marlowe they would have arranged a day-long drinking party with James Bond, Callan, George Smiley and Kim Philby, all of whom would have given their correct names to the police. It seems much more plausible that Marlowe was an aggressive drunk and had pulled a knife on Ingram Frizer (also drunk) during an argument over the bill. The bizarre 'spiriting away' theory can only be given credence by further arbitrary assertions (e.g. that Marlowe was Walsingham's lover) but, even if that was found to be true, it would not follow that Marlowe continued writing plays or that those plays were fathered by Shakespeare rather than, say, Chapman. Bate points out that Marlowe has no interest at all in politics, except that of a fascistic, world-dominating kind, whereas Shakespeare is fascinated by the political process in all its complexity.[14] The stylometric evidence for separate authorship is also strong, as can be seen from Thomas Merriam's results discussed on p. 159.

The case for Oxford is hampered from the start by the fact that he died in 1604, whereas new plays attributed to Will the player continued to appear for a number of years after that date. The most that can be said for it is that it gives a superficially more 'Hamlet-like' Shakespeare – the reason for its appeal to Sigmund Freud; but against this we cannot assert that Shakespeare was not himself distinctly Hamlet-like: we have too little evidence even to speculate about the matter. In any case, why should dramatists be expected to resemble their characters? Anti-Stratfordians lay great stress on the gap between the idealised Shakespeare of the text and the London actor-businessman and Stratford bourgeois of the records, but such divisions in a life are far from rare: one thinks of Samuel Richardson, simultaneously a novelist admired for his intimate understanding of the workings of the female heart and a ruthlessly efficient master printer, and of Wallace Stevens, the most refined of modernist poets and a successful insurance executive. Australia's finest twentieth-century lyric poet, John Shaw Neilson, the author of post-symbolist verse of rare delicacy, worked for several years as a quarryman, smashing rocks with a sledgehammer.

But even to formulate the question 'How can the Stratford booby have written these immortal plays?' is to beg it: the writer of the plays was clearly a person of exceptional natural gifts, wherever and however they arose. An implied assumption of anti-Stratfordian claims that would father the plays on a member of the aristocracy is that such endowments are primarily genetic and therefore more likely to emerge in noble families such as Oxford's or Rutland's. But the Tudor aristocracy was emphatically not the product of natural selection over many generations for literary and artistic skill but purely for political and military prowess. Darwinian imperatives were extremely severe in their case, since failure in either criterion was likely to lead to death on the battlefield or on the block. That the possession of an artistic sensibility might have been disadvantageous for survival is suggested by the cases of Wyatt, Surrey, Raleigh and Falkland – to look no further. The female line could hardly have contributed since their marriages were normally arranged ones with members of their own class. Genetic distinctiveness of the extreme kind assumed by these writers for Shakespeare is infinitely more likely to have arisen from the population at large than from the very small number of males bred for power who held the rank of earl or lord in Elizabethan England.

The same applies to the argument that only an aristocrat would have possessed the breadth of knowledge evident in the plays. There is a long tradition of books by members of various professions – lawyers, doctors, sailors, soldiers, schoolteachers, diplomats, royal functionaries and followers of various kinds of archaic sports – arguing that references to their particular mystery in the Shakespeare corpus reveal a knowledge so profound that the author must at one time have been a practitioner of the nominated profession/craft/sport. Assuming that these are accurate judgements, it needs to be explained how this knowledge was acquired. For a start, not all these activities could have been essayed by one person in the relatively brief period before Will the player emerges as a professional actor. On the other hand the humbly born polymath author is far from unusual: James Joyce in the twentieth century and Dickens in the nineteenth are both shining examples. It has never been suggested that Dickens had to be a lawyer to have written *Bleak House*, or Joyce a professor of linguistics to have written *Finnegans Wake*. In Shakespeare's case it is easy to imagine him socialising with Inns-of-Court students in the Devil's Tavern in order to clarify legal issues arising from his plays: with the students forming an influential part of his audience, these were things he simply had to get right. And so on for other kinds of specialised knowledge.

The absence (already mentioned) of surviving documents, letters or even books containing Shakespeare's name is another problem: one would expect a hard-working writing life to leave more material traces. On the other hand two historically attested fires, the burning down of the Globe in 1613 and the destruction of what remained of Shakespeare's London in 1666, provide a perfectly adequate explanation. As for any documents left in Stratford, it is quite likely that they were put to the hundred-and-one domestic uses to which paper fell victim at a time when it was a much needed but relatively expensive substance. (Few Shakespeareans will not have encountered the story of Warburton's cook destroying a large part of a volume of Jacobean plays in order to provide paper to support pie-crusts.) Moreover, the absence of authorial manuscripts is far from uncommon even among considerable writers. The dramatist Nathaniel Lee (1649–92) produced thirteen successful plays for the London stage, some of which were regularly revived for over a century, but, apart from the dubious case of a printed volume of his *Nero* with handwritten corrections, has not left a manuscript of any kind.

Another way in which the anti-Stratfordian case is unpersuasive is its failure to acknowledge the technical aspects of writing a play for the Elizabethan stage. The candidates are invariably amateurs. Actors through the ages have, on the whole, always been confident that the plays were written by a member of their own profession because of the many subtle ways in which scenes and bits of business are found to work theatrically, even with stages and audiences remote from those for which they were originally intended, and despite being written in a now archaic form of the English language. Beyond that, the writing of a play for the Elizabethan public stage was a highly technical activity. Bentley's *The Profession of Dramatist* and Andrew Gurr's standard studies[15] indicate some aspects of this: the need to tailor roles to particular players, the constraints of the censorship and licensing systems, the constant allowance that had to be made for hostile municipal authorities. A further complication was the need for plays to be effectively 'plotted' so as to permit thirty or more characters to be portrayed by a much smaller body of actors. David Bradley's *From Text to Performance in the Elizabethan Theatre: Preparing the Play for the Stage*[16] explores the formidable difficulties of this particular aspect of the dramatist's craft. Amateurs in Shakespeare's time did write plays but they were not tailor-made professional performances like those attributed to Will the player; rather they wrote for performance before captive audiences at universities (where they were usually in Latin and might last five or six hours), for the houses of the great, or for the printed or manuscript page. The only sensible reason ever suggested why members of the aristocracy might have wanted their plays to be performed on the public stage is as a programme of political propaganda masterminded from the court; but even in that case it would surely have been obvious that the task was better left to sympathetic professionals.

CIRCUMSTANTIAL EVIDENCE

The Shakespeare authorship controversy is an appropriate place to review the role of circumstantial evidence in scholarly reasoning, since most of the proposed demonstrations are of this kind. The presentation of circumstantial evidence usually takes the form of the bringing together of a series of indications which in themselves are not strong or convincing in the hope that they will be more impressive as a unity. One simple example, described in Chapter four, is the method of parallels as it used to be employed in attribution studies on Elizabethan drama. The error of this practice was pointed out by Byrne, who in her five rules, quoted earlier, laid down the conditions that had to be obeyed in work of this kind if it was to be to any degree persuasive.[17]

Circumstantial evidence is frequently associated with chains of reasoning similar to the Aristotelian sorites. These take the forms: if A is the case then B, if B is the case then C, and if C is the case then D, and so on. All such chains depend on the strength of the weakest link. If the probability that can be assigned to the various links is uniformly low, the overall probability (as the product of all the individual ones) is likely to be beneath consideration. And yet such arguments continue to appear. An example of a chain stretched to the point where its links barely cohere is given by Michell[18] from Colonel B. R. Ward's *The Mystery of 'Mr W. H.'* (1922). The stages in the argument may be summarised as follows:

(1) The phrase 'onlie begetter' in the dedication to the first edition of Shakespeare's sonnets refers, not to the author or the inspirer, but to the person who obtained the manuscript for the bookseller, Thomas Thorpe.
(2) This name is encoded in the phrase 'M^{r}.W.H.ALL.HAPPINESSE' found in Thomas Thorpe's dedication to the volume, and is in fact that of William Hall, 'one of Thorpe's occasional collaborators' (a theory of the Shakespearean scholar Sir Sidney Lee).
(3) In 1606, three years before the publication of the sonnets, William Hall the stationer had published a poem by the Jesuit Robert Southwell, which was printed by George Eld who also printed the sonnets.
(4) Southwell's place of refuge had been the house of Lord Vaux at Hackney.
(5) The Earl of Oxford also lived at Hackney.
(6) A William Hall was married in Hackney church in 1608. He may therefore have had access to Oxford's house.
(7) William Hall of Hackney may have been the same person as Thorpe's associate William Hall.
(8) Oxford's house 'King's Place' may have been the house at Hackney at which Vaux had sheltered Southwell. If so Southwell's manuscript may have been found there.
(9) The manuscript of the sonnets was found by William Hall of Hackney in Oxford's house or disposed of to him after Oxford's house was sold.
(10) The sonnets were entered on the Stationers' Register nine months after the marriage of William Hall of Hackney and may have marked the birth of his first child.
(11) Therefore Oxford, not Shakespeare, is the author of the sonnets.

Expressed as a chain of linked propositions this would run as follows. **If** Lee's interpretation of the meaning of the dedication is correct, **and if** the dedication also contains a covert allusion to William Hall, **and if** William Hall the stationer is the same person as William Hall of Hackney, **and if** William Hall of Hackney was able to obtain manuscripts from King's Place, **and if** one of these was the manuscript of the sonnets, **and if** possession of a manuscript of a work makes one (1) its author and (2) its 'onlie begetter', **and if** all countervailing evidence that Shakespeare was the author of the sonnets (including his name on the title-page) is totally incorrect, the conclusion would indeed follow. But it requires only one of these links to fail to sink the entire theory, and all of them are so extremely fragile that only the prior assumption that Oxford was the author of Shakespeare's works would have allowed them to be accepted for a moment. If very charitably we were to assign each of them a one in five probability of being true, and then multiplied these probabilities, we would have odds of 78,125 to one against. This is not the stuff that conclusions are made on and if the gallant colonel applied the same kind of reasoning to military intelligence received in the field his regiment must have waited a long time between victories.

Actually, this particular argument is a mixture of the chain and the skein. The difference has been clarified by a legal authority:

> It has been said that circumstantial evidence is to be considered as a *chain*, and each piece of evidence as a link in the chain; but that is not so, for then, if any one link broke the chain would fall. It is more like the case of a rope composed of several cords. One strand of the cord might be insufficient to sustain the weight, but three stranded together may be quite of sufficient strength.[19]

This suggests a different way of relating evidence and assessing probabilities. If we had three or four genuinely independent skeins we might even be in a position to combine rather than multiply out their probabilities. In the present case the link most directly affected is that which identifies William Hall of Hackney with the William Hall who procured the Southwell manuscript for Eld. The name itself must have been a common one: Hall is frequently encountered at the time as a surname and William is a very common forename. I would be surprised if there were fewer than a hundred adult males of this name in London during the years concerned, a probability itself sufficient to sink the argument. A skein-like element appears again in the connection of Robert Southwell and one of these William Halls with Hackney. But this skein is still only cobweb-thin: since recusant families had elaborate networks for transmitting texts in manuscript, work by Southwell may have come to William Hall the stationer from dozens of sources. What plausibility Ward's argument possesses comes from its blatant circularity. Oxford's authorship, which the demonstration is supposed to prove, has actually been assumed from the start. The question as presented to the reader is 'Is there documentary proof that Oxford was the author of the sonnets?' The real question is 'Since we already believe that Oxford was the author of the sonnets, can we think of some way in which they may have come into the hands of Thomas Thorpe?'

Virtuosi of circularity will frequently indulge in the advanced form which we might call 'looping the loop'. In this a whole series of assumptions are used to support each other progressively. Consider Schoenbaum on John Mackinnon Robertson's attempt to disprove the Shakespearean authorship of *Titus Andronicus*:

> Robertson's range extends far beyond the play that is his point of departure and return. He sees, as an aspect of his task, the identification of the 'unsigned work' of Peele, Greene, and Lodge. As he moves along, assumption provides a basis for further assumption. Having accepted the anonymous *George a Greene* as Greene's, Robertson uses it as evidence for that playwright's participation in *Edward III*. After tracing Peele in *Titus*, he can say that the *Titus*-word *remunerate* points to his hand in the *Troublesome Reign*.[20]

Here we only have to invoke Schoenbaum's addition to Byrne's five rules: 'parallels from plays of uncertain or contested authorship prove nothing'.[21] Robertson was in good company though; Edmond Malone, having 'decided that *Titus* could not be Shakespeare's, . . . used this exclusion as support for his theories regarding the authenticity of *Henry VI* – thus providing an ominous early illustration of the tendency of canonical investigators to set forth a hypothesis, then urge it as a fact in support of a subsequent hypothesis'.[22]

Arguments relying on circumstantial evidence often require strenuous arguing away of contradictory evidence. This may be done with a greater or lesser degree of ingenuity but the signs should be noted and each dismissal carefully assessed. Let us assume that a writer's recorded birth or death date is inconvenient for an argument. The suggestion might be made that the informant was misinformed or that there was a scribal error in the source (counting stonemasons as scribes when the evidence is on a tombstone) or that the evidence may have been deliberately falsified or 'weeded' for some reason, plausible or implausible. All of these things did occasionally happen; however, the majority of official records are accurately recorded and an argument that becomes over-reliant on the dismissal of such evidence should be viewed with suspicion. When arguments can only be justified by fanciful conspiracy theories (so frequent in writings on the Shakespeare claimants) they will persuade only the already committed.

THE GROUPIST ARGUMENT

I have left till last the theory that Shakespeare's works are not the product of a single predominating author but of a club of authors using Will the player as their agent and editor. Theories of this kind first emerged as the result of attempts to obviate difficulties in the cases for particular claimants. Since Oxford who died in 1604 was an implausible candidate for the authorship of the later plays and the Earl of Rutland, who was born in 1576, was too young to have written the early ones, it was tempting to hypothesise a group in which both were active. Michell (pp. 242–3) lists fourteen such groups put forward by various authors. Their membership may be summarised in terms of the number of times each individual appears: Bacon (8), Ralegh (6), Marlowe, Earl of Rutland (5), Earl of Oxford, Shakespeare (4), Daniel, Earl of Derby, Countess of Pembroke, Sir Philip Sidney, Earl of Southampton (3), Barnes, Greene, Nashe, Peele, Spenser (2); others singly (21). Michell adds to these a picture of Shakespeare as a universal plagiarist, receiving scenes and whole dramas from a variety of sources and stitching them together into actable plays:

> Shakspere was the channel through which Somebody, together with several others unknown, infiltrated their writings into the theatre and publishing house. These were not always finished plays, but speeches, lyrics and dramatic passages in the form, perhaps, of old-style masques. As a finder and broker of plays, Shakspere had access to the best writings of his contemporaries as well as to old works. Taking from here and there he made a modern drama out of the materials he had been given, bridging gaps with lines of his own writing. The result was highly successful. Shakspere was a professional and knew how to please both the actors and the theatre audience. At this sort of work he was, perhaps, a genius.[23]

This picture, though much more extreme, and implying the usual conspiracy theory, is not unrelated to the way in which Will the player probably worked on older plays to prepare them for a return to the repertoire. It also has elements in common with Bate's view of Shakespeare's memory as packed with reminiscences of earlier drama. But for Bate this is not a passive process; instead Shakespeare is transforming, rethinking, resisting, wrestling with this material in a fierce attempt to become a strong artist in the Bloomian sense. This is also what we see in his reworking of known sources, such as Bate's example of 'The barge she sat in' speech from *Antony and Cleopatra* in its remaking from the prose text of North's *Plutarch*.[24] Above all, this picture of the plays as Frankenstein's monsters put together from differently authored parts denies the possibility of a Shakespearean voice, and in so doing robs the plays of what is, for most of us, their main interest.

CHAPTER TWELVE

Arguing attribution

In the previous chapters we have looked at various aspects of the present and past practice of attribution studies. In the course of this exploration a number of general questions were raised about the nature of the attributionist project and the modes of argument employed in it. The time has now come to draw this scattered material together.

CRITERIA OF PROOF

The criteria for the acceptance of an attribution as proven have traditionally been based on legal models for the evaluation of evidence. The law (especially criminal law) is charged with making decisions about matters of fact and motive concerning events which were rarely the object of careful scrutiny at the time: so is attributional scholarship. The law, at least in countries with a common law tradition, is based on both adversarial and deliberative modes of argument, the first instanced in the plea of the barrister or attorney and the second in the summing up of the judge. Most scholarly books and articles can be classified under one or the other category. Both institutions have to assess the credibility of testimony and have developed elaborate protocols for doing this. Certain basic standards of proof are common to both. In criminal law, guilt has to be proved beyond reasonable doubt; in civil cases the balance of probability determines the findings. In attribution studies the second would be sufficient to let a received attribution stand but, for reasons given by Furbank and Owens, it would require the first to overturn an accepted attribution or to establish a new one from scratch.[1] Above all, both are rhetorical systems, based on persuasion and adjudication leading, in successful cases, to consensus. This 'forensic' view of literary scholarship has been the subject of much discussion over the last decade, especially in textual and editorial studies.[2] 'Where there can be no final proof', Gary Taylor writes, 'everything depends upon persuasion, and rhetoric is the agent of persuasion' (p. 44). Aristotle would have agreed entirely. Richard Filloy argues that 'satisfying an audience, as large as the world or as small as the individual, is the province of rhetoric; and those who do it well . . . may be fairly said to be reading rhetorically'.[3] An argument that does not persuade may still possibly be correct but will have failed in its purpose.

There is a tendency to assume that rhetorical methods of proof are somehow inferior to as well as different from scientific or mathematical ones. The fact, as any organic chemist who has been before a court on a bigamy charge can vouch, is that both are very effective in their own fields, but that each serves a different purpose, draws on different kinds of data, and has different ways of using that data. If Morton's kind of stylometry could ever validate itself as a science, questions of attribution might pass entirely into the mathematical realm; but this, as we saw in Chapter eight, is still only an aspiration. In any case, it is only the processing of scores in stylometry that is 'objective' or, more cautiously, may be so, because such work can still be well or poorly done: the entry into history to appropriate the text, the choice of ways of representing the text in quantitative form, and the return to history to submit quantitative conclusions to communal adjudication all involve qualitative judgements, as most practitioners are aware. Any attempt to create an 'hermetic' standing for stylometric findings denies both the intensely contingent nature of the materials and the researchers' own historicity as agents within an evolving and highly disputatious discipline. A stylometry that forgets that it is a study of the historical conducted from within history is deceiving itself. For Taylor, the only difference between a scholarly editor and a physicist is that 'physicists calculate their probabilities very precisely' (p. 44). Physics no less than literary scholarship depends 'upon the ability of a clique of adherents to persuade a majority of potential practitioners' (p. 53). The present situation in attribution studies is that evidence gained from quantitative analysis has to submit itself to a broader, rhetorically conducted system of assessment. Its influence within this process may be to sweep all before it; however, it is not a substitute for the adjudicatory process but a contributor to it, and is ultimately bound by its rules. The stylometrist is an expert witness – not a learned judge. Indeed, this pattern works at two levels, for the stylometrical conclusion has to persuade the community of stylometrists before it can even be presented to the wider constituency of humanists, and there are as many figures, tropes, enthymemes and rebuttals to be discovered in the pages of *Computers and the Humanities* as in *The Review of*

English Studies. It is possible, of course, for the roles of expert witness and adjudicator to be performed by one well-rounded scholar; but the widely varied kinds of expertise required for advanced work in the discipline make this a rare happening.

QUALITATIVE AND QUANTITATIVE CRITERIA

The value of a rhetorically based system of proof is that it can make use of qualitative as well as quantitative evidence. Few scientists today would grant universal applicability to Rutherford's quip that 'qualitative is just poor quantitative'. The biomathematician Ian Stewart points out that

> there are many circumstances in which qualitative information is what really counts, and quantitative measurements are a rather poor route toward finding that information. For example, the most important question about a bridge is, 'will it fall down?' and calculating its precise numerical breaking strain on a supercomputer is just an exceedingly complicated way to get a yes/no answer – and perhaps an unnecessarily complicated one.[4]

The drawback of qualitative judgements lies in a reduced capacity, compared with quantitative reasoning, to compel conviction.

Why attribution studies needs both kinds of judgement can be shown by a thought experiment. On a distant planet in a far-off galaxy two authors are born in the same city at the same time and given the same education. One grows up to be a great writer and the other a dreadful one; but, because of the common influences at work, their modes of writing are syntactically indistinguishable. Author A (the genius) writes inspiring works which contain sentences such as 'To be or not to be that is the question' and 'We hold these truths to be self-evident' while the works of the other contain equivalent statements in the form 'To be or not to be that is the pumpkin' and 'We hold these fish to be incontinent.' It would be immediately obvious to literary readers, on qualitative grounds alone, that two authors were involved; yet a quantitative investigation would have difficulty in distinguishing between them. In an analogy borrowed from Peter Groves, to deny the validity of these judgements would be equivalent to 'denying the reality of perspective in Renaissance art because it doesn't show up in a chemical analysis of the pigments'.[5] Of course, neither perspective nor individual style are present in the object as such: rather, some configuration of the object activates patterns of recognition and process in the form-composing brain. The perceptions involved in each case are genuine though the ability to perceive them may be possessed to a greater or a lesser degree and the actual experience may well differ from individual to individual. The problem for scholarship is not that such judgements are unquantifiable but how they are to be moderated, which must be through some kind of process of adjudication by those whom Taylor calls 'the readers who matter' (p. 47).

The thought-experiment also problematises the definitions of style used by stylometrists. Rudman claims that 'The statement that there are elements of style that cannot be quantified is moot. I believe that all elements of style can be isolated in their essence and therefore be quantified.'[6] But this is merely to set up a circular definition of style that excludes the unquantifiable. Holmes avoids the problem by acknowledging it:

> The stylometrist therefore looks for a unit of counting which translates accurately the 'style' of the text, where we may define 'style' as a set of measurable patterns which may be unique to an author.[7]

This is at least consistent but it discards many aspects of language that would be immediately evident to a reader and might well constitute that reader's principal reason for being interested in the text in the first place. How might purely quantitative tests distinguish the prose of Swift's *A Modest Proposal*, whose characteristic stylistic feature is its bitter, wounding irony, from Swift's unironic prose or from that of the political arithmeticians whom Swift parodies? (The thought of a neural network set to work to distinguish the ironic from the unironic is an intriguing one.) Rather than hijacking the useful word 'style', purely quantitative stylometrists need to find a new term for what they are investigating, which, as Holmes shows, is no more and no less than a particular subset of stylistic features which show a constant periodicity.

MARKERS AND REPRESENTATIONS

Alongside methods for the establishment of proof, a second salient issue affecting the status of attributional arguments is the way in which researchers represent the texts that are the subject of their investigations and the relative fullness of these representations. To clarify the problem of relative fullness we might consider three levels positioned between near-totality and near-emptiness. When Erasmus studied his Jerome-spuria or Bentley his Phalaris, using a combination of scholarly understanding and intuitive response to features of language, every word of the text was significant and no aspect of internal or external evidence excluded. This is our first level. In a present-day stylometric study using principal component analysis on a list of forty or fifty high-frequency words, the work would be represented by one specific kind of information about perhaps half the total number of tokens and a considerably smaller proportion of the total number of types; moreover, some information about such matters as syntax would still be retained vestigially through the word frequencies. This is our second level. Finally, let us consider a test of Morton's kind which looked only at a small number of isolated verbal habits, collectively comprising a very small proportion of the word types of the text, though, seeing these would mostly be common ones, a higher proportion of tokens. In this case there would be no pretence of *representing* the work as such; instead, the concentration would be entirely on discrete linguistic practices. This point is made not to suggest that any one of the three levels (or any intervening one on the scale they create) is better or worse than the others for the purpose of distinguishing authors – in a given situation it might well be the slimmest representation that gave the best result – but simply to establish fullness as one aspect of the wider question of ways of representation.

One measure of fullness would be reversibility, measured by the extent to which knowledge of the samples which represent the work allows us to reconstruct the nature of the work. With Erasmus and Bentley there would be no difficulty since the sample was the whole work. In our second instance the raw frequency lists and scatter plots would preserve some basic information about content and style. Calvino wittily demonstrates in *If On a Winter's Night a Traveller* how much a frequency list of a novel's vocabulary can convey of the character of the originating work. In the passage concerned, Lotaria, who has no interest in reading as such, performs precisely the operation we have just described:

> 'Look here. Words that appear nineteen times:
> blood, cartridge belt, commander, do, have, immediately, it,
> life, seen, sentry, shots, spider, teeth, together, your . . .
> 'Words that appear eighteen times:
> boys, cap, come, dead, eat, enough, evening, French, go,
> handsome, new, passes, period, potatoes, those, until . . .
> 'Don't you already have a clear idea what it's about?' Lotaria says.
> 'There's no question: it's a war novel, all action, brisk writing, with a certain underlying violence. The narration is entirely on the surface, I would say; but to make sure, it's always a good idea to take a look at the list of words used only once, though no less important for that.'[8]

A full frequency list, then, preserves quite a rich body of information about the text independent of any kind of processing to which it might be subjected. But a collection of frequencies for collocations would tell one next to nothing about the content or even the style of the originating text. In this case, the selecting process is profoundly entropic: it sheds nearly all the information that would be most likely to interest a reader of the work. A single distinguishing habit – say, a preference for 'someone' over 'somebody' – would tell us even less.[9]

Having made these distinctions it is tempting to look briefly at the possibility of a linkage between the quantitative concepts sample, distinguishing habit and frequency and their rhetorical counterparts synecdoche, metonymy and metaphor. The sample is a part of the overall data set chosen to represent the whole; the distinguishing habit a subordinate aspect of style which is always present in the work of the particular writer while not in any meaningful sense representing it. That a Middleton prefers 'push' to 'pish' is an arbitrary choice that has nothing to do with the part of him that thinks and composes dialogue for his characters. The rhetorical counterpart of the sample is the trope of synecdoche in which a part of something stands for the whole ('I went to see a leg show'); that of the distinguishing habit is metonymy, defined by Dupriez and Halsall as 'a trope which allows the designation of one thing by the name of some element belonging to the same whole, on the strength of some sufficiently obvious relationship'.[10] Metonymy is used when someone claims to be prepared to die for the flag or the crown (the iron boot of tyranny, on the other hand, is a metaphor). There is nothing in the intrinsic nature of a crown that makes it expressive of monarchy: its referential power comes from the fact that monarchs have chosen to wear them.

The frequency as a mathematical derivative of the verbal data is something different again. If we consider a table of numerical values and their extracted ratios, such as those given by Farringdon at the conclusion of the Fielding *New Essays*, and ask in what way it 'figures' the texts in the rhetorical sense of the word, one possible answer would be that it is another form of metonymy; but calling a frequency a metonymy does not explain very much: a bolder view, familiar to rhetoricians, is that mathematical *proportion* is a form of metaphor not of metonymy. Dupriez and Halsall define metaphor as 'a transfer from one meaning to another through a personal operation based on an impression or interpretation which readers must discover or experience for themselves' (p. 276). Once we begin to consider tables of frequencies (and any subsequent derivations) as metaphors for the work rather than an abstracted part of it, we cease to be concerned with any representative power they may possess. Instead, their function becomes one of designating or characterising but in a much more complex way than the distinguishing habit. The operation required of the reader is primarily a mathematical one, but not entirely, as it requires a negotiation between the quantitative and the qualitative, not just a reduction of the second into the first. The establishment even of a rough and ready equivalence between statistical categories and rhetorical ones is a further bridge beween the two systems of argument.

So once again the logic of attribution studies turns out to be a rhetoric. This does not mean that it is illogical, rather that it follows the recommendation of Aristotle in making logic the servant of rhetoric: rhetorical proofs still have to be logical. Quantitative evidence, although in many cases the most powerful we have, reveals its figurative nature when it enters the rhetorical system of proof. To do this it has to surrender its Platonic assumption that it stands apart from the world of contingency and accept its participation in the practical functions of language, which include the deliberative. Within the rhetorical system, the aim of quantitative reasoning is (1) to test hypotheses erected on the basis of qualitative reasoning, and (2) to propose conclusions to be deliberated. In cases where the qualitative evidence is weak, we will probably accept the quantitative as decisive; but where the qualitative appears to contradict the quantitative we will fear the pumpkin scenario. A judgement arrived at through quantitative reasoning that does not *persuade* through other than quantitative means may well be rejected for reasons that have been considered above and in Chapter eight. This situation seems likely to apply for as long as stylometry is creating its results on behalf of the community of literary and historical scholars and the institution of the law, and for their use. Were it ever to reinvent itself as a sub-discipline of genetics, neurobiology, experimental psychology, or cognitive linguistics this situation might need to be reconsidered; but there is little sign of that to date.

PROBABILITIES IN ATTRIBUTION

It remains to apply some of these conceptions to attributional practice. Both qualitative and quantitative processes of proof in the discipline offer their results in the form of probabilities. Statistical stylometry is often able, following Taylor, to be very precise about its probabilities because they are calculated, while rhetorical and black-box kinds of scholarly adjudication assign them to broad bands. The following band-categories are proposed for this purpose: (1) assured attribution, (2) confident attribution, (3) tentative attribution, and (4) plausible speculation. These have their exact mirror images in four categories of disattribution. Disattribution requires the additional categories of (5) confident discrediting of an existing attribution, and (6) informed suspicion.

- An assured attribution or deattribution is one that is genuinely beyond reasonable doubt: a case that is supported by strong evidence of several kinds, including the stylometric, and for which there is no arguable alternative.
- A confident attribution or deattribution might rest on one particular result (say a positive stylometric finding) with generally supportive internal and external evidence and with no tenable alternative, or by a range of good positive results with one anomalous negative that cannot at present be accounted for.
- A tentative attribution or deattribution would characteristically be the result of a process of arbitration between one body of evidence in favour and another against, with the decision coming down on a particular side only through the balance of probabilities. This kind of work needs to be done from time to time, though its results may not be particularly exciting.
- A plausible speculation is simply a piece of evidence or argument which falls a good way short of establishing an attribution but might prove valuable if further data were to emerge. It is submitted to the framer of some wider future argument, which it may encourage.

Anything below this level is not worth recording from the point of view of attribution and should simply be filed away privately as an unsupported hunch until further evidence is secured. Disattribution requires the following additional categories:

- Confident discrediting of an existing attribution is what has been done so effectively by Vieth with regard to Rochester and Furbank and Owens with regard to Defoe. It rests on historical investigation of the circumstances under which an attribution was originally made. When an attribution has been made without knowledge or authority, it simply lapses. Because this method does not consider the work as such, only what has been asserted about it, it may reject correct attributions along with insufficiently grounded ones.
- Informed suspicion. There are cases when a traditional attribution exists but is relatively weak and external, internal or stylistic evidence

casts some doubt on it. In this case one might legitimately wish to move the work into the limbo category of 'author unknown', which is that of the great majority of the anonymous and pseudonymous texts of the world.

Attributionists would do well to use these categories conservatively: experience shows a common tendency to overstate results and to cling defiantly to unsubstantiable causes. This brings us to another subject, that of *parti pris* in attribution studies.

BIAS IN ATTRIBUTION

That our search for the author takes place within the social institution of humanistic scholarship calls for us to be keenly aware of the human dynamics of that institution. For attribution studies to be more than a scholarly exercise undertaken in the hope of yielding some unpredictable future benefit or as a way of testing techniques, there has to be something one urgently needs to know. Either investigations arise from acutely felt problems or are undertaken with the intention of generating them. Countless cases of anonymous authorship will never be investigated because they are not part of a problem. The reasons for choosing to work on one case rather than another are generally ideological ones in the broader sense of the term. Certain authors and certain works matter to us much more than others, even if we are not always sure of the reasons why.

Once attribution becomes problem-driven there is also likely to be bias involved. More is at stake, both personally and institutionally, than simply identifying an author or mode of authorship. For biographers, in particular, the peripheral work, the dubious attribution or the tempting addition of new work to the canon might be vital to the interpretation of the religious belief, political stance or sexual orientation of the presumed author. (Did Virgil write the distinctly unheroic poem about the pleasures of lounging in bars called the 'Copa Surisca'? Did Milton write the anti-Trinitarian *De doctrina Christiana*? Was Puritan Marvell the author of the pro-Royalist Francis Villiers elegy and 'Tom May's death'?) It is exactly those works which authors themselves might have found embarrassing that are most likely to appear surreptitiously or anonymously. On the other hand, when *parti pris* also exists among their contemporaries, these same works are the ones most likely to be claimed for the corpus by those with an axe to grind.

The best way of dealing with bias in scholarship is to declare it. Where it is not declared the reader should always be alert for it. Erasmus's zeal against the Jerome 'forger' is clearly influenced by his intense dislike of the Augustinians – the order in which he had spent his own unhappy formative years. Researchers have a duty to explain why they are themselves interested in a particular problem. They should also make clear why they have faith in a particular methodology as likely to yield a solution to that problem. Filloy insists that the task of the researcher is not simply one of marshalling evidence but also involves continual reflection on the processes by which proof is pursued.

> To understand the process of persuasion, we must inquire further. What kinds of evidence argue successfully for acceptance? How do successful arguments build to conviction in our minds? When do the possibilities of coincidence or contrived similarity give way to satisfaction that the likelihood is overwhelming, that the text is genuine? In such an inquiry, categories of argument like the historical or stylistic are useful, but inquiry into how the components of persuasion are organized and identified in a given situation is the traditional province of rhetoric. A rhetorical approach to this problem cannot guarantee one correct way to make such a judgment, but it can provide the means to describe the process.[11]

We need to observe ourselves becoming convinced, or the reverse, and be clear in our minds how and why that has happened. In Filloy's discussion of Selden's *Table-talk* we can share the process of his coming to a conclusion and then questioning it, and then decide whether we want to agree. If this procedure involves some sacrifice of the formal impersonality of academic discourse this may not be a bad thing.[12]

Closely related to the question of how ideological bias influences the conduct of research is that of individual cognitive styles. Researchers may be characterised as lumpers or splitters, dashers or draggers, divergent or convergent thinkers, purifiers or syncretists, empiricists or generalisers, landscapers or miniaturists, visualisers or non-visualisers, intellectually rigid or flexible, hypostatisers or nominalists. (*Hypostasis* is the process of assuming an objective reality for abstractions: the *nominalist* insists that such formulations are only names, not things.) These probably inborn differences, by functioning independently of ideological allegiances, provide the inner turbulence that protects ideologies from premature ossification; but it will also be obvious that certain cognitive styles are going to be more congenial to one ideology than to another. An abstract, convergent thinker would have been far more at home in the intellectual world of mediaeval scholasticism or 1960s Structuralism than a divergent, visualising mind; while the latter would have responded far more effectively to the expectations of early nineteenth-century literary

Romanticism. Or to put it another way, an Aquinas born in 1795 could never have become a Keats or a Keats born in 1226 an Aquinas. Such inherent dispositions affect both our performance as scholars and our reaction to the work of others. Convergent thinkers will be most impressed by a carefully worked through argument; divergent thinkers by arguments that progress by associative leaps revealing unexpected connections. The two may well have problems of communication: nothing is more self-defeating than an argument between two people who are talking past each other because they perceive and categorise phenomena in different ways.[13] Here the most useful role may well be that of the more rounded adjudicator who simply points this out to the contestants, though this is not necessarily a recipe for popularity.

Particularly important for attribution studies are the two cognitive predispositions vulgarly known as lumping and splitting. These are in their origins inborn styles which from time to time will be empowered by a particular cultural moment: recent Postmodern decades have been better at splitting than lumping. Lumpers like to make connections and to compose wholes. Characteristically, they will be alert for evidence that allows new work to be added to an established authorial corpus and less concerned with anomalies that challenge the additions – indeed, they may argue, like the critics of ancient Pergamon, that anomaly and a certain level of inconsistency are the natural condition of an author's lifework. The splitter works from the other perspective, looking, like the Homeric and Biblical Analysts, for evidence that will divide a corpus (or a work) among more than one author. Here the greatest weight is given to the evidence of difference (on occasions quite minute difference). Shared bodies of data will often be interpreted by exponents of both tendencies. The lumper will look for features that characterise the work of 'Homer' and will try to gather as much material as possible under that broad umbrella while the splitter searches for inconsistencies within the work as evidence for collaborative composition. The scholar engaged in attribution studies is likely to be sent on expeditions of both kinds and should be aware of the limits beyond which either process becomes counter-productive (a matter of tact as much as definition). We should also bear in mind that a reaction from an extreme case of one process is quite likely to lead to an extreme case of the other: so, the exposure of a good deal of irresponsible lumping with regard to the Rochester and Defoe corpora may well have led to an excess of sceptical splitting. Of course, it is possible for both processes to work in harmony. We are entitled to accept *Timon of Athens* into the Shakespeare canon while acknowledging that a substantial part of it may be by Middleton. We are equally entitled to include it in the collected works of Middleton.

Differences in cognitive styles and ideological bias are facts of scholarly work. We should do our best to become aware of the extent to which they influence our own research and spare no pains to search out their influence over that of others. To recognise these things is not to derogate from the value of scholarship as a truth-seeking institution but is simply part of the critical process by which individual bias is recognised and corrected within the larger adjudicatory whole. Splits performed by a constitutional lumper and lumps composed by a natural splitter deserve special respect.

ATTRIBUTION AND INDIVIDUALITY

In Chapter three the attempt was made to address the diachronic activity of writing with the kinds of awareness created by our literary culture's deep, recent engagement with synchronic models of authorship. To begin with, attention was drawn to the collaborative nature of most historical acts of writing, even when they were issued to the world as the work of a single author. Under the rubric of precursory authorship we explored some of the processes by which texts grow by derivation from other texts, both written and oral. Under the notions of executive authorship and revisionary authorship we accommodated the agency of a dominant author and text creator to a pattern which still allowed for a variety of peripheral collaborations and interventions. Through the idea of declarative authorship we examined ways in which an authorial signifier might float free of the work towards other works or move from outside the work to possess it. While our perspective remained diachronic, we were searching for aspects of professional authorship that non-diachronic approaches had taught us should be there and, when we looked, that expectation turned out to be valid. In this spirit we were able to move from an author-centred to a work-centred definition of authorship as an entity accommodating a number of separable functions which could be performed by the same person or by several.

In subsequent chapters we turned to the question of how works can be made to reveal the contributions of all those individuals who have taken part in their formation at all identifiable stages; but this was to postpone not to solve the problem of how far the process of creation, by whomsoever and in whatever combination of participants it is undertaken, can leave ineradicable traces of individuality. The problem is most pressing but not necessarily most easily solved in the case of the executive author. Let us return to Mark Rose's claim quoted in Chapter three that 'authors do not really create in any literal sense, but rather produce texts through complex processes of adaptation and transformation'.[14] There are cases in which we might question this: some forms of creativity (often somewhat eccentric and marginal ones) are so dazzlingly idiosyncratic that it is impossible to derive them, even by a process of combination, from existing elements. Since the human brain is the unpredictable outcome of a fusing of two nuclei at the moment of conception, brains will arise possessing capacities not shared by other members of the human species. But in most cases it does seem reasonable to redirect our search for originality away from the idea of creation *ex nihilo* to this process of adaptation and combination, whether it be conducted on the heroic scale that produces great writing or in the much more modest ways that will give an ineradicable, albeit barely detectable, personal inflection to writing which is profoundly imitative – the residuum that frustrates even the most careful of attempts to produce a perfect simulacrum of a personal style.

Burrows sees 'the sorts of difference that enable good readers to distinguish between Smollett and Fielding though they write much like each other' as something 'dissipated among the many lesser vectors' created by eigen analysis which are not used in stylometric tests of authorship.[15] This alerts us to the important fact that attribution studies is not, for the most part, concerned with the delineation of individuality as such but with the humbler project of narrowing boundaries. Those branches employing external evidence characteristically operate by reducing contexts. The target work is placed at first in a larger frame, then in a series of progressively smaller ones, until a plausible author or authors is reached. We might start by assigning a newly discovered poem to the London literary world of the 1590s. We might then locate its author among a body of writers associated with the court or courtiers, and next within the circle of, say, the Earl of Southampton. This would then lead us to a small group of known writers or perhaps a particular member of that group but with no way of omitting the possibility that it might be by a previously unknown one. Research based on the study of a writer's ideas pursues a presumed uniqueness in the confluence of beliefs and the argued form in which they are held, a matter which while effective for active, well nourished minds might not allow us to distinguish one fundamentalist or new-ager from another. In effect we tighten the noose, eliminating alternative possibilities as we do so, the individual being the residuum of this process, like a chemical compound extracted from a rich and diverse ore; yet the author so identified is no more than the sum of the attributes that survive this process of exclusion – at best an identity but hardly an individuality.

The same problem is present in stylometry as that of uncertainty over just when quantitative distinctions between samples can be accepted as indicating different authorship, the point on which Ledger was quoted in Chapter eight (p. 141). In one of his tests Burrows found that difference of genre was able to override difference of authorship.[16] In this case samples from dramatic work by Scott and Byron grouped together on a plot that succeeded perfectly in distinguishing between their work in other genres. Smith warns likewise that 'counts of features in texts are affected by a variety of influences on the writer. Authorship itself is but one and not always the major one.'[17] Most recently Craig, using cluster analysis, tested the respective value of authorship, genre and date in establishing proximity measures for plays from the age of Shakespeare and assigning them to groups, finding that, while authorship is undoubtedly the most powerful of the three, its effect weakens as the size of the groups is increased.[18] But the problem is not one for stylometry and computational stylistics only but applies to all attributional arguments. Individuality may be approached by a progressive reduction of contexts or separating out of attributes or by the plotting of quantifiable features of style within a field of variation, but that is not the same thing as to characterise it positively and uniquely and does not guarantee that more than one individuality may not shelter under the same configurations of data. We may have sound biological reasons for believing that individuality itself exists while despairing of ever being able to account for it by inductive means alone. No accumulation of negatives can ever give us a positive.

Ian Lancashire with his model of individuality as a characteristic of the idiolect and the associational matrix runs into the same problem when he comes to describing it. The grounding of individuality in memory is as old as Locke and was famously illustrated by Sterne in *Tristram Shandy*.[19] The problem for attribution studies is, again, how connections formed in the idiolect are to be distinguished from those acquired from and shared with the sociolect, a matter which in Lancashire's or Foster's case would be pursued through the analysis of content rather than of the usage of function words. The moment questions of this kind are raised, one becomes aware of the extent to which philosophical problems underlying the attributionist enterprise remain unexamined. The reluctance of attributionists to reflect theoretically on their craft has already been commented on.

Traditional stylistics bypassed the problem of defining individuality by appealing directly to literary conceptions of style as 'l'homme même'. Instead of moving in towards the author through a process of exclusion, it began by accepting the work as an embodiment of the individuality of its author. The method as practised by an Erasmus was not one of searching for a singular essence but for a principle of coherence embracing the totality of style and ethos. It can still be effective with those writers who genuinely possess a distinctive personal style but offers less purchase with the drab herd. Precisely this distinction, when made by Congreve in *The Double-dealer*, is actually ironic: it is the fools who possess the style and the man of sense who holds back from personal display:

Lady Froth. I Vow *Mellefont's* a pretty Gentleman, but Methinks he wants a Manner.

Cynthia. A Manner! what's that, Madam?

Lady Froth. Some distinguishing Quality, as for example, the *Belle-air* or *Brilliant* of Mr. *Brisk*; the Solemnity, yet Complaisance of my Lord, or something of his own, that should look a little *Je-ne-scay quoysh*; he is too much a Mediocrity, in my mind.

Cynthia. He does not indeed affect either pertness, or formality; for which I like him . . . [20]

Mellefont's reticence springs from the same cultural causes as the stylistic sobriety of authors such as Addison, writing a little later, and might well baffle an investigator dependent on holistic assessment. Similarly, when Dryden speaks of humour as 'the ridiculous extravagance of conversation, wherein one man differs from all others', he is not asserting that all men so differ but that certain extravagant men, like Falstaff, depart from a generally observed norm.[21] But the point for our present discussion is not the problem of practice but what the holistic method as a method has to tell us about the nature of individuality as expressed in language. In this view, individuality is defined in a literary way as the sum of all the traces of expression, belief, attitude and personality transmitted by the work. The method of investigation is the literary one of close reading or the parallel sociolinguistic techniques employed by Barbara Johnstone that were discussed in Chapter one. This method, as we saw a little earlier, has the enormous advantage of representing the work in the fullness of its power to signify rather than figuring it through tables of frequencies or entries in the Stationers' Register. Its weakness, as we have also seen, is that the perceptions are themselves individual to the particular reader and would need to be subjected to a process of adjudication by other readers, who might well respond differently. The interrogation of one individuality by another must always be a dialogic process in which the interrogator can never stand outside the dialogue.

It may well appear at this point that the best way of proceeding would be to rely on holistic methods to identify problem works and propose hypotheses concerning their authorship but then to turn to techniques of differentiation to confirm or disprove them: much excellent work has been and will continue to be done on exactly this basis. No one would deny that certainty, insofar as it can be aspired to, is most likely to emerge from the patient examination of differences and similarities in the handling of elements that are common to all candidates for the authorship of an anonymous work. Insofar as our interest extends no further than distinguishing the work of author A from that of author B (and so on through the alphabet) this limitation can be accepted without too many gripes. The alternative method of looking for features unique to the target text and the work of a particular author, while the source of some spectacular individual finds, is vulnerable both to the statistical likelihood that such exclusive correspondences will exist for all pairs of reasonably prolific authors and to the fact that the discovery of countervailing instances would immediately throw the result into question. And yet it is worth asking whether attributionists should devote more attention to investigating what is truly unique in the work of authors. Donald Foster's attempt to put this method into practice remains controversial; but many who question the particular finding of 'A funeral elegy' would probably feel that in his concentrating on the singular and idiosyncratic rather than individual preferences among the common stock of words and ideas his heart is in the right place. When Constant Mews writes

> It was when reading afresh the *Epistolae duorum amantium* in 1993, this time with greater awareness of Abelard's vocabulary as a logician, that I encountered words and ideas that sent a shiver down my spine[22]

we share the excitement that attends the unmediated recognition of uniqueness. Mews himself would be the first to concede that his case for the attribution of the new letters needed a good deal more arguing (which he proceeds to give) than this; but the case suggests that more attention to the unique would not do any harm. Looking across to the sociolinguists, whose concerns are at times very close to those of attributionists, we find that they too have been taking steps in this direction.

Long before Johnstone's challenge to the Saussurean assumptions of sociolinguistics, workers in that discipline had recognised that random sampling was impractical for their special kind of enquiry. J. K.

Chambers advances an alternative to the random sample which he calls the 'judgement sample', citing a passage from one of the anthropological writings of Margaret Mead in illustration. Any particular individual, according to Mead,

> can be accurately placed, in terms of a very large number of variables – age, sex, order of birth, family background, life experience, temperamental tendencies . . . , political and religious position, exact situational relationship to the investigator, configurational relationship to every other informant, and so forth. Within this extensive degree of specification, each informant is studied as a perfect example, an organic representation of his complete cultural experience.[23]

The concern of the mainstream sociolinguist at this point would be to search for correlations between the linguistic variable (e.g. individual preferences between a standard phoneme and its regional alternative) and social variables of the kind described, scores being summed as instances of the frequency of the deviant against the standard form.[24] By reversing the major emphasis, at least temporarily, from the field to the individual, a richer sense is obtained of kinds of variation which older versions of the discipline used to dismiss as anomalous.

Barbara Johnstone's innovation, discussed in Chapter one, was to call for sociolinguistics to move from a deterministic to a voluntarist orientation by redefining linguistic variables from being causes of individual performance to being options from which the individual chooses. Apart from that, her analyses are always of language at work in social situations, and her interest ceases with describing the language of a series of individuals: she is not herself concerned whether that knowledge might be used in determining the authorship of anonymous texts. Her case studies, presented in pairs, are generally of contrasted kinds of speakers, not of similar ones. However, she does devote one important part of her study to the examination of personal variations introduced to phone-questionnaire scripts by those administering them to respondents, this being a field in which deviation from the agreed form of words is severely discouraged.[25] If there was a real-life counterpart to our earlier fable of the philosopher king and his invented language it should surely be in this strictly disciplined mode of linguistic behaviour; but in practice, and despite the best efforts of supervisors, such communications are never without their individual inflections, and would be less effective if they were since the respondent is always more likely to co-operate with a caller who comes over as a distinct and attractive personality. Johnstone speaks of her own reaction to one such intrusion:

And yet, even knowing that they are interacting with a business entity, people still hear an individual. Fran-with-Olan-Mills had a low physical voice for a woman, somewhat like my own. She drew out the vowel in 'Hi,' pronouncing it as a diphthong, and she spoke the word with a combination of speed and intonation that made her sound, to my ears, as if she weren't from my area. Overall, she sounded intelligent and likeable. After hanging up on her, I felt a little bad about having done so, as I always do (though not bad enough to keep me from hanging up again the next time somebody from Olan Mills calls). (p. 93)

The methodological interest of Johnstone's work to attributionists lies in its directing of attention to those aspects of language which are most strongly expressive of individuality, as typified by her father's inimitable 'aaahh', so vivid in her memory (pp. 4–5). By asserting that one of the fundamental tasks of language is the indication of selfhood, she encourages the search for the features that mark it. Attributionists have always been aware of those aspects of individual style which are genuinely transgressive of rules and of the frames that constitute them and have sometimes enrolled them as 'fingerprints' but, like sociolinguists, have as often disregarded them for not offering a basis for comparative evaluation. Yet it is the assemblage of minor components, or, to use a musical analogy, the particular sonority of the overtones generated by a text as much as the nature of its deployment of the commonalities of culture and language that creates what the reader recognises as its individuality. It will do us no harm to listen more attentively to those overtones.

The other matter that calls for consideration is the obvious fact that the subject matter of attribution studies is not individuality as it exists in the unexaminable neurological ground of consciousness but various effects or derivatives of individuality. The first of these derivates is the subjective apprehension of our own individuality which all of us experience intuitively – the consciousness of our being an I and of perceiving the world from the perspective of that I.[26] This enters attribution studies in relationships of identification such as that between Erasmus and the writing of Jerome in which one subjectivity is able to reconstruct another with such particularity and fullness that the boundaries between them seem to dissolve. The actor's identification with a part is another form of this. But such a relationship, as we saw, can never be other than dialogic with the rules written by the attributionist and to that extent always open to review by others.

What we are much more likely to be concerned with in attribution studies is a second derivative, which we may describe as the social performance of individuality through language and action. This will characteristically be transformed by the attributionist into a third derivative that takes the form of a scholarly remodelling of the performance into a configuration more amenable to analysis, which may be either mathematical or contextual. The work of attribution studies, in its modern conception, is predominantly concerned with these two last-named derivatives, not in any meaningful sense with the *Ding an sich*. This being the case, it seems reasonable to propose that the attributionist's business is never really with individuality as such but with the less problematical category of identity. Identity is what we are able to construct from the data available in the anonymous or pseudonymous work and those of the candidates: like the summing up that followed Johnstone's brief telephone conversation it belongs to the realm of the contingent and possible, but may nonetheless be highly revealing. If the repertoire is rich enough and the notation of the scores (whether numerical or ideational) accurate enough, an identity may turn out to be unique according to all available measures; yet, uniqueness can never be proved – even in stylometric work the best we can do is to run up extremely high probabilities for it, and in historical contextualisation to create a case that lies beyond reasonable doubt.

The arrival through various kinds of analysis at the recognition of a putatively unique identity is the defining moment of attribution studies in its modern conception, and provides us with our best chance of establishing a disciplinary consanguinity between the very diverse body of techniques that have been considered in this book; and yet identity, even highly distinctive identity, is not the same as individuality, but simply the testable product of individuality. Individuality is something distinct from its performance. It is the ultimately unexaminable state in which each of us forms ourselves for, and is formed by, the world; it is both stable and unstable; it is social and it is anti-social; it builds our reality and is built by it; it is the origin of writing and its conclusion. If we can ever apprehend it directly in a writer it is only in those experiences of oneness Erasmus felt after a lifetime's reading of Jerome; otherwise it has to be approached through poetry, not scholarship. Attribution studies is probably wise not to pursue it too intently but to be content with the lesser achievement of cataloguing the derivatives that mark particular individualities. Nonetheless it will do it no harm to acknowledge that its necessarily prosaic deliberations take place in the shadow of enormous mysteries.

Notes

INTRODUCTION

1 (Oxford University Press, 1993); reprinted as *The Culture and Commerce of Texts: Scribal Publication in Seventeenth-century England* (Amherst: University of Massachusetts Press, 1998).

2 (Oxford University Press, 1999).

3 *The Golden Age of Australian Opera: W. S. Lyster and his Companies 1861–1880* (Sydney: Currency Press, 1981); *James Edward Neild: Victorian Virtuoso* (Carlton, Vic.: Melbourne University Press, 1989).

4 Roland Barthes, 'The death of the author', in *Image, Music, Text: Essays*, selected and translated by Stephen Heath (London: Fontana, 1977), pp. 142–8; Michel Foucault, 'What is an author?' (1969), trans. Joseph V. Harari, in David Lodge, ed. *Modern Criticism and Theory: A Reader* (London: Longman, 1988), pp. 197–210; Seán Burke, *The Death and Return of the Author* (Edinburgh University Press, 1992).

1 INDIVIDUALITY AND SAMENESS

1 Michael E. Hobart and Zachary S. Schiffman, *Information Ages: Literacy, Numeracy and the Computer Revolution* (Baltimore: Johns Hopkins University Press, 1998), p. 27.

2 *Boswell's Life of Johnson*, ed. George Birkbeck Hill, rev. L. F. Powell, 6 vols. (Oxford: Clarendon Press, 1934), iii. p. 280.

3 *The Linguistic Individual: Self-Expression in Language and Linguistics* (New York: Oxford University Press, 1996), pp. 12–15.

4 *Selected Writings of Edward Sapir in Language, Culture and Personality*, ed. David C. Mandelbaum (Berkeley and Los Angeles: University of California Press, 1958), p. 542.

5 Mary Thomas Crane, *Shakespeare's Brain: Reading with Cognitive Theory* (Princeton University Press, 2001), pp. 11–12.

6 II. ii. 197–202, in *The Complete Plays of William Congreve*, ed. Herbert Davis (University of Chicago Press, 1967), p. 60.

7 'Non-traditional authorship attribution studies: ignis fatuus or Rosetta stone?', *BSANZ Bulletin* 24 (2000), 170.

2 HISTORICAL SURVEY

1 For the foundation of the library, see Rudolf Pfeiffer, *History of Classical Scholarship*, 2 vols. (Oxford: Clarendon Press, 1968, 1976), i. pp. 87–104 and *passim*, and, anecdotally, Luciano Canfora, *The Vanished Library: A Wonder of the Ancient World*, trans. Martin Ryle (London: Hutchinson Radius, 1989).
2 *Poetics*, 26:6 in *The Poetics of Aristotle*, ed. and trans. S. H. Butcher, 4th edn (London: Macmillan, 1936), p. 111.
3 Vitruvius Pollio, *De architectura*, Book VII, Preface, sect. 5 ff. Only one competitor was judged to have composed his own poem. A parallel case from seventeenth-century England is recorded in *The Rev. Oliver Heywood, B.A. 1630–1702; His Autobiography, Diaries, Anecdote and Event Books*, ed. J. Horsfall Turner, 4 vols. (Brighouse and Bingley: [Printed for the Editor], 1882–5), i. p. 189. A candidate minister who tried to present a printed sermon as his own 'was traced by the scent of an intelligent hearer even as he was preaching it'.
4 Canfora, *Vanished Library*, pp. 45–6.
5 Anthony Grafton, *Forgers and Critics: Creativity and Duplicity in Western Scholarship* (Princeton University Press, 1990). Grafton also illustrates that forgers have to possess the skills of good attributionists if they are to be successful. In this way forgery both tests and advances attribution.
6 *The Attic Nights of Aulus Gellius*, with an English translation by John C. Rolfe (London: Heinemann, 1954), pp. 244–9.
7 For Gellius' reliance on Varro's now lost *De comediis Plautinis*, the extent of which is not clear from his own text, see Leofranc Holford-Strevens, *Aulus Gellius* (London: Duckworth, 1988), pp. 115–18.
8 As by Aben Ezra, who, as cited by Spinoza, merely listed a few key phrases from passsages that demonstrated the impossibility of Mosaic authorship, adding that those who understood their mystery (i.e. were already cognisant of the problem) would 'know the truth' (*Tractatus Theologico-politicus*, trans. Samuel Shirley (Leiden: E. J. Brill, 1991), p. 162).
9 Letter 107 in Jerome, *Select Letters*, trans. F. A. Wright (London: Heinemann, 1933), p. 365.
10 Bruce M. Metzger, *The Canon of the New Testament: Its Origin, Development, and Significance* (Oxford: Clarendon Press, 1987), pp. 182–3.
11 Ibid., pp. 251–4.
12 *The Apocalypse in the Middle Ages*, ed. Richard K. Emmerson and Bernard McGinn (Ithaca, NY: Cornell University Press, 1992), p. 6.
13 Metzger, *Canon of the New Testament*, pp. 171–4.
14 Foucault, 'What is an author?', p. 204.
15 See, for example, his discussion of the Epistle to the Hebrews in J. P. Migne, *Patrologia Latina*, xxiii. cols. 647–50.
16 The nature of these debates is summarised in A. J. Minnis, *Mediaeval Theory of Authorship: Scholastic Literary Attitudes in the Later Middle Ages*, 2nd edn (Aldershot: Scolar Press, 1988), pp. 95–6.

17 James Willis, *Latin Textual Criticism* (Urbana: University of Illinois Press, 1972), pp. 126–30, regards them as inept.
18 Minnis, *Mediaeval Theory of Authorship*, p. 96.
19 *The Treatise of Lorenzo Valla on the Donation of Constantine. Text and Translation into English*, ed. and trans. Christopher B. Coleman (New Haven: Yale University Press, 1922), pp. 131–3.
20 *Patristic Scholarship. The Edition of St Jerome*, ed., trans. and annotated by James F. Brady and John C. Olin, vol. LXI of *Collected Works of Erasmus* (University of Toronto Press, 1992), p. 71.
21 *Textual Scholarship: An Introduction* (New York: Garland, 1992), p. 295; see also his remarks on the 'hermeneutics of suspicion' on p. 296. Erasmus's ideal of reading comes close to that which is the subject of George Poulet's 'Criticism and the experience of interiority', in *The Structuralist Controversy: The Languages of Criticism and the Sciences of Man*, ed. Richard Macksey and Eugenio Donato (Baltimore: Johns Hopkins University Press, 1972), pp. 56–88.
22 *The Sleepwalkers: A History of Man's Changing Vision of the Universe* (Harmondsworth: Penguin, 1964), p. 340.
23 Grafton, *Forgers and Critics*, praises the 'wealth of the data' (p. 93) deployed in Isaac Casaubon's study of the authorship of the Hermetic corpus (pp. 89, 93–4).
24 Metzger, *Canon of the New Testament*, p. 240.
25 *Epistolae Pauli et aliorum apostolorum ad Graecam veritatem castigatae et . . . enarratae* (Paris, 1532), fol. clxxxixr.
26 Metzger, *Canon of the New Testament*, pp. 240–1.
27 Spinoza, *Tractatus Theologico-politicus*, p. 205.
28 Ibid., pp. 169–73, 190.
29 *Histoire critique du vieux testament* (Paris, 1678), pp. a1v–a2r; *A Critical History of the Old Testament* (London, 1682), pp. a1v–a2r.
30 Simon, *Histoire critique*, p. a2r. See also p. 23: 'Ces Livres étant revues par le Sanhedrin, ou par d'autres personnes inspirées de Dieu, avoient toute l'autorité necessaire qu'on pouvoit desirer dans une affair de cette importance.'
31 Spinoza, *Tractatus Theologico-politicus*, pp. 206–8.
32 See for instance the chapter on the textual history of Tom Stoppard's *Travesties* in Philip Gaskell, *From Writer to Reader: Studies in Editorial Method* (Oxford: Clarendon Press, 1978), pp. 245–62.
33 Homer, *The Iliad*, trans. E. V. Rieu (Harmondsworth: Penguin, 1950), p. xi.
34 There is a summary of this research and an analysis of its implications in Walter J. Ong, *Orality and Literacy: The Technologizing of the Word* (London: Methuen, 1982), pp. 17–30.
35 See below, pp. 207–8.
36 Pfeiffer, *Classical Scholarship*, ii. p. 158, citing Bentley's *Remarks upon a Late Discourse of Free-Thinking* in *Works*, ed. Alexander Dyce (London, 1836–8; repr. New York: AMS Press, 1966), iii. p. 304; Samuel Butler, *The Authoress of*

the Odyssey: where and when she wrote, who she was, the use she made of the Iliad, and how the poem grew under her hands, introd. David Grene (University of Chicago Press, 1967), reprinting the second edition (London, 1922).

37 For this history see David C. Douglas, *English Scholars 1660–1730*, 2nd rev. edn (London: Eyre & Spottiswoode, 1951); Graham Parry, *The Golden Age Restor'd: The Culture of the Stuart Court, 1603–42* (Manchester University Press, 1981); and Kevin Sharpe, *Sir Robert Cotton 1586–1631: History and Politics in Early Modern England* (Oxford University Press, 1979). While many early seventeenth-century scholars were tacitly or openly involved with the parliamentary opposition to Charles I and Charles II, several of their eighteenth-century successors were Jacobites or Nonjurors.

38 This tradition is discussed in Love, *Scribal Publication in Seventeenth-century England*; Arthur F. Marotti, *Manuscript, Print, and the English Renaissance Lyric* (Ithaca: Cornell University Press, 1995); Henry Woudhuysen, *Sir Philip Sidney and the Circulation of Manuscripts 1558–1640* (Oxford: Clarendon Press, 1996); Peter Beal, *In Praise of Scribes: Manuscripts and their Makers in Seventeenth-century England* (Oxford: Clarendon Press, 1998); and Margaret Ezell, *Social Authorship and the Advent of Print* (Baltimore: Johns Hopkins University Press, 1999).

39 *The Works of John Wilmot, Earl of Rochester*, ed. Love, pp. 258–9.

40 *The Works of Aphra Behn*, ed. Janet Todd, 7 vols. (London: William Pickering, 1992–6), i. pp. 269–71.

41 For a more up-to-date judgement on the authorship of the plays concerned, see *Annals of English Drama 975–1700*, ed. Alfred Harbage, 2nd edn rev. S. Schoenbaum (London: Methuen, 1964) and 3rd edn rev. S. Wagonheim (London: Routledge, 1989) – there was some dissatisfaction with the third edition. Harbage also published an article 'Elizabethan-Restoration palimpsest', *MLR* 35 (1940), 287–319, in which he identified a number of Restoration plays as adaptations of lost Caroline and Jacobean forerunners. Judith Milhous and Robert D. Hume review a body of post-1660 attributions in their 'Attribution problems in English drama 1660–1700', *Harvard Library Bulletin* 31 (1983), 5–39. Langbaine's underrated achievement is discussed in Paulina Kewes, *Authorship and Appropriation: Writing for the Stage in England 1660–1710* (Oxford University Press, 1998), pp. 207–18.

42 Cf. Ong, *Orality and Literacy*, pp. 21–3 and Kewes, *Authorship and Appropriation*, *passim*. Accusations of plagiarism were also made increasingly in the course of quarrels between authors.

43 Cited in Grafton, *Forgers and Critics*, p. 78 from a fragment of a dialogue by Porphyry.

44 In *Notes and Observations on the Empress of Morocco Revised* (London, 1674); further discussed in Chapter four.

45 *The Life of John Milton . . . with Amyntor; or a Defence of Milton's Life* (London, 1761), pp. 68–79. For the accusation against Milton, see William Riley Parker, *Milton*, 2nd edn rev. Gordon Campbell, 2 vols. (Oxford: Clarendon Press, 1996), ii. pp. 964–6.

46 Discussed in Roger Thompson, *Unfit for Modest Ears: A Study of Pornographic, Obscene and Bawdy Works Written or Published in England in the Second Half of the Seventeenth Century* (London: Macmillan, 1979).
47 Discussed at pp. 107, 135 below. The no less famous case of the *Federalist* is of a different nature, since it was not the identity of the authors but the extent of their contribution that was uncertain.
48 New and enlarged edition by James Kennedy, W. A. Smith and A. F. Johnson, 9 vols. (Edinburgh: Oliver and Boyd, 1926), i. p. xi.

3 DEFINING AUTHORSHIP

1 *Authors and Owners: The Invention of Copyright* (Cambridge, MA: Harvard University Press, 1993), p. 8.
2 *Theories of Discourse* (Oxford: Basil Blackwell, 1986), p. 3.
3 *The Predicament of Culture: Twentieth-century Ethnography, Literature, and Art* (Cambridge, MA: Harvard University Press, 1988), p. 268.
4 *The World, the Text, and the Critic* (New York: Vintage, 1991), p. 4.
5 Ibid., p. 152.
6 *Terence's comedies made English with his life and some remarks at the end. By several hands* (London, 1694), sig. a3r–v. Laurence Eachard and Sir Roger L'Estrange were among those involved.
7 'Ephemeris id est totius diei negotium', sect. vii.
8 *Books and Readers in the Early Church: A History of Early Christian Texts* (New Haven: Yale University Press, 1995), p. 120.
9 A recent example was the discovery by Alexander Demandt of the text of Theodor Mommsen's lectures on the Roman imperial period in the transcript of Paul and Sebastian Hensel, compensating for the never written fourth volume of Mommsen's *History of Rome*. Arthur Kirsch has used the same method to reconstitute talks given by W. H. Auden in 1946 (*Lectures on Shakespeare* (Princeton University Press, 2001)). While the ideas conveyed are probably those of the authors, the same cannot be claimed for details of expression.
10 Unpublished translation by Constant Mews from the Latin text in Bernhard Bischoff, 'Aus der Schule Hugos von St Viktor', in his *Mittelalterliche Studien*, 3 vols. (Stuttgart: Anton Hiersemann, 1967), ii. pp. 186–7.
11 Roger North, *The Life of the Lord Keeper North*, ed. Mary Chan (Lewiston, NY: E. Mellen Press, 1995), p. 386. It does not seem that the pamphlet was ever written.
12 Arthur Sherbo, 'Isaac Reed's diaries, 1762–1804: a source book', *N&Q* 245 (June 2000), 213–16 (215).
13 Bob Hohler, 'Ghostwriter on Clinton book loses his spirit', *Boston Globe*, 8 July 1999, A3.
14 Schoenbaum, *IE*, p. 226.
15 Harvey Sachs, *Virtuoso: The Life and Art of Niccolò Paganini, Franz Liszt, Anton Rubinstein . . .* ([London]: Thames & Hudson, 1982), p. 110.

16 Adam Fox, 'Ballads, libels, and popular ridicule in Jacobean England', *Past and Present* 145 (1994), 47–83.
17 (New York: Mysterious Press, 1996), p. 435.
18 'W. B. Yeats and the resurrection of the author', *Library*, 6th ser. 16 (1994), 101–34.
19 'Middle English romance and its audiences', in Mary-Jo Arn and Hannecke Wirtjes, with Hans Jansen, *Historical and Editorial Studies in Medieval and Early Modern English* (Groningen: Wolters-Noordhoff, 1985), pp. 41–2.
20 Quintilian, *Institutio oratoria*, III.iii.1. Some authorities distinguished *iudicium* from *inventio.*
21 *The Works of John Dryden*, gen. eds. H. T. Swedenberg, jr and Alan Roper, 19 vols. to date (Berkeley and Los Angeles: University of California Press, 1956–), I. p. 53.
22 Malcolm Bowie, 'Unceasingly blessed', *TLS*, 19 Nov. 1999, 3.
23 *Architectural Remains of Richmond, Twickenham, Kew, Petersham and Mortlake, drawn in lithography by Thomas R. Way with notes compiled by Frederic Chapman* (London, 1900), p. 26.
24 A transition explored in Kewes, *Authorship and Appropriation.*
25 Rose, *Authors and Owners*, p. 1. For a general discussion of the topic of this section from the perspective of film, see James Dudley Andrew, *Concepts in Film Theory* (Oxford University Press, 1984). Andrew distinguishes between adaptation, intersection and transforming.
26 *J. M. Synge: Plays*, ed. Ann Saddlemyer (Oxford University Press, 1968), p. 103.
27 *Josephus: The Historian and his Society* (London: Duckworth, 1983), p. 236; citing Henry St John Thackeray, *Josephus: The Man and the Historian* (New York, 1929).
28 Examples will be found in the numerous volumes of *Paris Review* interviews and in Kate Grenville and Sue Woolfe, *Making Stories: How Ten Australian Novels Were Written* (North Sydney: Allen & Unwin, 1993), esp. pp. 59–72.
29 *Letters from Orinda to Poliarchus* (London, 1705), p. 62; also in *The Collected Works of Katherine Philips: The Matchless Orinda.* 3 vols. ii: *The Letters*, ed. Patrick Thomas (Stump Cross, Essex: Stump Cross Books, 1990), pp. 70–1.
30 In his dedication to Buckhurst of 'Of dramatick poesie, an essay' (1668) (*Works*, xvii. p. 3).
31 As shown in preliminary unpublished statistical testing by John Burrows.
32 One traditional critique of the Mosaic authorship of *Genesis* was discussed in Chapter two above, p. 16 and n.
33 Ronald Hayman, *A Life of Jung* (London: Bloomsbury, 1999), pp. 434–7.
34 A. C. Elias, jr, '*Senatus Consultum*: revising verse in Swift's Dublin circle, 1729–1735', in *Reading Swift: Papers from the Third Münster Symposium on Jonathan Swift* [1994], eds. Hermann J. Real and Helgard Stöver-Leidig (Munich: Wilhelm Fink, 1998), p. 249, citing Laetitia Pilkington, *Memoirs*, ed. A. C. Elias, jr (Athens: University of Georgia Press, 1997), i. p. 283.
35 For the table-book, see Richard H. Rouse and Mary A. Rouse, 'Wax tablets', *Language & Communication* 9 (1989), 175–91.

36 Ann Burns with Barbara Hoffert, 'First novels', *Library Journal*, 15 March 1988, 31–5.
37 Quoted in Jason Steger, 'The word servant', *Age*, 18 Mar. 2000, Extra, 3.

4 EXTERNAL EVIDENCE

1 'Salmons in both, or some caveats for canonical scholars', in E&F, pp. 77–8.
2 (Oxford University Press, 1999).
3 'Printers of the mind: some notes on bibliographical theories and printing-house practices', *SB* 22 (1969), 7.
4 'Internal evidence and the attribution of Elizabethan plays', in E&F, p. 189 and n.*.
5 Kevin Sharpe, *Reading Revolutions: The Politics of Reading in Early Modern England* (New Haven: Yale University Press, 2000), pp. 253–4.
6 Among the attempts to unveil Traven are Karl S. Guthke, *B. Traven, Biographie eines Ratsels* (1933); Will Wyatt, *The Man who was B. Traven* (1980); Judy Stone, *The Mystery of B. Traven* (1977) and Frederik Hetmann, *Der Mann der sich verbarg* (1983). The dominant identification is that with Ret Marut. See also *B. Traven. Life and Work*, ed. Ernst Schürer and Philip Jenkins (University Park: Pennsylvania State University Press, 1987).
7 Donald Foster describes successful pursuits of the identities of publishers' readers in *Author Unknown: Tales of Literary Detection* (New York: Henry Holt, 2000), pp. 28–9, 38–40 and 44.
8 Letter to author, 7 July 2000.
9 David V. Erdman, 'The signature of style', in E&F, pp. 47–50.
10 Samuel Taylor Coleridge, *Essays on His Times from 'The Morning Post' and 'The Courier'*, ed. David V. Erdman, i. p. xxviii, vol. 3 of *The Collected Works*, 14 vols. (London: Routledge & Kegan Paul, 1969–99).
11 Dirk Spennemann and Jane Downing, 'Literary detection: discovering the identity of a "Master mariner"', *Margin*, 47 (April 1999), 8–13. Further details of the authors' painstaking search are given in their 'Unmasking transient colonial authors: the case of Handley Bathurst Sterndale', *BSANZ Bulletin* 23 (1999), 148–63.
12 See Alvar Ellegård, *Who was Junius?* (Stockholm: Almqvist & Wiksell, 1962), discussed further in Chapters six and eight.
13 *The Dramatic Works of Richard Brinsley Sheridan*, ed. Cecil Price, 2 vols. (Oxford: Clarendon Press, 1973), ii. p. 518.
14 Love, *James Edward Neild*, p. 62.
15 Settle, *Notes and Observations*, p. A2r.
16 Harold Love, 'The authorship of the postscript of *Notes and Observations on the Empress of Morocco*', *N&Q* 211 (Jan.–June 1966), 27–8.
17 David Dyregrov, 'Jo. Haines as librettist for Purcell's *Fairy Queen*', *Restoration and 18th Century Theatre Research*, 2nd ser. 7 (1992), 29–46.
18 Ibid., p. 34.

19 'Eliza Haywood's last ("lost") work: *The History of Miss Leonora Meadowson* (1788)', *BSANZ Bulletin* 23 (1999), 131–47.
20 (Oxford University Press, 1999) and (Oxford: Clarendon Press, 1992).
21 *Pre-Restoration Stage Studies* (Cambridge, MA: Harvard University Press, 1927), pp. 349–50; cited in Schoenbaum, *IE*, p. 224.
22 'The author of *The Hibernian Father*: an early colonial playwright', *Australian Literary Studies* 2 (1966), 278–88.
23 Public Record Office STAC8 261/25. For further evidence of the same kind see Fox, 'Ballads, libels and popular ridicule'.
24 Harold N. Hillebrand, 'Thomas Middleton's *The Viper's Brood*', *Modern Language Notes* 42 (1927), 35–8. See also Schoenbaum, *IE*, pp. 208–10 and pp. 136–8 below.
25 (Repr. London: The British Library, 1998.)
26 *Boswell's Life of Johnson*, i. p. 416.
27 *Thomas Percy's 'Life of Dr. Oliver Goldsmith'*, ed. Richard L. Harp (Salzburg: Institut für Englische Sprache und Literatur, Universität Salzburg, 1976), p. 61. Laslett argues that while Homer's picture of the family life of Hector cannot be treated as historical data the incidental detail of his helmet's crest being of horsehair is likely to be accurate ('The wrong way through the telescope: a note on literary evidence in sociology', *British Journal of Sociology* 27 (1976), 321–2).
28 Kenneth Curry, 'Two new works of Robert Southey', *SB* 5 (1952–3), 199.
29 Zachary Leader, 'Raising Ron Cain: How Amis and Larkin mocked their own movement', *TLS*, 5 May 2000, 13–15.
30 *The Letters of Kingsley Amis*, ed. Zachary Leader (London: HarperCollins, 2000), p. 241.
31 Preface to *Valentinian* (1685), pp. A4r, A3v.
32 *The Roxburghe Ballads*, ed. J. Woodfall Ebsworth, 9 vols. in 8 (New York: AMS Press, 1966), iv. p. 589. The line in question is 'What King would choose to be a *Catiline*?'
33 Bodl. MS don. b 8, p. 490.
34 Christopher Tiffin, review of Juliet Flesch, *Love Brought to Book: A Bio-bibliography of 20th-century Australian Romance Novels*, *BSANZ Bulletin* 22 (1998), 61–2.
35 Carol Billman, *The Secret of the Stratemeyer Syndicate: Nancy Drew, The Hardy Boys, and the Million Dollar Fiction Factory* (New York: Ungar, 1986), pp. 157–9.
36 *Horizon* 1 (1940), 353–4; see also *The Collected Essays, Journalism and Letters of George Orwell*, ed. Sonia Orwell and Ian Angus, 4 vols. (London: Secker and Warburg, 1968), i. pp. 460–85.
37 'Rebellions antidote: a new attribution to Aphra Behn', *N&Q* 236 (June 1991), 175–7. The poem has two signatures, J.C.B. and A.B. The assumption that, because Coffee addresses Tea as 'dear Sister', Tea's lines must have been written by a woman is unpersuasive.
38 *SB* 9 (1957), 163–78.
39 Frank Molloy, 'Attribution and pseudonyms: the case of Victor J. Daley', *BSANZ Bulletin* 24 (2000), 116–28.

40 'H marks the spot of first desert explorer', *Weekend Australian*, 2–3 Dec. 2000, 1–2. The discovery was made by a respected rock-art specialist, Robert Bednarik.
41 'Latin title-page mottoes as a clue to dramatic authorship', *The Library*, 4th ser. 26 (1946), 28–36.
42 'George Gascoigne, *The Noble Arte of Venerie*, and Queen Elizabeth at Kenilworth', in *Joseph Quincy Adams Memorial Studies*, ed. James G. McManaway, Giles E. Dawson and Edwin E. Willoughby (Washington: Folger Shakespeare Library, 1948), pp. 653–4.
43 Williams, 'An initiation into initials', 170; see also Franklin B. Williams, 'Renaissance names in masquerade', *PMLA* 69 (1954), 314–23.
44 Woudhuysen, *Sir Philip Sidney*, pp. 266–78.
45 My quotations are from the five-volume reprint of Walter's original eleven in the Wordsworth Classic Erotica series (Ware, Hertfordshire, 1995–6). Pagination is continuous throughout.
46 *My Secret Life*, ed. and introd. Gordon Grimley (St Albans: Panther Books, 1972), pp. 8–9. Ian Gibson's attempt to revive Legman's attribution in *The Erotomaniac* (London: Faber, 2001) is unpersuasive.
47 *The Lost Theatres of London* (London: Hart-Davis, 1968), pp. 553–6.
48 To be precise, Charterhouse had a headmaster and the wider institution, which also incorporated an almshouse, had a Master.
49 *Grand dictionnaire universel du xixe siècle*, art. 'Chemins de fer' (Paris, 1867), iii. cols. 1132–3.
50 (Melbourne: The Text Publishing Company, 1994), pp. vi–vii. Typesetting is credited to 'The Condom Company'.
51 Samuel Butler in *The Way of All Flesh*, published posthumously in 1903, describes a similar work (in this case imaginary) written by his hero, Ernest Pontifex, which takes the form of 'a series of semi-theological, semi-social essays purporting to have been written by six or seven different people and viewing the same class of subjects from different standpoints' (*Ernest Pontifex or The Way of All Flesh*, ed. Daniel F. Howard (London: Methuen, 1964), p. 341).
52 J. W. Johnson, 'Did Lord Rochester write *Sodom*?', *Papers of the Bibliographical Society of America* 81 (1987), 119–53; Harold Love, 'But did Rochester *really* write *Sodom*?', *Papers of the Bibliographical Society of America* 87 (1993), 319–36.
53 Text in Love, 'But did Rochester *really* write *Sodom?*', 335.
54 There is a convenient summary of recent scholarship on the poem in James A. Freeman, 'The Latin lover revived: a rational ending for the *Pervigilium Veneris*', *Classical and Modern Literature: a Quarterly* 19 (1999), 109–21. The best edition is that of Laurence Catlow (Brussels: Latomus, 1980).

5 INTERNAL EVIDENCE

1 *The Canon of Thomas Middleton's Plays: Internal Evidence for the Major Problems of Authorship* (London: Cambridge University Press, 1975), p. 5.
2 'The uses and abuses of internal evidence', in E&F, p. 7.

3 Sherbo, 'The uses and abuses of internal evidence', p. 8.
4 See on this Peter Clark, *British Clubs and Societies 1580–1800* (Oxford University Press, 2000).
5 See Love, *Scribal Publication in Seventeenth-century England*, pp. 177–230.
6 See, on this topic, Charles Reid, *The Music Monster* (London: Quartet, 1984), pp. 84–8.
7 However, problems remain which are considered in Paul Werstine, 'Plays in manuscript', in *A New History of Early English Drama*, ed. John D. Cox and David Scott Kastan (New York: Columbia University Press, 1997), pp. 490–1.
8 Stanley Wells, Gary Taylor et al., eds. *William Shakespeare: A Textual Companion* (Oxford: Clarendon Press, 1987), pp. 124–5.
9 *Man's Unconquerable Mind: Studies of English Writers, from Bede to A. E. Houseman and W. P. Ker* (London: Cape, 1939; repr. 1964), pp. 204–49 and Note pp. 407–8.
10 Caroline Spurgeon, *Shakespeare's Imagery and What it Tells us* (Cambridge University Press, 1935); see also her 'Imagery in the Sir Thomas More fragment', *Review of English Studies* 6 (1955), 257–70; Edward A. Armstrong, *Shakespeare's Imagination: A Study of the Psychology of Association and Inspiration* (London: Drummond, 1946); Crane, *Shakespeare's Brain*.
11 'Deciding the authorship of a doubtful text: the case of John Selden's *Table-talk*', *Quarterly Journal of Speech* 70 (1984), 41–52.
12 'On the authorship of *Two Dissertations concerning Sense and the Imagination, with an Essay on Consciousness*', *N&Q* 247 (2000), 197.
13 'The three texts of "Piers Plowman", and their grammatical forms', *MLR* 14 (1919), 129–51; part-reprinted in E&F, pp. 142–3.
14 William McColly and Dennis Weier, 'Literary attribution and likelihood-ratio tests: the case of the Middle English *Pearl*-poems', *CHum* 17 (1983), 65–75, conclude on the basis of stylometric analysis that 'granting the assumptions on which the criterion-word variables are based, these tests indicate almost without doubt that the five works *Cleanness*, *Sir Gawain*, *Patience*, *Pearl*, and *St Erkenwald* are from the hands of five different authors' (p. 68); however, they also concede that 'the null hypothesis of equal Poisson parameters, upon which the likelihood-ratio test depends, may be too restrictive for a simple application in problems where all authors are unknown' (p. 69). The safest interpretation of their result is that it failed to confirm the hypothesis of common authorship without formally disproving it.
15 *Australasian* (Melbourne), 10 Feb. 1872, 178, quoted in Love, *James Edward Neild*, p. 312.
16 Henry Fielding, *New Essays by Henry Fielding: His Contributions to the 'Craftsman' (1734–1739) and Other Early Journalism*, ed. Martin Battestin, with a stylometric analysis by Michael G. Farringdon (Charlottesville: Virginia University Press, 1989).
17 R. H. Barker, *Thomas Middleton* (New York: Columbia University Press, 1958), pp. 70–1; cited in Schoenbaum, *IE*, p. 211.

18 Fielding, *New Essays by Henry Fielding*, p. xxxvii.
19 'Bibliographical clues in collaborate plays', *The Library*, 4th ser. 13 (1932), 24.
20 Schoenbaum, *IE*, pp. 191–2.
21 Roger Lonsdale, ed., *The Poems of Thomas Gray, William Collins, Oliver Goldsmith* (London: Longmans, 1969).
22 An 'unusual' expression does not have to be striking in its unusualness – indeed, that might in itself encourage imitation. As experimentation with the LION archive will quickly show, many mundane combinations of words are unique to particular works and authors.
23 Harold Stein, 'A note on the versification of *Childe Harold*', *Modern Language Notes* 42 (1927), 34.
24 Fogel, 'Salmons in both', 94.
25 See below, pp. 147–51.
26 *Editing Wyatt: An Examination of Collected Poems of Sir Thomas Wyatt together with Suggestions for an Improved Edition* (Cambridge: Cambridge Quarterly (Publications), 1972), p. 160.
27 See C. A. J. Coady, *Testimony: A Philosophical Study* (Oxford: Clarendon Press, 1992).
28 'Marvell, R.F. and the authorship of "Blake's victory"', *English Manuscript Studies* 5 (1995), 110–11.
29 *Problems and Methods of Literary History with Special Reference to Modern French Literature: A Guide for Graduate Students* (Boston: Ginn & Company, 1922), p. 161.

6 STYLISTIC EVIDENCE

1 Johnstone, *The Linguistic Individual*, pp. 186, 187.
2 Foster, *Author Unknown*, pp. 65–9, 188–220.
3 *Literary Revision: The Inexact Science of Getting it Right* (New Haven: Beinecke Library, 1990), pp. 55–6.
4 'The uses and abuses of internal evidence', p. 19, citing *Boswell's Life of Johnson*, iv. p. 190 n. 2.
5 *The Casuist Uncas'd*, 2nd edn (London, 1680), pp. A2v–A3r.
6 Also the view of Nigel Smith, *Perfection Proclaimed: Language and Literature in English Radical Religion 1640–1660* (Oxford University Press, 1989) and Clement Hawes, *Mania and Literary Style: The Rhetoric of Enthusiasm from the Ranters to Christopher Smart* (Cambridge University Press, 1996).
7 *The Literary Culture of Nonconformity in Later Seventeenth-century England* (Leicester University Press, 1987), p. 246.
8 *The Works of Tacitus*, Vol. I (London, 1728), Discourse II, sect. 13, pp. 30–1.
9 (Oxford: Clarendon Press, 1969), pp. 355–6.
10 A body of over 5,000 polemic works published during the years of the Fronde (1648–54). For an example of the problems associated with texts of this kind see Hubert Carrier, 'La critique d'attribution au confluent des méthodes

de l'histoire littéraire: l'exemple des Mazarinades de Cyrano de Bergerac' in Luc Fraisse, ed. *L'Histoire littéraire: ses méthodes et ses résultats: Mélanges offerts à Madeleine Bertaud* (Geneva: Droz, 2001), pp. 153–66.

11 A number of these examples come from Ellegård's discussion in *Who was Junius?*, pp. 110–19.

12 'The shares of Fletcher and his collaborators in the Beaumont and Fletcher canon (I)', *SB* 8 (1956), 145.

13 2 vols. (London, 1794).

14 *The Collaboration of Webster and Dekker* (New Haven: Yale University Press, 1909); Schoenbaum, *IE*, pp. 74–6.

15 Ellegård, *Who was Junius?*, pp. 116–18.

16 This effect was identified by Jakob Stoll, 'Zur Psychologie der Schreibfehler', *Fortschritte der Psychologie* 2 (1913), 1–133 as one of the fundamental causes of scribal errors; but it equally affects speakers.

17 Coleridge, *Essays on His Times*, i. p. xxxi.

18 Erdman, 'The signature of style', pp. 65–8.

19 *Literary Review* (Dec. 1999/Jan. 2000), 19–20.

20 '*A funeral elegy*: W[illiam] S[hakespeare]'s "best-speaking witnesses"', *Shakespeare Studies* 25 (1997), 129–34.

21 *The Watchman*, no. 1, Tuesday 1 March 1796, ed. Lewis Patten as vol. 2 of *The Collected Works*, p. 31.

22 *Essays on His Times*, i. pp. xxxi–xxxii. These images would repay cognitive analysis of the kind given to Shakespeare by Mary Crane.

23 Erdman, 'The signature of style', p. 61.

24 A. C. Partridge, *Orthography in Shakespeare and Elizabethan Drama* (London: Edward Arnold, 1964), pp. 141–63; Donald W. Foster, *Elegy by W.S.: A Study in Attribution* (Newark: University of Delaware Press, 1989), pp. 80–154.

25 Partridge, *Orthography in Shakespeare*, p. 147.

26 Sherbo, 'The uses and abuses of internal evidence', 21.

27 (Amsterdam: Elsevier, 1993); also as *Forensic Science International* 58 (1993).

28 W. M. Drobisch, 'Ein statisticher Versuch über die formen des lateinischer Hexameters', *Berichte über die Verhandlungen der Königl.-Sächsischen Gesellschaft der Wissenschaften, Philologische-Historische Klasse* 18 (1866), 75–139. Summarised in C. B. Williams, *Style and Vocabulary: Numerical Studies* (London: Griffin, 1970), pp. 116–20 with statistical interpretations and additional data from Longfellow's English hexameters in *Evangeline*.

29 The history of these attempts is reviewed in Schoenbaum, *IE*, pp. 3–62.

30 Discussed in Williams, *Style and Vocabulary*, pp. 113–15.

31 Karl Wentersdorf, 'Shakespearean chronology and the metrical tests', in W. Fischer and K. Wentersdorf, eds., *Shakespeare-Studien* (Marburg: N. G. Elwert, 1951); John G. Fitch, 'Sense-pauses and relative dating in Seneca, Sophocles and Shakespeare', *American Journal of Philology* 102 (1981), 289–307; Barron Brainerd, 'The chronology of Shakespeare's plays: a statistical study', *CHum* 14 (1980), 221–30.

32 Marina Tarlinskaja, *Shakespeare's Verse: Iambic Pentameter and the Poet's Idiosyncrasies* (New York: Peter Lang, 1987); Peter Groves, *Strange Music: The Metre of the English Heroic Line* (Victoria, B.C.: *English Literary Studies*, 1998).
33 See Ward E. Y. Elliott and Robert J. Valenza, 'And then there were none: winnowing the Shakespeare claimants', *CHum* 30 (1996), 191–245 and 'The professor doth protest too much, methinks: problems with the Foster "response"', *CHum* 32 (1998), 425–90; Donald W. Foster, 'Response to Elliott and Valenza, "And then there were none"', *CHum* 30 (1996), 247–55 and 'The Claremont Shakespeare authorship clinic: how severe are the problems?', *CHum* 32 (1998), 491–510.
34 Elliott and Valenza, 'And then there were none', 201, citing Tarlinskaja, *Shakespeare's Verse*, Chapter six.
35 Foster, 'The Claremont Shakespeare authorship clinic', 504.
36 Ibid., 506.
37 For generative metrics see Morris Halle and Samuel J. Keyser, 'Illustration and defence of a theory of the iambic pentameter', *College English* 33 (1971), 154–76; Paul Kiparsky, 'The rhythmic structure of English verse', *Linguistic Inquiry* 8 (1977), 189–247; Paul Kiparsky and Gilbert Youmans, eds., *Rhythm and Meter* (San Diego: Academic Press, 1989).
38 Groves, *Strange Music*, pp. 92–5.
39 Derek Attridge, *The Rhythms of English Poetry* (London: Longmans, 1982).
40 *A History of English Prose Rhythm* (London: Macmillan, 1912).
41 Fielding, *New Essays by Henry Fielding*, pp. xxxiv–xxxv.
42 Ibid., p. xxix.
43 See P. N. Furbank and W. R. Owens, *The Canonisation of Daniel Defoe* (New Haven: Yale University Press, 1988), pp. 100–21 and *passim*. A fatal error on Moore's part was using wrong ascriptions as evidence for others, thus progressively corrupting whatever intuitive ear for Defoe's style he may have begun with.
44 'Internal evidence and the attribution of Elizabethan plays', *Bulletin of the New York Public Library* 65 (1961), 112; cited in Fielding, *New Essays by Henry Fielding*, p. xxxii.
45 E.g. in Johnstone, *The Linguistic Individual*, pp. 36–7.
46 *Rasselas and Other Tales*, ed. Gwin J. Kolb, vol. XVI of *The Yale Edition of the Works of Samuel Johnson* (New Haven and London: Yale University Press, 1958–), p. 7. On Johnson's style see in particular Alvin Kernan, *Printing Technology, Letters & Samuel Johnson* (Princeton University Press, 1987), pp. 172–81.
47 *The Disputed Assignment of Memoirs of an English Officer to Daniel Defoe*, 2 vols. (Stockholm: Almqvist & Wiksell, 1974), i. p. 30.
48 *PMLA* 31 (1916), 326–58.
49 Hoy, 'The shares of Fletcher and his collaborators (I)', 145.
50 Peter B. Murray, *A Study of Cyril Tourneur* (Philadelphia: University of Pennsylvania Press, 1964), pp. 158–89.
51 Schoenbaum, *IE*, pp. xvi–xvii.

7 GENDER AND AUTHORSHIP

1 See pp. 75–6.
2 *The Way Women Write* (New York: Teachers College Press, 1977), p. 137.
3 John Clute, introd. to James Tiptree, jr [Alice B. Sheldon], *Her Smoke Rose Up Forever. The Great Years of James Tiptree, Jr.* (Sauk City: Arkham House, 1990), p. xi.
4 Silverberg's introduction to Tiptree's 1975 collection *Warm Worlds and Otherwise*, quoted by Clute in his introduction to *Her Smoke Rose Up Forever*, p. xi. Compare the insistence of a reviewer of the *Era* of 14 November 1847 that 'no woman *could* have penned the "Autobiography of Jane Eyre"' (*The Brontes: The Critical Heritage*, ed. Miriam Allott (London: Routledge, 1974), p. 79).
5 Summarised from Jacqueline Pearson, *The Prostituted Muse: Images of Women and Women Dramatists 1642–1737* (Hemel Hempstead: Wheatsheaf, 1988), pp. 63–5.
6 *Henry Handel Richardson: The Letters*, ed. Clive Probyn and Bruce Steele with Rachel Solomon, 3 vols. (Melbourne University Press, 2000), i. pp. 581–2 (letters 332, 333).
7 *Works and Days: From the Journal of Michael Field*, ed. T. and D. C. Sturge Moore (London: John Murray, 1933), p. 16. A new edition by Sharon Bickle of the correspondence between Bradley and Cooper is in preparation.
8 Flavia Alaya, *William Sharp-Fiona Macleod* (Cambridge, MA: Harvard University Press, 1970).
9 Quoted in Grenville and Woolfe, *Making Stories*, pp. 67–8.
10 Preface to *The Luckey Chance* in *The Works of Aphra Behn*, vii. p. 217.
11 *Computation into Criticism: A Study of Jane Austen's Novels and an Experiment in Method* (Oxford: Clarendon Press, 1987).
12 *A Woman's Friendship*, ed. Elizabeth Morrison (Sydney: University of New South Wales Press, 1988), p. 39.
13 See John Burrows and Harold Love, 'Attribution tests and the editing of seventeenth-century poetry', *Yearbook of English Studies* 29 (1999), 151–75 and 'Did Aphra Behn write "Caesar's Ghost"?', in David Garrioch, Harold Love, Brian McMullin, Ian Morrison and Meredith Sherlock, eds., *The Culture of the Book: Essays from Two Hemispheres in Honour of Wallace Kirsop* (Melbourne: Bibliographical Society of Australia and New Zealand, 1999), pp. 148–72.
14 Rita Carter with Christopher Frith, *Mapping the Mind* (Berkeley: University of California Press, 1998), p. 71. See also Jeffrey E. Clarke and Eran Zaidel, 'Anatomical-behavioural relationships: corpus callosum morphometry and hemispherical specialization', *Behavioural Brain Research* 64 (1994), 185–202.
15 See on this bilaterality Bennett A. Shaywitz, Sally E. Shaywitz, et al., 'Sex differences in the functional organization of the brain for language', *Nature* 373 (16 Feb. 1995), 607–9.
16 Carter, *Mapping the Mind*, pp. 71, 77–9.

17 Doreen Kimura, 'Sex differences in the brain', *Scientific American* (Sept. 1992), 84.
18 Review of Norman Mailer, *Genius and Lust: A Journey through the Major Writings of Henry Miller* (New York: Grove Press, 1976) in *The New York Times Book Review*, 26 Oct. 1976, 2.
19 Hiatt, *The Way Women Write*, pp. 2–6.
20 Alicia Skinner Cook, Janet J. Fritz, et al., 'Early gender roles in the functional use of language', *Sex Roles* 12 (1985), 909–15; repr. in Carol Nagy Jacklin, ed. *The Psychology of Gender*, 4 vols. (Aldershot: Edward Elgar, 1992), iv. pp. 308–14.
21 Anthony Mulac, John M. Wiemann, Sally J. Widenmann & Toni W. Gibson, 'Male/female language differences and effects in same-sex and mixed-sex dyads: the gender-linked language effect', *Communication Monographs* 55 (1988), 315–35; repr. in Jacklin, *The Psychology of Gender*, iv. pp. 356–76.
22 *The Folkstories of Children* (Philadelphia: University of Pennsylvania Press, 1981).
23 *Becoming a Reader: The Experience of Fiction from Childhood to Adulthood* (Cambridge University Press, 1991), pp. 90–3; see also Vivian Paley, *Boys and Girls: Superheroes in the Doll Corner* (University of Chicago Press, 1984), esp. p. 135.
24 'Computers and the study of literature', in Christopher S. Butler, ed. *Computers and Written Texts* (Oxford: Blackwells, 1992), p. 180.
25 Keith Walker has kindly presented me with a copy of L. G. Pockock, *The Landfalls of Odysseus* (Christchurch, NZ: Whitcombe and Tombs, 1955), which supports a modified form of Butler's belief that the work was composed at Trapani in Sicily but ignores the gender issue.
26 Butler, *The Authoress of the Odyssey*, p. 4.
27 (London: HarperCollins, 1994).
28 *Slip-shod Sibyls: Recognition, Rejection and the Woman Poet* (Harmondsworth: Penguin, 1995), pp. 147–72.
29 '*Anna Boleyn* and the authenticity of Fielding's feminine narratives', *Eighteenth-century Studies* 21 (1988), 427–53.
30 Robin Lakoff's earlier but often cited *Language and Woman's Place* (New York: Harper & Row, 1975) relied on intuitive assessments of usage.
31 These findings are summarised in Hiatt, *The Way Women Write*, pp. 121–37.
32 'A computer-assisted investigation of gender-related idiolect in Octavio Paz and Rosario Castellanos', *CHum* 26 (1992), 103–17.
33 A theme developed in his *Fighting for Life: Contest, Sexuality, and Consciousness* (Ithaca: Cornell University Press, 1981).

8 CRAFT AND SCIENCE

1 *Science* 214 (1887), 237–49.
2 'A mechanical solution of a literary problem', *Popular Science Monthly* 60 (1901), 97–105. Mendenhall's data-collection, performed by women research assistants, was ingeniously mechanised. As one assistant read out the numbers

of letters in each word the other would punch the corresponding key of a recording device (p. 102).

3 *Who Wrote Shakespeare?* (London: Thames & Hudson, 1996), p. 229.

4 'Letter frequency as a discriminator of authors', *N&Q* 239 (1994), 467–9. The data is given fuller statistical processing in his 'Heterogeneous authorship in early Shakespeare and the problem of *Henry V*', *LLC* 13 (1998), 15–28 and with Robert A. J. Matthews, 'Neural computation in stylometry II: an application to the works of Shakespeare and Marlowe', *LLC* 9 (1994), 1–6.

5 (Cambridge University Press, 1944).

6 Frederick Mosteller and David L. Wallace, *Inference and Disputed Authorship: The Federalist* (Reading, MA.: Addison-Wesley Pub. Co., 1964); 2nd edition as *Applied Bayesian and Classical Inference: The Case of the 'Federalist' Papers* (New York: Springer-Verlag, 1984).

7 *A Statistical Method for Determining Authorship*, Gothenberg Studies in English 13 (University of Gothenberg, 1962) and *Who Was Junius?* Ellegård's work was the model for Hargevik's critique of a Defoe attribution in *The Disputed Assignment of Memoirs of an English Officer.*

8 6th edn (New York: W. H. Freeman and Co., 1999); (Oxford: Pergamon Press, 1982).

9 *CHum* 28 (1994), 87–106.

10 There is a good account of this production in *The Revenger's Tragedy*, ed. Brian Gibbons (London: Black, 1990), pp. xxxiii–xxxvi.

11 Schoenbaum, *IE*, pp. 208–10.

12 'The authorship of *The Revenger's Tragedy*', *Studies in Philology* 23 (1926), 157–68.

13 Murray, *A Study of Cyril Tourneur*, pp. 158–89.

14 Lake, *The Canon of Thomas Middleton's Plays.*

15 M. W. A. Smith, '*The Revenger's Tragedy*: the derivation and interpretation of statistical results for resolving disputed authorship', *CHum* 21 (1987), 21–55.

16 M. W. A. Smith, 'The authorship of *The Revenger's Tragedy*', *N&Q* 236 (1991), 508–13.

17 'Invalidation reappraised', *CHum* 30 (1997), 417–31.

18 Hugh Craig, 'Authorial attribution and computational stylistics: if you can tell authors apart, have you learned anything about them?', *LLC* 14 (1999), 103–13.

19 In *A Spiritual Spicerie* (London, 1638) Braithwaite writes: 'This moved mee sometimes to fit my buskin'd Muse for the Stage; with other occasionall Presentments or Poems; which being free-borne, and not mercenarie, received gracefull acceptance . . . For so happily had I crept into *Opinion* . . . as nothing was either presented by mee . . . to the *Stage*; or committed by mee to the *Presse*; which past not with good approvement in the estimate of the world' (pp. 429–30). These 'buskin'd' plays [i.e. tragedies] remain unidentified.

20 (New York: Scribner, 1978).

21 For a summary of forty major distributions, see Merran Evans, Nicholas Hastings and J. Brian Peacock, *Statistical Distributions*, 3rd edn (New York: Wiley, 2000).

22 M. W. A. Smith, 'An investigation of Morton's method to distinguish Elizabethan playwrights', *CHum* 19 (1985), 11. See also his 'An investigation of the basis of Morton's method for the determination of authorship', *Style* 19 (1985), 341–59 and 'Merriam's applications of Morton's method', *CHum* 21 (1987), 59–60. The criticised results are defended in Merriam, 'Invalidation reappraised'.
23 Burrows, 'Computers and the study of literature', p. 173.
24 Andrew Q. Morton, 'Authorship: the nature of the habit', *TLS*, 17–23 Feb. 1989, 164, 174.
25 David I. Holmes, 'The evolution of stylometry in humanities scholarship', *LLC* 13 (1998), 114; see also Michael L. Hilton and David I. Holmes, 'An assessment of cumulative sum charts for authorship attribution', *LLC* 8 (1993), 73–80 and D. I. Holmes and F. J. Tweedie, 'Forensic stylometry: a review of the cusum controversy', *Revue informatique et statistique dans les sciences humaines* 31 (1995), 19–47. Holmes lists a number of other studies critical of this aspect of Morton's work.
26 Hilton and Holmes, 'An assessment of cumulative sum charts', 78–9.
27 'Stylometry and method. The case of Euripides', *LLC* 10 (1995), 271–2. There are also likely to be other forms of variation within a stylistic signature – e.g. from genre to genre and character to character.
28 'An exploration of differences in the Pauline epistles using multivariate statistical analysis', *LLC* 10 (1995), 85.
29 See McColly and Weier in Chapter five, n. 14 above.
30 Ledger, 'An exploration of differences', 86.
31 M. W. A. Smith, 'An investigation of Morton's method', 7.
32 See Jill M. Farringdon et al., *Analysing for Authorship: A Guide to the Cusum Technique* (Cardiff: University of Wales Press, 1996) and Merriam, 'Invalidation reappraised'. Morton's original methods are effectively used in D. P. O'Brien and A. C. Darnell, *Authorship Puzzles in the History of Economics: A Statistical Approach* (London: Macmillan, 1982) to test a number of assumptions which had been made by previous writers on external or internal grounds. In most of the cases considered they are able to offer a persuasive resolution.
33 Morton, *Literary Detection*, p. 105.
34 Holmes, 'Authorship attribution', 99.
35 Burrows, 'Computers and the study of literature', 181. The mathematical basis of the method is described in José Nilo G. Binongo and M. W. A. Smith, 'The application of principal component analysis to stylometry', *LLC* 14 (1999), 445–65; see also J. F. Burrows and D. H. Craig, 'Lyrical drama and the "turbid mountebanks": styles of dialogue in Romantic and Renaissance tragedy', *CHum* 28 (1994), 63–86 and D. I. Holmes and R. S. Forsyth, 'The *Federalist* revisited: new directions in authorship attribution', *LLC* 10 (1995), 111–27.
36 *LLC* 7 (1992), 91–110.
37 Humanists may prefer, like the author, to approach this complex topic through an introductory text concerned with its rapidly ramifying

commercial use. Recommended is Kate A. Smith, *Introduction to Neural Networks and Data Mining for Business Applications* (Melbourne: Eruditions, 1999). This covers the more advanced self-organising feature maps and Adaptive Resonance Theory as well as the standard model here considered.

38 Described in K. Smith, *Neural Networks*, pp. 45–51.

39 Bradley Kjell, 'Authorship determination using letter pair frequency features with neural network classifiers', *LLC* 9 (1994), 119–24; Holmes, 'The evolution of stylometry', 115; Holmes and Tweedie, 'Forensic stylometry'.

40 'Neural computation in stylometry I: an application to the works of Shakespeare and Fletcher', *LLC* 8 (1993), 203–9; Merriam and Matthews, 'Neural computation in stylometry II'; Merriam, 'Letter frequency as a discriminator of authors', 469.

41 Johan F. Hoorn et al., 'Neural network identification of poets using letter sequences', *LLC* 14 (1999), 311–38.

42 Ledger, 'An exploration of differences', 86.

43 For Foster's account of this discovery see *Author Unknown*, pp. 53–94.

44 See p. 91 above.

45 Among these the case for William Stradling is compelling. See Lisa Hopkins, '"Elegy by W. S.": another possible candidate?', *Philological Quarterly* 76 (1997), 159–68.

46 Foster, '*A funeral elegy*', 129–34.

47 'Empirically determining Shakespeare's idiolect', *Shakespeare Studies* 25 (1997), 172.

48 Armstrong, *Shakespeare's Imagination*; see also Schoenbaum, *IE*, pp. 186–9. Chambers, 'Shakespeare and the play of *More*', 213–38 and pp. 83–4 below.

49 Sarah A. Tooley, 'Some women novelists', *The Woman at Home* 5 (1897–8), 205.

50 Holmes, 'The evolution of stylometry'; Rudman, 'The state of authorship attribution studies: some problems and solutions', *CHum* 31 (1997–8), 351–65 and 'Non-traditional authorship attribution studies: ignis fatuus or Rosetta stone?'

51 The complaint about the number of different tests used arises from a desire for the field to establish a range of generally accepted methodologies. The tests in themselves may have been poorly or expertly applied.

52 Schoenbaum, *IE*, p. 147.

53 See the papers cited in Chapter six, n. 33 plus Ward E. Y. Elliott and Robert J. Valenza, 'Glass slippers and seven-league boots: C-prompted doubts about ascribing *A funeral elegy* and *A lover's complaint* to Shakespeare', *Shakespeare Quarterly* 48 (1997), 177–207.

54 Schoenbaum, *IE*, p. 48.

55 Also a criticism made by P. N. Furbank and W. R. Owens: see 'Dangerous relations', *The Scriblerian and the Kit-Kats* 33 (1991), 242–4 and *The Canonisation of Daniel Defoe*, pp. 176–83.

56 Spoken remark attributed to Ward Elliott in Foster, 'Response to Elliott and Valenza', 254.
57 Robert Matthews, 'Digging the dirt on age', *New Scientist*, 13 March 1999, 18.
58 Morton, *Literary Detection*, p. 22.
59 Fielding, *New Essays by Henry Fielding*, p. 549.
60 '*Edmund Ironside* and "stylometry"', *N&Q* 239 (1994), 469.
61 Furbank and Owens, 'Dangerous relations', 242.
62 Morton, *Literary Detection*, p. 39.
63 McMenamin, *Forensic Stylistics*, p. 46.
64 Sams, '*Edmund Ironside*', 472.
65 Furbank and Owens, 'Dangerous relations', 242.
66 Morton, *Literary Detection*, p. 105 and earlier. His proposed model of memory (p. 16) was a department store with small, frequently requested items near the front door and large and less often required ones at the back, which does not take us very far.
67 Ian Lancashire, 'Paradigms of authorship', *Shakespeare Studies* 26 (1998), 299. The theme is more fully developed in his 'Empirically determining Shakespeare's idiolect', 171–85.
68 Merriam, 'Letter frequency as a discriminator of authors', 468.
69 Ibid., 469.
70 Craig, 'Authorial attribution', p. 104.
71 Rudman, 'Non-traditional authorship attribution studies', 176.

9 BIBLIOGRAPHICAL EVIDENCE

1 (London: Edward Arnold, 1977).
2 (Wetheral: Plains Books, 1990).
3 In Davison, *The Book Encompassed*, pp. 57–68.
4 2 vols. (London: Cassell, 1973).
5 Richard S. Forsyth and David I. Holmes, 'Feature-finding for text classification', *LLC* 11 (1996), 163.
6 Considered by Wallace Notestein and Frances Relf in the introduction to their edition *Commons Debates for 1629* (Minneapolis: University of Minnesota, 1921), pp. xi–lxv.
7 *The Poems and Letters of Andrew Marvell*, ed. H. M. Margoliouth, 3rd edn rev. Pierre Legouis with the collaboration of E. E. Duncan-Jones (Oxford: Clarendon Press, 1971), ii. p. 323.
8 Leah H. Marcus, 'From oral delivery to print', in Arthur F. Marotti and Michael D. Bristol, eds. *Print, Manuscript and Performance: the Changing Relations of the Media in Early England* (Columbus: Ohio State University Press, 2000), pp. 37–8.
9 The tradition of *samizdat* publication in the former Soviet Union is a more recent example of the same phenomenon.
10 *Piers Plowman. Vol. 1. The A Version: Will's visions of Piers Plowman and Do-well*, ed. George Kane; *Vol. 2. The B Version: Will's visions of Piers Plowman, Do-well, Do-better and Do-best*, ed. George Kane and E. Talbot Donaldson; *Vol. 3. The C*

Version: Will's visions of Piers Plowman, Do-well, Do-better and Do-best, ed. George Russell and George Kane (London: Athlone Press, 1988–97). Vols. i and ii were originally published in 1960 and 1975 respectively.

11 This was also to be true of early compositors.

12 The contributions to this debate are reviewed in Joseph Rudman, 'Non-traditional authorship attribution studies in the *Historia Augusta*: some caveats', *LLC* 13 (1998), 151–7.

13 *Texts and Transmission: A Survey of the Latin Classics*, ed. L. H. Reynolds (Oxford: Clarendon Press, 1983), p. 344.

14 *On Editing Shakespeare* (Charlottesville: University Press of Virginia, 1966), pp. 11–12. Cf. the diagram in Wells, Taylor et al., *William Shakespeare: A Textual Companion*, p. 31. For a valuable revisionist perspective on the question see Peter W. M. Blayney, 'The publication of playbooks', in Cox and Kastan, *A New History of Early English Drama*, pp. 383–422, esp. 392–4.

15 George R. Price, 'The authorship and the manuscript of *The Old Law*', *Huntington Library Quarterly* 16 (1952–3), 117–39.

16 Hoy, 'The shares of Fletcher and his collaborators', see Chapter six, pp. 117–18.

17 Wells, Taylor et al., *William Shakespeare: A Textual Companion*, pp. 401–2.

18 'Multiple authorship and the question of authority', *Text* 5 (1991), 286.

19 For a range of similar cases, see Gaskell, *From Writer to Reader*.

20 *Spectator*, 15 July 2000, 21. D. J. Taylor, 'A true ghost story' in the same journal for 21 October 2000, asserts that 'at least half of the 20 books included in this week's hardback bestseller list . . . were produced with the help of collaborators' (12).

21 In Davison, *The Book Encompassed*, pp. 69–82.

22 See John Carter and Graham Pollard, *An Enquiry into the Nature of Certain Nineteenth Century Pamphlets*, 2nd edn, ed. Nicolas Barker and John Collins; with Nicolas Barker and John Collins, *A Sequel to An Enquiry into the Nature of Certain Nineteenth Century Pamphlets by John Carter and Graham Pollard: The Forgeries of H. Buxton Forman and T. J. Wise Re-examined*, 2 vols. (London: Scolar Press, 1983).

23 North, *The Life of the Lord Keeper North*, p. 60.

24 H. Robbins Landon, *Horns in High C: A Memoir of Musical Discoveries and Adventures* (London: Thames & Hudson, 1999), p. 90 and Alan Tyson and H. C. Robbins Landon, 'Who composed Haydn's Op 3?' *The Musical Times* 105 (July 1964), 506–7.

25 'A verse miscellany of Aphra Behn: Bodleian Library MS Firth c. 16', *English Manuscript Studies* 2 (1990), 189–227.

26 Rochester's *Poems on Several Occasions*, ed. James Thorpe (Princeton University Press, 1950); David M. Vieth, *Attribution in Restoration Poetry: A Study of Rochester's 'Poems' of 1680*, Yale Studies in English, no. 153 (New Haven: Yale University Press, 1963).

27 For collections of dated watermarks see Gaskell, *A New Introduction to Bibliography*, p. 398; for setting styles R. A. Sayce, 'Compositorial practices

and the localization of printed books, 1530–1800', *The Library*, 5th ser. 21 (1966), 1–45.

28 2 vols. (Oxford: Clarendon Press, 1963).

29 Donald F. Bond, 'The first printing of the *Spectator*', *Modern Philology* 47 (1950), 164–77.

30 *The Schollers Purgatory, Discovered in the Stationers Common-wealth* (London, 1624), p. 121.

31 Ong, *Orality and Literacy*, pp. 117–38.

32 *The Works of John Wilmot, Earl of Rochester*, ed. Love, pp. 614–15.

33 *The Works of the Right Honourable the Earls of Rochester, and Roscommon*, 3rd edn (London, 1709), p. (*A*2v).

34 *The Works of John Wilmot, Earl of Rochester*, ed. Love, pp. 612–13.

35 Joseph Bédier, *Etudes critiques* (Paris: A. Colin, 1903), p. 86. Discussed in Morize, *Problems and Methods of Literary History*, pp. 158–69 and Gustave Rudler, *Les Techniques de la critique et de l'histoire littéraires en littérature française moderne* (Oxford University Press, 1923), pp. 42–7.

10 FORGERY AND ATTRIBUTION

1 Janet Martin, 'John of Salisbury as a classical scholar', in *The World of John of Salisbury*, ed. Michael Wilks (Oxford: Blackwells, 1994), pp. 179–201.

2 Grafton, *Forgers and Critics*, p. 24.

3 See pp. 18–19 above; Nicholas of Cusa, *The Catholic Concordance*, ed. and trans. Paul E. Sigmund (Cambridge University Press, 1991), pp. 216–22.

4 See John Marenbon, *The Philosophy of Peter Abelard* (Cambridge University Press, 1997), pp. 82–93. Marenbon accepts both the correspondence and the autobiographical *Historia calamitatum* as genuine. Newly attributed letters between the pair have been published by Constant Mews as *The Lost Love Letters of Heloise and Abelard: Perceptions of Dialogue in Twelfth-century France* (New York: St Martin's Press, 1999). The authenticity of the original correspondence is defended in Mews, pp. 47–53.

5 See Richard Bentley, *A Dissertation upon the Epistles of Phalaris, Themistocles, Socrates, Euripides, and Others; and the Fables of Æsop*, published with William Wotton, *Reflections upon Ancient and Modern Learning*, 2nd edn (London, 1697) and *A Dissertation upon the Epistles of Phalaris. With an Answer to the Objections of the Honourable Charles Boyle* (London, 1699).

6 Pfeiffer, *Classical Scholarship*, ii. p. 91.

7 Grafton, *Forgers and Critics*, pp. 54–5, 60–1, 99–123.

8 Petronius, *Titi Petronii Arbitri equitis Romani Satyricon cum fragmentis Albæ Græcæ recupertatis ann. 1688 nunc demum integrum* (Rotterdam: François Nodot, 1693).

9 For a survey see Paul Baines, *The House of Forgery in Eighteenth-century Britain* (Aldershot: Ashgate, 1999).

10 For Bertram's forgeries, see John Whitehead, *This Solemn Mockery: The Art of Literary Forgery* (London: Arlington Books, 1973), pp. 54–9.

11 Defoe's intention in this pretence is one of the topics of Robert Mayer, *History and the Early English Novel: Matters of Fact from Bacon to Defoe* (Cambridge University Press, 1997).
12 Facsimile, ed. James Sutherland (Los Angeles: William Andrews Clark Memorial Library, University of California, 1960), p. 3. See also Philip Pinkus, *Grub Street Stripped Bare; the Scandalous Lives and Pornographic Works of the Original Grub St Writers* (London: Constable, 1968), pp. 75–6.
13 Bentley, *A Dissertation upon the Epistles of Phalaris*, p. 7.
14 Ed. Bernard Bergonzi (Harmondsworth: Penguin, 1968), p. 492.
15 See Jerald and Sandra Tanner, eds., *Hofmann's Confession* (Salt Lake City: Utah Lighthouse Ministry, 1987) and Linda Sillitoe and Allen Roberts, *Salamander: The Story of the Mormon Forgery Murders* (Salt Lake City: Signature Books, 1988). Hofmann's numerous other highly skilled forgeries included a spurious Emily Dickinson holograph poem and the printed *Oath of a Freeman.*
16 For verbals see p. 140.
17 Discussed in McMenamin, *Forensic Stylistics*, pp. 77–110 and *passim.*
18 Ibid., p. 92.
19 See *Communist Forgeries: Hearing before the Subcommittee to Investigate the Administration of the Internal Security Act . . . June 2, 1961* (Washington: U.S. Government Printing Office, 1961) for the CIA's view of the matter – that organisation being itself deeply involved in the same activity.
20 For Jung, see pp. 45–6.
21 Petronius, *Titi Petronii Arbitri*, pp. *3v–*6v.
22 'Faking the past: computer analysis of literary imitations', unpublished conference paper ('Shady Book', Bibliographical Society of Australia and New Zealand conference, Canberra, 28 September 1991).
23 (Norman: University of Oklahoma Press, 1994).
24 The charge of impressionism is one of several brought by Irving N. Rothman against Furbank and Owens in his uneven 'Defoe de-attributions scrutinized under Hargevik criteria: applying stylometrics to the canon', *Papers of the Bibliographical Society of America* 94 (2000), 375–98. It is not clear that Rothman has fully understood Hargevik's intricate statistical argument.
25 *Doutes proposé sur l'âge du Dante par P. H. J. (Père Hardouin, Jésuite) avec notes par C. L.* (Paris, 1847).
26 These terms are offered to the writers of those phrase books of Latin for modern use, so popular recently, as insults suitable for shouting at football matches, particularly when Celtic are playing Rangers or at any game involving Notre Dame.
27 For the Benedictines see Hardouin, *Prolegomena*, pp. 194–5. The identity of Archontius is discussed in Mathurin Veyssière de la Croze, *Vindiciae veterum scriptorum* (Rotterdam, 1708), pp. 20–2.
28 (London, 1819).
29 Hardouin, *Prolegomena*, pp. 37–9.
30 Hobart and Schiffman, *Information Ages*, p. 103; see also pp. 87–90.

31 (Oxford: Basil Blackwell; Stratford-upon-Avon: Shakespeare Head Press, 1925); *Ben Jonson*, ed. C. H. Herford and Percy Simpson, 11 vols. (Oxford: Clarendon Press, 1954), i. pp. 139, 133.
32 Roman Polanski's film *The Ninth Gate* (1999) concludes with an ingenious variation on this scenario.

11 SHAKESPEARE AND CO.

1 Jonathan Bate, *The Genius of Shakespeare* (London: Picador, 1997), pp. 65–100 offers a commonsensical refutation of this and a number of related contentions.
2 'Was the 1609 *Shake-speares Sonnets* really unauthorized?', *Review of English Studies* ns 34 (1983), 157–71.
3 Documented in Gerald Eades Bentley, *The Profession of Dramatist in Shakespeare's Time, 1590–1642* (Princeton University Press, 1971; corr. repr. 1986), pp. 264–92. Of Fletcher, Bentley notes: 'he is known to have had a hand in about 69 plays, but only nine of them were published in his lifetime' (p. 275) – a much lower ratio than in Shakespeare's case.
4 Bentley, *The Profession of Dramatist*, p. 266.
5 Bentley's careful examination of these and other contractual obligations of house-dramatists illuminates much that has been found puzzling in the professional conduct of Shakespeare.
6 Bate comments intriguingly on Shakespeare's conscious and unconscious reworkings of predecessors, particularly Marlowe, as part of the process of finding his own identity as a playwright (*Genius of Shakespeare*, pp. 106–32).
7 See *Shakespeare's Lost Play: Edmund Ironside*, ed. Eric Sams (London: Fourth Estate, 1985); Sams, 'Edmund Ironside'; *King Edward III*, ed. Giorgio Melchiori (Cambridge University Press, 1998); Eric Sams, ed., *Shakespeare's Edward III: An Early Play Restored to the Canon* (New Haven: Yale University Press, 1996).
8 For 'If I die' see *William Shakespeare: The Complete Works. Original-spelling edition*, gen. eds. Stanley Wells and Gary Taylor (Oxford: Clarendon Press, 1986), p. 883. Quotations from the plays are from this edition. For 'A funeral elegy' see pp. 147–51.
9 Love, *James Edward Neild*, pp. 146–7 and *passim*.
10 Michell, *Who Wrote Shakespeare?*, p. 109.
11 Ibid., pp. 250 and 97–105.
12 Cf. pp. 204–5.
13 Bate, *The Genius of Shakespeare*, p. 90.
14 Ibid., pp. 108–9, 112.
15 *The Shakespearian Playing Companies* (Oxford: Clarendon Press, 1996) and *The Shakespearean Stage, 1574–1642*, 3rd edn (Cambridge University Press, 1992).
16 (Cambridge University Press, 1992).
17 Byrne, 'Bibliographical clues'; see pp. 90–1.
18 Michell, *Who Wrote Shakespeare?*, pp. 179–81.

19 Franklin Fiske Heard, *Oddities of the Law* (London: The Eastern Press, 1921), p. 135, citing Pollock, C. B., in *Regina* v. *Exall*, 4 Foster & Finlason, 929.
20 Schoenbaum, *IE*, p. 113.
21 Ibid., p. 192.
22 Ibid., p. 22.
23 Michell, *Who Wrote Shakespeare?*, p. 252.
24 Bate, *The Genius of Shakespeare*, pp. 10–13.

12 ARGUING ATTRIBUTION

1 Furbank and Owens, *The Canonisation of Daniel Defoe*, p. 31.
2 See in particular, David Greetham, 'Textual forensics', *PMLA* 111 (1996), 32–51 (from an issue more generally concerned with the subject of evidence) and 'Facts, truefacts, factoids; or, why are they still saying those nasty things about epistemology?', *Yearbook of English Studies* 29 (1999), 1–23 and Gary Taylor, 'The rhetoric of textual criticism', *Text: Transactions of the Society for Textual Scholarship* 4 (1988), 39–57.
3 Filloy, 'Deciding the authorship of a doubtful text', 51.
4 *Life's Other Secret: The New Mathematics of the Living World* (London: Penguin, 1998), p. 246.
5 Groves, *Strange Music*, p. 47.
6 Rudman, 'Non-traditional authorship attribution studies: ignis fatuus or Rosetta stone?', 197, n. 35.
7 Holmes, 'Authorship attribution', 87.
8 Italo Calvino, *If On a Winter's Night a Traveller* (London: Minerva, 1982), p. 187.
9 Such a habit should not be called a 'fingerprint' because it is rarely unique to an individual.
10 Bernard Dupriez, *A Dictionary of Literary Devices. Gradus, A–Z*, trans. and adapted Albert W. Halsall (University of Toronto Press, 1991), pp. 280–1.
11 Filloy, 'Deciding the authorship of a doubtful text', 42.
12 See on this point Taylor, 'The rhetoric of textual criticism', 53–4.
13 One famous case was that of the atom scientists Enrico Fermi and Leo Szilard whose cognitively disjunctive collaboration is described in William Lanouette, 'The odd couple and the bomb', *Scientific American* 283 (2000), 86–91.
14 Rose, *Authors and Owners*, p. 8.
15 Burrows, 'Computers and the study of literature', 181.
16 Burrows, 'Not unless you ask nicely', 101–2.
17 M. W. A. Smith, 'Attribution by statistics: a critique of four recent studies', *Revue informatique et statistique dans les sciences humaines* 26 (1990), 242. The subject of this last remark was McColly and Weier's attempt to determine whether the five 'Pearl' poems were by one, two or a number of authors.
18 'Is the author really dead? An empirical study of authorship in English Renaissance drama', *Empirical Studies of the Arts* 18 (2000), 119–34. Genre in this context refers to the traditional dramatic genres only.

19 Locke grounds personal identity in 'the consciousness of present and past Actions' (*An Essay concerning Humane Understanding*, 2nd edn (London, 1694), Book II, Chap. XXVII, p. 185). Sterne's debt to Locke is explored in John Traugott, *Tristram Shandy's World: Sterne's Philosophical Rhetoric* (Berkeley: University of California Press, 1954).

20 William Congreve, *The Complete Plays of William Congreve*, ed. Herbert Davis (University of Chicago Press, 1967), p. 139.

21 Dryden, 'An essay of dramatick poesie' (*Works*, xvii. p. 59). Of course inept writers can sometimes be distinctive in their limitations while the talented chameleon baffles us!

22 Mews, *The Lost Love Letters of Heloise and Abelard*, p. x. For a similar moment of discovery see Foster, *Author Unknown*, p. 65: 'Here at last was a writer who set the lights flashing and the bells ringing.'

23 'National character', in *Anthropology To-day*, ed. A. L. Kroeber (University of Chicago Press, 1953), pp. 645–6; cited in J. K. Chambers, *Sociolinguistic Theory: Linguistic Variation and its Social Significance* (Oxford: Basil Blackwell, 1995), p. 41. I am aware of criticisms which have been made of Mead's findings in her own anthropological work and which would need to be taken into account in any evaluation of this method.

24 J. K. Chambers, *Sociolinguistic Theory*, pp. 22–5.

25 Johnstone, *The Linguistic Individual*, pp. 92–127.

26 Perceptively explored under the notion of 'extended consciousness' in Antonio Damasio, *The Feeling of What Happens: Body and Emotion in the Making of Consciousness* (London: Heinemann, 1999), pp. 195–233.

Select bibliography

Alaya, Flavia. *William Sharp–Fiona Macleod* (Cambridge, MA: Harvard University Press, 1970).

Appleyard, J. A. *Becoming a Reader: The Experience of Fiction from Childhood to Adulthood* (Cambridge University Press, 1991).

Armstrong, Edward A. *Shakespeare's Imagination: A Study of the Psychology of Association and Inspiration* (London: Drummond, 1946).

Baines, Paul. *The House of Forgery in Eighteenth-century Britain* (Aldershot: Ashgate, 1999).

Barthes, Roland. 'The death of the author', in *Image, Music, Text: Essays*, selected and translated by Stephen Heath (London: Fontana, 1977), pp. 142–8.

Bate, Jonathan. *The Genius of Shakespeare* (London: Picador, 1997).

Beal, Peter. *In Praise of Scribes: Manuscripts and their Makers in Seventeenth-century England* (Oxford: Clarendon Press, 1998).

Bédier, Joseph. *Etudes critiques* (Paris: A. Colin, 1903).

Behn, Aphra. *The Works of Aphra Behn*, ed. Janet Todd, 7 vols. (London: William Pickering, 1996).

Bentley, Gerald Eades. *The Profession of Dramatist in Shakespeare's Time, 1590–1642* (Princeton University Press, 1971; corr. repr. 1986).

Bentley, Richard. *A Dissertation upon the Epistles of Phalaris. With an Answer to the Objections of the Honourable Charles Boyle* (London, 1699).

Billman, Carol. *The Secret of the Stratemeyer Syndicate: Nancy Drew, The Hardy Boys, and the Million Dollar Fiction Factory* (New York: Ungar, 1986).

Binongo, José Nilo G. and M. W. A. Smith. 'The application of principal component analysis to stylometry', *LLC* 14 (1999), 445–65.

Boswell, James. *Boswell's Life of Johnson*, ed. George Birkbeck Hill, rev. L. F. Powell, 6 vols. (Oxford: Clarendon Press, 1934).

Brainerd, Barron. 'The chronology of Shakespeare's plays: a statistical study', *CHum* 14 (1980), 221–30.

Burke, Séan. *The Death and Return of the Author* (Edinburgh University Press, 1992).

Burns, Ann with Barbara Hoffert. 'First novels', *Library Journal*, 15 March 1988, 31–5.

Burrows, John. *Computation into Criticism: A Study of Jane Austen's Novels and an Experiment in Method* (Oxford: Clarendon Press, 1987).

'Computers and the study of literature', in Christopher S. Butler, ed. *Computers and Written Texts* (Oxford: Blackwells, 1992), pp. 167–204.

'Not unless you ask nicely: the interpretative nexus between analysis and information', *LLC* 7 (1992), 91–110.

'A computational approach to the Rochester canon', in *The Works of John Wilmot, Earl of Rochester*, ed. Harold Love (Oxford University Press, 1999), pp. 681–705.

Burrows, John and D. H. Craig. 'Lyrical drama and the "turbid mountebanks": styles of dialogue in Romantic and Renaissance tragedy', *CHum* 28 (1994), 63–86.

Burrows, John and Anthony J. Hassall. '*Anna Boleyn* and the authenticity of Fielding's feminine narratives', *Eighteenth-century Studies* 21 (1988), 427–53.

Burrows, John and Harold Love. 'Attribution tests and the editing of seventeenth-century poetry', *Yearbook of English Studies* 29 (1999), 151–75.

'Did Aphra Behn write "Caesar's Ghost"?', in David Garrioch et al., eds. *The Culture of the Book: Essays from Two Hemispheres in Honour of Wallace Kirsop* (Melbourne: Bibliographical Society of Australia and New Zealand, 1999), pp. 148–72.

Butler, Samuel. *The Authoress of the Odyssey: where and when she wrote, who she was, the use she made of the Iliad, and how the poem grew under her hands*, introd. David Grene (University of Chicago Press, 1967), repr. of 2nd edn (London, 1922).

Byrne, Muriel St Clare. 'Bibliographical clues in collaborate plays', *The Library*, 4th ser. 13 (1932), 21–48.

Carrier, Hubert. 'La critique d'attribution au confluent des méthodes de l'histoire littéraire: l'exemple des Mazarinades de Cyrano de Bergerac', in Luc Fraisse, ed. *L'Histoire littéraire: ses méthodes et ses résultats. Mélanges offerts à Madeleine Bertaud* (Geneva: Droz, 2001), pp. 153–66.

Carter, John and Graham Pollard. *An Enquiry into the Nature of Certain Nineteenth Century Pamphlets*, 2nd edn, ed. Nicolas Barker and John Collins; with Nicolas Barker and John Collins, *A Sequel to An Enquiry into the Nature of Certain Nineteenth Century Pamphlets by John Carter and Graham Pollard: The Forgeries of H. Buxton Forman and T. J. Wise Re-examined*, 2 vols. (London: Scolar Press, 1983).

Carter, Rita with Christopher Frith. *Mapping the Mind* (Berkeley: University of California Press, 1998).

Chambers, R. W. 'The three texts of "Piers Plowman", and their grammatical forms', *MLR* 14 (1919), 129–51.

'Shakespeare and the play of *More*', in *Man's Unconquerable Mind: Studies of English Writers, from Bede to A. E. Houseman and W. P. Ker* (London: Cape, 1939; repr. 1964), pp. 204–49 and Note pp. 407–8.

Clark, Peter. *British Clubs and Societies 1580–1800* (Oxford University Press, 2000).

Coady, C. A. J. *Testimony: A Philosophical Study* (Oxford: Clarendon Press, 1992).

Congreve, William. *The Complete Plays of William Congreve*, ed. Herbert Davis (University of Chicago Press, 1967).

Cox, John D. and David Scott Kastan, eds. *A New History of Early English Drama* (New York: Columbia University Press, 1997).

Craig, Hugh. 'Authorial attribution and computational stylistics: if you can tell authors apart, have you learned anything about them?', *LLC* 14 (1999), 103–13.

'Is the author really dead? An empirical study of authorship in English Renaissance drama', *Empirical Studies of the Arts* 18 (2000), 119–34.

Crane, Mary Thomas. *Shakespeare's Brain: Reading with Cognitive Theory* (Princeton University Press, 2001).

Damasio, Antonio. *The Feeling of What Happens: Body and Emotion in the Making of Consciousness* (London: Heinemann, 1999).

Davis, Tom. 'The analysis of handwriting: an introductory survey', in Peter Davison, ed. *The Book Encompassed: Studies in Twentieth-century Bibliography* (Cambridge University Press, 1992), pp. 57–68.

Deloffre, Frédéric. 'Quelques réflexions sur la critique d'attribution', in Luc Fraisse, ed. *L'Histoire littéraire: ses méthodes et ses résultats. Mélanges offerts à Madeleine Bertaud* (Geneva: Droz, 2001), pp. 247–71.

Dixon, Peter and David Mannion. 'Goldsmith's periodical essays: a statistical analysis of eleven doubtful cases', *LLC* 8 (1993), 1–19.

Dryden, John. *The Works of John Dryden*, gen. eds. H. T. Swedenberg, jr and Alan Roper, 19 vols. to date (Berkeley and Los Angeles: University of California Press, 1956–).

Duncan-Jones, Elsie. 'Marvell, R. F. and the authorship of "Blake's victory"', *English Manuscript Studies* 5 (1995), 110–11.

Dyregrov, David. 'Jo. Haines as librettist for Purcell's *Fairy Queen*', *Restoration and 18th Century Theatre Research*, 2nd ser. 7 (1992), 29–46.

Elias, A. C., jr. '*Senatus Consultum*: revising verse in Swift's Dublin circle, 1729–1735', in *Reading Swift: Papers from the Third Münster Symposium on Jonathan Swift* [1994], eds. Hermann J. Real and Helgard Stöver-Leidig (Munich: Wilhelm Fink, 1998), pp. 249–67.

Ellegård, Alvar. *A Statistical Method for Determining Authorship*, Gothenberg Studies in English 13 (University of Gothenberg, 1962).

Who was Junius? (Stockholm: Almqvist & Wiksell, 1962).

Elliott, Ward E. Y. and Robert J. Valenza. 'And then there were none: winnowing the Shakespeare claimants', *CHum* 30 (1996), 191–245.

'Glass slippers and seven-league boots: C-prompted doubts about ascribing *A funeral elegy* and *A lover's complaint* to Shakespeare', *Shakespeare Quarterly* 48 (1997), 177–207.

'The professor doth protest too much, methinks: problems with the Foster "response"', *CHum* 32 (1998), 425–90.

Erasmus, Desiderius. *Patristic Scholarship. The Edition of St Jerome*, ed., trans. and annotated by James F. Brady and John C. Olin, vol. LXI of *Collected Works of Erasmus* (University of Toronto Press, 1992).

Erdman, David V. 'The signature of style', in E&F, pp. 45–68.
Erdman, David V. and Ephim G. Fogel, eds. *Evidence for Authorship: Essays on Problems of Attribution* (Ithaca: Cornell University Press, 1966) [Collecting papers originally published in the *Bulletin of the New York Public Library*, 1957–61].
Ezell, Margaret. *Social Authorship and the Advent of Print* (Baltimore: Johns Hopkins University Press, 1999).
Farringdon, Jill M. et al. *Analysing for Authorship: A Guide to the Cusum Technique* (Cardiff: University of Wales Press, 1996).
Fielding, Henry. *New Essays by Henry Fielding: His Contributions to the 'Craftsman' (1734–1739) and Other Early Journalism*, ed. Martin Battestin, with a stylometric analysis by Michael G. Farringdon (Charlottesville: Virginia University Press, 1989).
Filloy, Richard. 'Deciding the authorship of a doubtful text: the case of John Selden's *Table-talk*', *Quarterly Journal of Speech* 70 (1984), 41–52.
Finlay, Michael. *Western Writing Implements in the Age of the Quill Pen* (Wetheral: Plains Books, 1990).
Fitch, John G. 'Sense-pauses and relative dating in Seneca, Sophocles and Shakespeare', *American Journal of Philology* 102 (1981), 289–307.
Fogel, Ephim G. 'Salmons in both, or some caveats for canonical scholars', in E&F, pp. 69–101.
Forsyth, Richard S. and David I. Holmes. 'Feature-finding for text classification', *LLC* 11 (1996), 163–74.
Forsyth, Richard S. and Emily K. Tse. 'Cicero, Sigonio, and Burrows: investigating the authenticity of the *Consolatio*', *LLC* 14 (1999), 375–400.
Foster, Donald W. 'Master W. H., R.I.P.', *PMLA* 102 (1987), 42–54.
Elegy by W.S.: A Study in Attribution (Newark: University of Delaware Press, 1989).
'Primary culprit: an analysis of a novel of politics', *New York*, 26 Feb. 1996, 50–7.
'Response to Elliott and Valenza, "And then there were none"', *CHum* 30 (1996), 247–55.
'*A funeral elegy*: W[illiam] S[hakespeare]'s "best-speaking witnesses"', *Shakespeare Studies* 25 (1997), 115–40.
'The Claremont Shakespeare authorship clinic: how severe are the problems?', *CHum* 32 (1998), 491–510.
Author Unknown: Tales of Literary Detection (New York: Henry Holt, 2000).
Foucault, Michel. 'What is an author?' (1969), trans. Joseph V. Harari, in David Lodge, ed. *Modern Criticism and Theory: A Reader* (London: Longman, 1988), pp. 197–210.
Fox, Adam. 'Ballads, libels and popular ridicule in Jacobean England', *Past and Present* 145 (1994), 47–83.
Fuegi, John. *The Life and Lies of Bertolt Brecht* (London: HarperCollins, 1994).
Furbank, P. N. and W. R. Owens. *The Canonisation of Daniel Defoe* (New Haven: Yale University Press, 1988).

'Dangerous relations', *The Scriblerian and the Kit-Kats* 33 (1991), 242–4.
Gaskell, Philip. *From Writer to Reader: Studies in Editorial Method* (Oxford: Clarendon Press, 1978).
Gellius, Aulus. *The Attic Nights of Aulus Gellius*, with an English translation by John C. Rolfe (London: Heinemann, 1954).
Gibson, Ian. *The Erotomaniac* (London: Faber, 2001).
Grafton, Anthony. *Forgers and Critics: Creativity and Duplicity in Western Scholarship* (Princeton University Press, 1990).
Greer, Germaine. *Slip-shod Sibyls: Recognition, Rejection and the Woman Poet* (Harmondsworth: Penguin, 1995).
Greetham, David. *Textual Scholarship: An Introduction* (New York: Garland, 1992).
'Textual forensics', *PMLA* 111 (1996), 32–51.
Grenville, Kate and Sue Woolfe. *Making Stories: How Ten Australian Novels Were Written* (North Sydney: Allen & Unwin, 1993).
Groves, Peter. *Strange Music: The Metre of the English Heroic Line* (Victoria, B.C.: *English Literary Studies*, 1998).
Halkett, Samuel and John Laing. *A Dictionary of the Anonymous and Pseudonymous Literature of Great Britain* (Edinburgh, 1882–3); later as *Dictionary of Anonymous and Pseudonymous English Literature*, new and enlarged edition by James Kennedy, W. A. Smith and A. F. Johnson, 9 vols. (Edinburgh: Oliver & Boyd, 1926).
Harbage, Alfred. 'Elizabethan-Restoration palimpsest', *MLR* 35 (1940), 287–319.
Hardouin, Jean. *Ad censuram scriptorum veterum prolegomena* (London, 1766).
Doutes proposé sur l'âge du Dante par P. H. J. (Père Hardouin, Jésuite) avec notes par C. L. (Paris, 1847).
Hargevik, Stieg. *The Disputed Assignment of Memoirs of an English Officer to Daniel Defoe*, 2 vols. (Stockholm: Almqvist & Wiksell, 1974).
Hiatt, Mary. *The Way Women Write* (New York: Teachers College Press, 1977).
Hillebrand, Harold N. 'Thomas Middleton's *The Viper's Brood*', *Modern Language Notes* 42 (1927), 35–8.
Hilton, Michael L. and David I. Holmes. 'An assessment of cumulative sum charts for authorship attribution', *LLC* 8 (1993), 73–80.
Hobart, Michael E. and Zachary S. Schiffman. *Information Ages: Literacy, Numeracy and the Computer Revolution* (Baltimore: Johns Hopkins University Press, 1998).
Holford-Strevens, Leofranc. *Aulus Gellius* (London: Duckworth, 1988).
Holmes, David I. 'The analysis of literary style: a review', *The Journal of the Royal Statistical Society* (Series A), 148(4) (1985), 328–41.
'Authorship attribution', *CHum* 28 (1994), 87–106.
'The evolution of stylometry in humanities scholarship', *LLC* 13 (1998), 111–17.
Holmes, David I. and R. S. Forsyth. 'The *Federalist* revisited: new directions in authorship attribution', *LLC* 10 (1995), 111–27.
Holmes, David I. and F. J. Tweedie. 'Forensic stylometry: a review of the cusum controversy', *Revue informatique et statistique dans les sciences humaines* 31 (1995), 19–47.

Hoorn, Johan F. et al. 'Neural network identification of poets using letter sequences', *LLC* 14 (1999), 311–38.

Hopkins, Lisa. '"Elegy by W. S.": another possible candidate?', *Philological Quarterly* 76 (1997), 159–68.

Hoy, Cyrus. 'The shares of Fletcher and his collaborators in the Beaumont and Fletcher canon (I)', *SB* 8 (1956), 129–46; (II) 9 (1959), 143–62; (III) 11 (1958), 85–106; (IV) 12 (1959), 91–116; (V) 13 (1960), 77–108; (VI) 14 (1961), 45–67; (VII) 15 (1962), 71–90.

Hume, Robert D. *Reconstructing Contexts: The Aims and Principles of Archaeo-Historicism* (Oxford University Press, 1999).

Irizarry, Estelle. 'A computer-assisted investigation of gender-related idiolect in Octavio Paz and Rosario Castellanos', *CHum* 26 (1992), 103–17.

Jacklin, Carol Nagy, ed. *The Psychology of Gender*, 4 vols. (Aldershot: Edward Elgar, 1992).

Jerome. *Select Letters*, trans. F. A. Wright (London: Heinemann, 1933).

Johnson, J. W. 'Did Lord Rochester write *Sodom*?', *Papers of the Bibliographical Society of America* 81 (1987), 119–53.

Johnstone, Barbara. *The Linguistic Individual: Self-Expression in Language and Linguistics* (New York: Oxford University Press, 1996).

Keeble N. H. *The Literary Culture of Nonconformity in Later Seventeenth-century England* (Leicester University Press, 1987).

Kenny, Anthony J. *The Computation of Style: An Introduction to Statistics for Students of Literature and Humanities* (Oxford: Pergamon Press, 1982).

A Stylometric Study of the New Testament (Oxford: Clarendon Press, 1986).

Kewes, Paulina. *Authorship and Appropriation: Writing for the Stage in England 1660–1710* (Oxford University Press, 1998).

Kjell, Bradley. 'Authorship determination using letter pair frequency features with neural network classifiers', *LLC* 9 (1994), 119–24.

Laan, Nancy. 'Stylometry and method. The case of Euripides', *LLC* 10 (1995), 271–8.

Lake, David. *The Canon of Thomas Middleton's Plays: Internal Evidence for the Major Problems of Authorship* (London: Cambridge University Press, 1975).

Lakoff, Robin. *Language and Woman's Place* (New York: Harper & Row, 1975).

Lancashire, Ian. 'Empirically determining Shakespeare's idiolect', *Shakespeare Studies* 25 (1997), 171–85.

'Paradigms of authorship', *Shakespeare Studies* 26 (1998), 296–301.

Langbaine, Gerard. *Momus triumphans, or, the plagiaries of the English stage: expos'd in a catalogue of all the comedies, tragi-comedies, masques, tragedies, opera's, pastorals, interludes, &c. both ancient and modern, that were ever yet printed in English . . .* (London, 1687); as *An Account of the English Dramatic Poets* (1691).

Ledger, Gerard. 'An exploration of differences in the Pauline epistles using multivariate statistical analysis', *LLC* 10 (1995), 85–97.

Ledger, Gerard and Thomas Merriam. 'Shakespeare, Fletcher, and the two noble kinsmen', *LLC* 9 (1994), 235–48.

Leed, Jacob. *The Computer and Literary Style* (Kent, OH: Kent State University Press, 1996).
Lonsdale, Roger, ed. *The Poems of Thomas Gray, William Collins, Oliver Goldsmith* (London: Longmans, 1969).
Love, Harold. *The Golden Age of Australian Opera: W. S. Lyster and his Companies 1861–1880* (Sydney: Currency Press, 1981).
James Edward Neild: Victorian Virtuoso (Carlton, Vic.: Melbourne University Press, 1989).
'Scribal texts and literary communities: the Rochester circle and Osborn b. 105', *SB* 42 (1989), 219–35.
'A Restoration lampoon in transmission and revision: Rochester's(?) "Signior Dildoe"', *SB* 46 (1993), 250–62.
'But did Rochester *really* write *Sodom*?', *Papers of the Bibliographical Society of America* 87 (1993), 319–36.
Scribal Publication in Seventeenth-century England (Oxford University Press, 1993); reprinted as *The Culture and Commerce of Texts: Scribal Publication in Seventeenth-century England* (Amherst: University of Massachusetts Press, 1998).
'How personal is a Personal Miscellany? Sarah Cowper, Martin Clifford and the "Buckingham Commonplace Book"', in R. C. Alston, ed. *Order and Connexion: Studies in Bibliography and Book History* (Cambridge: D. S. Brewer, 1997), pp. 111–26.
McAleer, Joseph. *Popular Reading and Publishing in Britain 1914–1950* (Oxford: Clarendon Press, 1992).
Passion's Fortune: The Story of Mills and Boon (Oxford University Press, 1999).
McColly, William and Dennis Weier. 'Literary attribution and likelihood-ratio tests: the case of the Middle English *Pearl*-poems', *CHum* 17 (1983), 65–75.
McKenzie, D. F. 'Printers of the mind: some notes on bibliographical theories and printing-house practices', *SB* 22 (1969), 1–75.
McManaway, James G. 'Latin title-page mottoes as a clue to dramatic authorship', *The Library*, 4th ser. 26 (1946), 28–36.
McMenamin, Gerald R. *Forensic Stylistics* (Amsterdam: Elsevier, 1993); also as *Forensic Science International* 58 (1993).
Marcus, Leah H. 'From oral delivery to print', in Arthur F. Marotti and Michael D. Bristol, eds. *Print, Manuscript and Performance: The Changing Relations of the Media in Early England* (Columbus: Ohio State University Press, 2000), pp. 33–48.
Marotti, Arthur F. *Manuscript, Print, and the English Renaissance Lyric* (Ithaca: Cornell University Press, 1995).
Mason, H. A. *Editing Wyatt: An Examination of Collected Poems of Sir Thomas Wyatt together with Suggestions for an Improved Edition* (Cambridge: Cambridge Quarterly (Publications), 1972).
Mendenhall, Thomas. 'The characteristic curves of composition', *Science* 214 (1887), 237–49.
'A mechanical solution of a literary problem', *Popular Science Monthly* 60 (1901), 97–105.

Merriam, Thomas. 'An investigation of Morton's method: a reply', *CHum* 21 (1987), 57–8.

'Neural computation in stylometry I: an application to the works of Shakespeare and Fletcher', *LLC* 8 (1993), 203–9.

'Letter frequency as a discriminator of authors', *N&Q* 239 (1994), 467–9.

'Invalidation reappraised', *CHum* 30 (1997), 417–31.

'Heterogeneous authorship in early Shakespeare and the problem of *Henry V*', *LLC* 13 (1998), 15–28.

Merriam, Thomas and Robert A. J. Matthews. 'Neural computation in stylometry II: an application to the works of Shakespeare and Marlowe', *LLC* 9 (1994), 1–6.

Metzger, Bruce M. *The Canon of the New Testament: Its Origin, Development, and Significance* (Oxford: Clarendon Press, 1987).

Mews, Constant. *The Lost Love Letters of Heloise and Abelard: Perceptions of Dialogue in Twelfth-century France* (New York: St Martin's Press, 1999).

Michell, John. *Who Wrote Shakespeare?* (London: Thames & Hudson, 1996).

Milhous, Judith and Robert D. Hume. 'Attribution problems in English drama 1660–1700', *Harvard Library Bulletin* 31 (1983), 5–39.

Milnes, Tim. 'On the authorship of *Two Dissertations concerning Sense and the Imagination, with an Essay on Consciousness*', *N&Q* 247 (2000), 196–98.

Minnis, A. J. *Mediaeval Theory of Authorship: Scholastic Literary Attitudes in the Later Middle Ages*, 2nd edn (Aldershot: Scolar Press, 1988).

Molloy, Frank. 'Attribution and pseudonyms: the case of Victor J. Daley', *BSANZ Bulletin* 24 (2000), 116–28.

Morize, André. *Problems and Methods of Literary History with Special Reference to Modern French Literature: A Guide for Graduate Students* (Boston: Ginn & Company, 1922).

Morton, Andrew Q. *Literary Detection: How to Prove Authorship and Fraud in Literature and Documents* (New York: Scribner, 1978).

'Authorship: the nature of the habit', *TLS*, 17–23 Feb. 1989, 164, 174.

Mosteller, Frederick and David L. Wallace. *Inference and Disputed Authorship: The Federalist* (Reading, MA: Addison-Wesley Pub. Co., 1964); 2nd edition as *Applied Bayesian and Classical Inference: The Case of the 'Federalist' Papers* (New York: Springer-Verlag, 1984).

Murray, Peter B. *A Study of Cyril Tourneur* (Philadelphia: University of Pennsylvania Press, 1964).

North, Roger. *The Life of the Lord Keeper North*, ed. Mary Chan (Lewiston, NY: Edward Mellen Press, 1995).

O'Brian, D. P. and A. C. Darnell. *Authorship Puzzles in the History of Economics: A Statistical Approach* (London: Macmillan, 1982).

O'Donnell, Mary Ann. 'A verse miscellany of Aphra Behn: Bodleian Library MS Firth c. 16', *English Manuscript Studies* 2 (1990), 189–227.

Oliphant, E. H. C. 'The authorship of *The Revenger's Tragedy*', *Studies in Philology* 23 (1926), 157–68.

Ong, Walter J. *Fighting for Life: Contest, Sexuality, and Consciousness* (Ithaca: Cornell University Press, 1981).

Orality and Literacy: The Technologizing of the Word (London: Methuen, 1982).

Oppenheim, Helen. 'The author of *The Hibernian Father*: an early colonial playwright', *Australian Literary Studies* 2 (1966), 278–88.

Orwell, George. 'Boys' weeklies', *Horizon* 1 (1940), 353–4.

The Collected Essays, Journalism and Letters of George Orwell, ed. Sonia Orwell and Ian Angus, 4 vols. (London: Secker and Warburg, 1968).

Owens, W. R. and P. N. Furbank. *A Critical Bibliography of Daniel Defoe* (London: Pickering & Chatto, 1998).

Partridge, A. C. *Orthography in Shakespeare and Elizabethan Drama* (London: Edward Arnold, 1964).

Pearsall, Derek. 'Middle English romance and its audiences', in Mary-Jo Arn and Hannecke Wirtjes, with Hans Jansen, *Historical and Editorial Studies in Medieval and Early Modern English* (Groningen: Walters-Noordhoff, 1985), pp. 37–47.

Pearson, David. *Provenance Research in Book History: A Handbook* (Repr. London: The British Library, 1998).

Pearson, Jacqueline. *The Prostituted Muse: Images of Women and Women Dramatists 1642–1737* (Hemel Hempstead: Wheatsheaf, 1988).

Petronius. *Titi Petronii Arbitri equitis Romani Satyricon cum fragmentis Albæ Græcæ recupertatis ann. 1688 nunc demum integrum* (Rotterdam, 1693).

Petti, Anthony G. *English Literary Hands from Chaucer to Dryden* (London: Edward Arnold, 1977).

Pfeiffer, Rudolf. *History of Classical Scholarship*, 2 vols. (Oxford: Clarendon Press, 1968, 1976).

Pierce, Frederick Erastus. *The Collaboration of Webster and Dekker* (New Haven: Yale University Press, 1909).

Pinkus, Philip. *Grub Street Stripped Bare; the Scandalous Lives and Pornographic Works of the Original Grub St Writers* (London: Constable, 1968).

Poulet, George. 'Criticism and the experience of interiority', in Richard Macksey and Eugenio Donato, eds., *The Structuralist Controversy: The Languages of Criticism and the Sciences of Man* (Baltimore: Johns Hopkins University Press, 1972), pp. 56–88.

Price, George R. 'The authorship and the manuscript of *The Old Law*', *Huntington Library Quarterly* 16 (1952–3), 117–39.

Reed, Joseph W. *Literary Revision: The Inexact Science of Getting it Right* (New Haven: Beinecke Library, 1990).

Rendell, Kenneth W. *Forging History: The Detection of Fake Letters and Documents* (Norman: University of Oklahoma Press, 1994).

Reynolds, L. H., ed. *Texts and Transmission: A Survey of the Latin Classics* (Oxford: Clarendon Press, 1983).

Rochester. *The Works of John Wilmot, Earl of Rochester*, ed. Harold Love (Oxford University Press, 1999).

Rose, Mark. *Authors and Owners: The Invention of Copyright* (Cambridge, MA: Harvard University Press, 1993).

Rothman, Irving N. 'Defoe de-attributions scrutinized under Hargevik criteria: applying stylometrics to the canon', *Papers of the Bibliographical Society of America* 94 (2000), 375–98.

Rouse, Richard H. and Mary A. Rouse. 'Wax tablets', *Language and Communication* 9 (1989), 175–91.

Rudler, Gustave. *Les Techniques de la critique et de l'histoire littéraires en littérature française moderne* (Oxford University Press, 1923).

Rudman, Joseph. 'The state of authorship attribution studies: some problems and solutions', *CHum* 31 (1997–8), 351–65.

'Non-traditional authorship attribution studies in the *Historia Augusta*: some caveats', *LLC* 13 (1998), 151–7.

'Non-traditional authorship attribution studies: ignis fatuus or Rosetta stone?', *BSANZ Bulletin* 24 (2000), 163–76.

Said, Edward. *The World, the Text, and the Critic* (New York: Vintage, 1991).

Sams, Eric. '*Edmund Ironside* and "stylometry"', *N&Q* 239 (1994), 469–72.

Sams, Eric, ed. *Shakespeare's Edward III: An Early Play Restored to the Canon* (New Haven: Yale University Press, 1996).

Sapir, Edward. *Selected Writings of Edward Sapir in Language, Culture and Personality*, ed. David C. Mandelbaum (Berkeley and Los Angeles: University of California Press, 1958).

Schoenbaum, Samuel. *Internal Evidence and Elizabethan Dramatic Authorship: An Essay in Literary History and Method* (London: Edward Arnold, 1966) [with valuable bibliography, pp. 231–56].

'Internal evidence and the attribution of Elizabethan plays', in E&F, pp. 188–203.

Settle, Elkanah. *Notes and Observations on the Empress of Morocco Revised* (London, 1674).

Sharpe, Kevin. *Reading Revolutions: The Politics of Reading in Early Modern England* (New Haven: Yale University Press, 2000).

Shaywitz, Bennett A., Sally E. Shaywitz et al. 'Sex differences in the functional organization of the brain for language', *Nature* 373 (16 Feb. 1995), 607–9.

Sherbo, Arthur. 'The uses and abuses of internal evidence', in E&F, pp. 6–24.

Simon, Richard. *Histoire critique du vieux testament* (Paris, 1678).

Smith, Kate A. *Introduction to Neural Networks and Data Mining for Business Applications* (Melbourne: Eruditions, 1999).

Smith, M. W. A. 'An investigation of Morton's method to distinguish Elizabethan playwrights', *CHum* 19 (1985), 3–21.

'An investigation of the basis of Morton's method for the determination of authorship', *Style* 19 (1985), 341–59.

'Merriam's applications of Morton's method', *CHum* 21 (1987), 59–60.

'*The Revenger's Tragedy*: the derivation and interpretation of statistical results for resolving disputed authorship', *CHum* 21 (1987), 21–55.

'A procedure to determine authorship using pairs of consecutive words: more evidence for Wilkins's participation in *Pericles*', *CHum* 23 (1989), 113–29.

'Attribution by statistics: a critique of four recent studies', *Revue informatique et statistique dans les sciences humaines* 26 (1990), 233–50.

'The authorship of *The Revenger's Tragedy*', *N&Q* 236 (1991), 508–13.

'The authorship of *Timon of Athens*', *Text: Transactions of the Society for Textual Scholarship* 5 (1991), 195–240.

Spedding, Patrick. 'Eliza Haywood's last ("lost") work: *The History of Miss Leonora Meadowson* (1788)', *BSANZ Bulletin* 23 (1999), 131–47.

Spennemann, Dirk H. R. and Jane Downing. 'Literary detection: discovering the identity of a "Master mariner"', *Margin* 47 (April 1999), 8–13.

'Unmasking transient colonial authors: the case of Handley Bathurst Sterndale', *BSANZ Bulletin* 23 (1999), 148–63.

Spinoza, Benedictus de. *Tractatus Theologico-politicus*, trans. Samuel Shirley (Leiden: E. J. Brill, 1991).

Stainer, C. L. *Jonson and Drummond their Conversations: A few Remarks on an 18th Century Forgery* (Oxford: Basil Blackwell; Stratford-upon-Avon: Shakespeare Head Press, 1925).

Stein, Harold. 'A note on the versification of *Childe Harold*', *Modern Language Notes* 42 (1927), 34–5.

Stillinger, Jack. 'Multiple authorship and the question of authority', *Text* 5 (1991), 285–93.

Sutton-Smith, Brian. *The Folkstories of Children* (Philadelphia: University of Pennsylvania Press, 1981).

Tarlinskaja, Marina. *Shakespeare's Verse: Iambic Pentameter and the Poet's Idiosyncrasies* (New York: Peter Lang, 1987).

Taylor, Gary. 'The rhetoric of textual criticism', *Text: Transactions of the Society for Textual Scholarship* 4 (1988), 39–57.

Thompson, Roger. *Unfit for Modest Ears: A Study of Pornographic, Obscene and Bawdy Works Written or Published in England in the Second Half of the Seventeenth Century* (London: Macmillan, 1979).

Tooley, Sarah H. 'Some women novelists', *The Woman at Home* 5 (1897–8), 161–211.

Tweedie, Fiona J., David I. Holmes and Thomas N. Corns. 'The provenance of *De Doctrina Christiana*, attributed to John Milton: a statistical investigation', *LLC* 13 (1998), 77–87.

Tweedie, Fiona J., S. Singh and D. I. Holmes. 'Neural network applications in stylometry: the *Federalist Papers*', *CHum* 30 (1996), 1–10.

Valla, Lorenzo. *The Treatise of Lorenzo Valla on the Donation of Constantine. Text and Translation into English*, ed. and trans. Christopher B. Coleman (New Haven: Yale University Press, 1922).

Vieth, David M. *Attribution in Restoration Poetry: A Study of Rochester's 'Poems' of 1680*, Yale Studies in English, 153 (New Haven: Yale University Press, 1963).

Wells, Stanley, Gary Taylor et al., eds. *William Shakespeare: A Textual Companion* (Oxford: Clarendon Press, 1987).

Wentersdorf, Karl. 'Shakespearean chronology and the metrical tests', in ed. W. Fischer and K. Wentersdorf, *Shakespeare-Studien* (Marburg: N. G. Elwert, 1951).
Whitehead, John. *This Solemn Mockery: The Art of Literary Forgery* (London: Arlington Books, 1973).
Williams, C. B. *Style and Vocabulary: Numerical Studies* (London: Griffin, 1970).
Williams, Franklin B. jr. 'Renaissance names in masquerade', *PMLA* 69 (1954), 314–23.
'An initiation into initials', *SB* 9 (1957), 163–78.
Wood, Anthony. *Athenae Oxonienses: An Exact History of all the Writers and Bishops who have had their Education in the Famous University of Oxford*, 2 vols. (London: Tho: Bennet, 1691–2).
Woudhuysen, Henry. *Sir Philip Sidney and the Circulation of Manuscripts 1558–1640* (Oxford: Clarendon Press, 1996).
Yule, G. Udny. *The Statistical Study of Literary Vocabulary* (Cambridge University Press, 1944).

Index

Printed in Great Britain
by Amazon

61382366R00168